Jazz Up Your Web Site

PAUL E. ROBICHAUX

PRIMA PUBLISHING

P is a registered trademark of Prima Publishing, a division of Prima Communications, Inc. In a Weekend is a trademark of Prima Publishing, a division of Prima Communications, Inc. Prima Publishing is a registered trademark of Prima Communications, Inc. Prima Publishing, Rocklin, California 95677.

Publisher: Matthew H. Carleson
Managing Editor: Dan J. Foster
Acquisitions Editor: Jenny Watson
Development Editors: Barb Terry, Chris Katsaropoulos
Project Editor: Geneil Breeze
Editorial Assistant: Kevin W. Ferns
Technical Reviewer: Bo Williams
Interior Design: Danielle Foster
Interior Layout: Marian Hartsough
Cover Design: Prima Design Team
Indexer: Katherine Stimson

ISBN: 0-7615-1137-7
Library of Congress Catalog Card Number: 97-66856
Printed in the United States of America

99 BB 10 9 8 7 6 5 4 3 2

This book is dedicated to my wonderful wife, Arlene,
whose patience and love were sorely tested
but well-proven during the writing of this book.
I couldn't have done it without you!

Contents at a Glance

CONTENTS

SATURDAY AFTERNOON
Adding Graphics, Backgrounds, and Accents 155

SATURDAY EVENING
Adding Animation, Sound, and Video. 191

ACKNOWLEDGMENTS

Books are always a team effort. I was fortunate to have a talented and skilled group of editors on this project. Jenny Watson, my acquisitions editor, was patient and persevered throughout the entire project. Fellow writer Bo Williams shared his insight as the technical editor. Barb Terry and Chris Katsaropoulos developed the book, and Geneil Breeze tied all the edits together and made sure the book got laid out properly. Their efforts produced the polished final result you're holding in your hands, and my hat's off to them.

My employers, Larry and Janie Layten of LJL Enterprises, were extremely accommodating in allowing me to schedule seemingly random vacations when deadlines approached and redo the Web site on short notice. My thanks to them.

I'd also like to thank my volunteer reviewers, a group of Webheads who took the time to give the concepts (and text!) of this book a reality check as I was writing it. In alphabetical order, my thanks to Brian Day, Jack Garrison, Moe Kunkle, Lee Seitz, and Paul Stephanouk. Many software vendors and programmers gave us permission to include their work on the accompanying CD; in addition to thanking them, I'd like to particularly thank Shannon Karl of USRobotics and Bill Holding of Avid for loaning me the video hardware used in Appendix C.

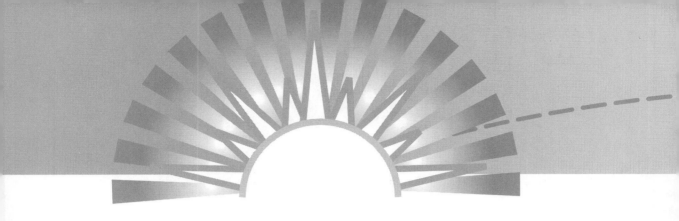

ABOUT THE AUTHOR

Paul Robichaux has been an Internet user since 1986 and a software developer since 1983. He designed his first Web site in 1993 using duct tape, a Unix workstation, and way too much Diet Coke. Since then, he's designed sites for small companies, Fortune 500 companies, nonprofits, and family members. Paul's currently a software consultant for LJL Enterprises, where he divides his time between writing cryptography and data security software for Macintosh and Windows. In his spare time, he writes books and Macintosh software. He still manages to spend plenty of time with his wife and young son. He can be reached via e-mail at **paulr@hiwaay.net**.

INTRODUCTION

You've taken the time out of your busy schedule to start putting your own Web pages together. Whether you've done it with a plain text editor and raw HTML or a sophisticated graphical editor like FrontPage 97 or Home Page, you've been wondering how you can dress up your site and give it that Webmaster touch that you've seen on some of your favorite sites.

You might think that you need months or even years to master the intricate skills needed to create a top-notch site. Good news—you can learn the basics *in a weekend!*

Who Is This Book For?

In the original days of the Internet, you had to be a wizard to use it—there were special commands to learn, arcane tools to use, and lots of pitfalls to avoid. The explosive growth of the Internet since 1994 or so is largely due to the World Wide Web. As the net has become more popular, the tools used to surf it—and create content for others to surf—have become more widespread and easier to use.

One mistake many new net users make is in thinking that you have to be some sort of computer genius to create Web pages. This impression is mostly due to not knowing how easy it really is to create content for the Web.

Of course, one of the reasons for the Web's incredible popularity is that *anyone* with something to say can create Web pages. You don't have to be a television network, Fortune 500 company, or newspaper editor to reach thousands of people with your information—you can do it from your den, your office, or your laptop.

Even though creating simple Web sites is easy, there are still many tips, tricks, and traps involved in adding spice and "jazz" to your pages. This book is for anyone who wants to improve his or her Web site by making it more attractive and easier to use.

What Can I *Really* Learn in a Weekend?

A surprising amount! It would take years to learn all the fundamentals of good graphic design. People spend years and years learning the principles of typography, layout, and art design. Likewise, some people have invested many long hours in perfecting the design and content of their sites. However, you don't have to be one of them!

This book can't possibly teach you everything you need to design an award-winning site, but it can teach you fundamental skills and techniques that you can use to start improving and enhancing your pages *right away!* Although you may not be able to go from zero to guru in a weekend, you *can* learn how to revamp your existing pages to take advantage of animation, video, sound, Java, ActiveX, and advanced HTML layout features.

The result? A great-looking home for your content. You still have to figure out what you want to put on your pages, but you'll even learn tips for that.

What Do I Need to Know?

You might be surprised to find out how little you need to know before you start jazzing up your Web pages. There are really only three things you absolutely need to know:

❖ You should already be comfortable using your computer, either with Windows 95 or MacOS.

❖ You should know how to use the Web browser of your choice. You can use this book equally well whether you prefer Netscape's Navigator, Microsoft's Internet Explorer, or another browser.

❖ You should have basic familiarity with HTML. If you've ever seen the HTML code for a page, that qualifies. If you've already created some home pages, or otherwise had exposure to HTML, so much the better!

If you want to look at the sample sites we talk about in each chapter, you should know how to use your computer to get on the Internet. If you want to use a particular image editor or Web page authoring tool (like FrontPage 97, Claris Home Page, or HotDog Pro), you can use it as we go along, but we'll focus on what to do, not how to do it.

What Do I Need to Use This Book?

Because this book is about enhancing your Web pages, it would be great if you already had Web pages. If not, don't despair; you can whip up some in a jiffy as you go.

Of course, you'll need a computer. Any machine running Windows 95, Windows NT, or the MacOS will do just fine. If you have a CD-ROM,

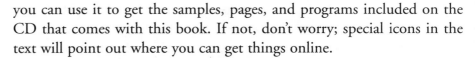

you can use it to get the samples, pages, and programs included on the CD that comes with this book. If not, don't worry; special icons in the text will point out where you can get things online.

You'll need a Web browser to view your pages, as well as the samples and examples included in each chapter. I recommend using the latest versions of either Netscape Navigator or Microsoft Internet Explorer. You can use whatever browser is convenient, but these two have the most complete implementation of the HTML standard.

To connect to the Internet, you'll need a modem or a full-time connection; if you want to put your pages on the Web, you'll need a place to put them, probably through your Internet service provider.

If you already have a preferred HTML editor, you can use it to work on your pages; if not, you can use one of the editors provided on the CD. Likewise, you'll need an image-editing program that can generate GIF images, like Photoshop or Paint Shop Pro; again, several are on the CD for your use.

What's in This Book?

In this book, the weekend begins on Friday evening. In fact, the weekend is broken up into seven sessions; each session should take you three or four hours at most to work through. The sessions are mostly independent, although you'll get the most out of the book if you go through them in order. Don't be afraid to skip around if there's something you're particularly interested in learning about. You can always go backwards, or forwards, later.

Each session has at least one part; some have more. Here's what you'll be doing during each part of the weekend.

○ *Friday Evening: Designing an Effective Web Page.* In this session, you'll learn the basics of good design, including how to design attractive, readable pages that draw readers in. You'll learn how to plan your site design for maximum impact, and you'll finally find out what all that talk about HTML extensions *really* means.

⚙ *Saturday Morning: Designing Pages with Tables; Designing Pages with Frames; and Designing Web Forms.* Tables, frames, and forms are the three keys to putting some jazz into your pages. Each has its own session, where you'll learn how they work, how to build them, and how to use them in your pages. At the end of each session, we'll look at some real-world sites and dissect them to show you how to put what you've learned into action.

⚙ *Saturday Afternoon: Adding Graphics, Backgrounds, and Accents.* After the basic design for your site is complete, you can start adding graphics to accent, decorate, and communicate. Learn how to build effective graphics that don't hog bandwidth or choke slow modems.

⚙ *Saturday Evening: Adding Animation, Sound, and Video.* It's Saturday evening—time to add graphics, sound, animation, and video to make your pages come alive! You'll learn how to spice up your pages; a separate appendix (Appendix C) covers the nuts and bolts of setting up your computer to record your own video and sound.

⚙ *Sunday Morning: Activating Your Web Site.* Now that your pages have taken shape, it's time to apply some radical tricks, including making it easier for popular Web search engines to find and index your pages. ActiveX and Java are the hottest things going in the Web world right now. Although you have to be a programmer to write Java or ActiveX controls, using someone else's controls in your pages is easy and legal. Learn how to make your pages fully active.

⚙ *Sunday Afternoon: Applying the Finishing Touches.* There's more to jazzing up your Web pages than stuffing them full of good-looking content—how about adding password protection, making it easy for search engines to find you, and accepting advertising? You'll learn how to do these, and more, on Sunday afternoon.

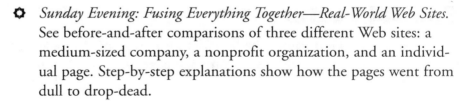

✪ *Sunday Evening: Fusing Everything Together—Real-World Web Sites.* See before-and-after comparisons of three different Web sites: a medium-sized company, a nonprofit organization, and an individual page. Step-by-step explanations show how the pages went from dull to drop-dead.

Of course, nothing says that you have to do these sessions over a weekend. You can do them whenever it's convenient for you, whether that's one weekend or a month of Sundays. Best of all, each chapter is overstuffed with links and tips that you can come back to later, so your learning won't end after the weekend is over.

What's on the CD?

The CD for this book features an array of Windows and Macintosh tools, graphics, sounds, and miscellaneous goodies that you can use to pump up your Web site. Here's a small sample of what you'll find:

✪ *HTML editors.* Choose from several, including 1-4-All, Aardvark Pro, Agile, Aspire-X, Coffee Cup, and FlexED.

✪ *Drawing, graphic, and multimedia utilities.* LiquidFX, WebPainter, the GoldWave audio editor, plus FlashView, itsagif, MapThis, Mapedit, and Animagic GIF.

✪ *Art and music.* Image collections from Octagamm, ToonWorld, and Havana Street (plus Richard Moeur's ultracool Traffic Sign collection), plus sounds and music from Michael Cox.

✪ *Java and ActiveX.* The AusComp control suite for Java and ActiveX, plus Java applets like RiadaCartel and KzmAdvertise.

✪ *Miscellaneous utilities.* SubmitBlaster, Banner*Show and Guestbook*Star.

Special Features

Throughout the book, you'll notice some special features that will help you get the most from each chapter.

Notes, tips, and cautions will give you valuable information right when you need it; they appear in the body of the text, like this:

NOTE By the end of 1997, some estimates predict that more than 75 million people worldwide will have access to the Web. That's a lot of potential visitors to your page!

Two kinds of icons are used throughout the book. The Find It On the Web icon tells you where to go to get a program, tool, or page mentioned in the text, like this:

FIND IT ON ▶
THE WEB   If you want to get a head start on the video chapter, go to
http://www.quicktime.apple.com and get the appropriate version of
QuickTime for your computer.

Likewise, when you see the On the CD icon, you'll know that it tells you where to go to get a program, tool, or page mentioned in the text, like this:

ON THE

CD

If you're looking for a good HTML editor, the CD includes trial versions of several, including Aardvark Pro, Agile, and Coffee Cup.

Finding More Online

Appendix B has a long list of online references covering everything discussed in our sessions, plus a whole lot more. In addition, this book has its own Web site. It's currently located at **http://fly.hiwaay.net/~paulr**, but if it ever moves you can find it by doing a Web search for "Robichaux" and "jazz"—not many pages use them together!

Designing an Effective Web Page

It's Friday evening, and you're ready to start learning how to jazz up your Web pages with graphics, sound, animation, Java, and—most important—good design principles.

Before you plunge in to the mechanics of making your page sizzle, though, there are some design fundamentals you should know about. This session will teach you:

- What a Web page *really* is—a collection of images, sounds, text, or whatever else you include, not just a single static file
- Some key HTML features you can use in your pages to make them look good in the major browsers
- The three key measures of an effective Web page
- How to design your pages to score well on each measure

Before you dig in, you might be wondering how much HTML you need to know. If you've already built even a simple Web page, then you know enough already to master the secrets of jazzing up your pages. If not, don't worry—notes in the text will point out other books and Web pages that can help you get up to speed.

NOTE Steve Callihan's *Create Your First Web Page in a Weekend* (Prima Publishing; ISBN 0-7615-0692-6) is an excellent place to start learning about building Web pages if you're not already comfortable with the lingo.

Web Page Basics

Because you're reading this book, it's safe to assume that you've seen Web pages before and that you've probably experimented with creating your own pages. Instead of another "teach-yourself-HTML-in-your-spare-time" tutorial, I'd rather talk about some often-overlooked basics of what Web pages are and how they move around on the net. Don't worry; we'll get to HTML in the next section.

What's a Web Page?

Let's start with the most basic of all basics: what *is* a Web page, anyway? There's a simple answer: a Web page is just another kind of file, like a letter to your mom or that copy of Doom you break out and play when the kids are in bed. The file's written in the *Hypertext Markup Language* (HTML), and Web browsers like Internet Explorer and Netscape Navigator know how to interpret the HTML to display a nicely formatted page of text, graphics, and hyperlinks.

The answer to this question might seem really obvious, but the simple answer actually hides some interesting nuggets. See, a Web page can include the contents of other files, too; for example, any time you use an image tag to display an image, you're really telling the Web browser to grab that image file and treat it like part of your page.

What looks like a single page to the person reading it might actually consist of dozens of individual files, on one computer or on computers all over the Internet.

Of course, if you just want to display content in the simplest possible way, you would use a single file. In fact, the pages you've designed in the past might be this way. After reading this book, your outlook will probably shift—when you design your pages, you'll have to focus on what the end user sees, not on the assortment of files that make it up. This is especially important when your pages contain many small images, icons, and labels—as they will by the time you get to Sunday morning!

You might be wondering how the browser knows how to download and display all the pieces of a complex page. Let's see how the downloading and display process works.

HTTP: How Web Pages Move

Hypertext Transfer Protocol (HTTP) is a special Internet language for transferring Web pages between you and a Web server. HTTP provides a set of rules for conversations between servers and browsers. You can use HTTP to transfer any kind of data; most often, though, it's used to move Web pages around.

When you type a URL like **http://www.primapublishing.com/ index.html** into your Web browser, you're telling it to fetch the file named index.html from the Internet Web site named **www.primapublishing.com**. The browser obligingly goes off to do your bidding. (I'm ignoring the occasional network error you're likely to see when surfing the net!) When the browser is finished fetching the page, it scans through the page looking at the HTML. Each time the browser finds a reference to an image or object stored on another computer, it fetches that item and displays it too.

NOTE Depending on how your browser's configured, the browser may download all the images and text contained in a page before displaying anything, or it may display each item as it loads. On Saturday afternoon, you'll learn how to control this process on your pages.

Every time the browser has to get another item for display, it must make a new connection to the remote server, ask for the item it wants, and wait for it to arrive. This process can be slow, especially when you're getting pages from a busy server or are using a modem to connect to the Internet. When you select a hyperlink from the page you're on (or choose an item from your hotlist), the whole process begins again with a new page.

Bandwidth and Your Pages

You'll often hear experienced Internet users talk about *bandwidth*. This is nothing more than a fancy word for capacity. For example, a 747 jumbo jet has more bandwidth than one of those little propeller-driven commuter planes. In the Internet's case, bandwidth is used to discuss or describe information-carrying capacity requirements. A *high-bandwidth* link is just a fast link; similarly, a high-bandwidth site is one that requires a lot of bandwidth to deliver its content.

It's tempting to assume that everyone has the same bandwidth as you do. If you're lucky enough to have a fast T-1 connection at your school or office, it's easy to design big pages with many great-looking graphics. But you'll aggravate people using modems because your high-bandwidth site is much slower over their links.

Of course, the number of images, sounds, Java applets, and so on that you put in your pages will influence the amount of bandwidth that it needs to be effective. What you may *not* realize is that the type, color, and size of your images can dramatically influence their file size in unexpected ways.

Images, Colors, and Size

Most images used in Web pages are compressed with the *Graphics Interchange Format* (GIF). GIF compresses images while maintaining all the original picture information; this *lossless* compression preserves the original quality of the image. GIF compression works by spotting patterns in each horizontal row of an image and then using special codes to represent patterns that have already occurred. The page shown in Figure 1.1 shows

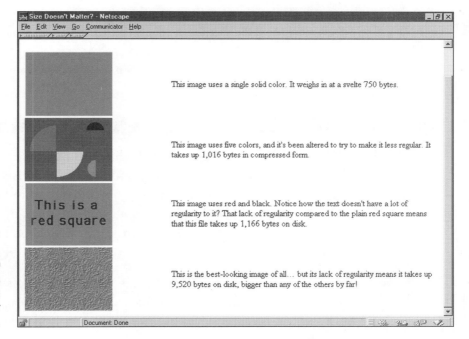

This image uses a single solid color. It weighs in at a svelte 750 bytes.

This image uses five colors, and it's been altered to try to make it less regular. It takes up 1,016 bytes in compressed form.

This is a
red square

This image uses red and black. Notice how the text doesn't have a lot of regularity to it? That lack of regularity compared to the plain red square means that this file takes up 1,166 bytes on disk.

This is the best-looking image of all... but its lack of regularity means it takes up 9,520 bytes on disk, bigger than any of the others by far!

Figure 1.1

All these shapes are the same size, but their file size varies.

several different images, made up of different patterns. Their compressed sizes vary even though the images are all 160×120.

There's a complex relationship between the number of colors you use in an image, the size of the image on-screen, and the image content, but it boils down to one simple rule: the GIF compression scheme will compress any regular feature of the image. The more regular patterns your image has, the more it will compress. The plain square shown earlier in Figure 1.1 has the best compression, but even the second image—with all its circles—compresses well because circles are regular patterns.

The fewer colors you use in an image, the better GIF compression works. Most image editors have a function that allows you to strip the color palette (or set of colors) used in an image down to the minimum necessary for displaying that image; you should take advantage of this capability if your editor supports it.

NOTE I'll talk more about the specifics of different Web graphic formats in the Saturday afternoon session "Adding Graphics, Backgrounds, and Accents."

HTML: It's Not Just for Geeks Any More

HTML is designed to be readable by humans but still easy for a computer to read and translate. This compromise means that there are many arcane requirements for how you lay out and structure HTML; in addition, the official HTML specifications lay out the language's standards and tell you how to write HTML that can be understood by any program that follows the standard.

FIND IT ON ▶ THE WEB
The full HTML 3.2 specifications are on the Web at **http://www.w3 .org/pub/WWW/MarkUp/Wilbur/**. They make for dry reading, but you can learn much about the intent behind the language by browsing through them. You can also get a sneak peek at HTML's future by checking out the proposed changes at **http://www.w3.org/pub/WWW/MarkUp/Cougar/**.

Throughout this session, and the rest of the book, I'm going to assume that you're using some kind of HTML editor, whether it's a bare bones tool like Windows Notepad or a sophisticated editor such as Symantec's Visual Page or Claris's Home Page. Because each editor is different, I usually won't talk about how to do things with a specific editor; instead, I'll focus on why you should, or shouldn't, use particular HTML features or tags and trust you to know how to make your editor do your bidding.

ON THE

CD
The CD for this book includes several HTML editors in the IBM\Webtools directory. If you aren't completely happy with the one you're using, check out 1-4-All, Aardvark Pro, Agile, Aspire-X, WebMedia, or any of the others to see whether they better meet your needs.

Most modern editors handle some, or even all, of the bookkeeping needed for producing legal HTML. They take care of things like matching pairs of tags, including all the required HTML sections, and so on. Even with this help, though, it's still useful to know a bit about specific HTML features to make best use of them in your jazzed-up pages. Let's start with a brief overview of the language and then examine specific things you need to know.

Understanding What HTML Is For

HTML is a descendant of a language called SGML, the *Standard Generalized Markup Language.* SGML was designed so that authors and designers could precisely specify the *structure* of a document independently of its content. SGML includes features for defining document types, so that I could write a document type declaration, or DTD, that matches the structure of this book. The DTD provides a computer-readable description of the structure of each document—in this book, each section represents part of a weekend; there are appendices and an index, some sessions have illustrations and figures, and so on.

This might seem an odd approach to take; after all, normally the author of a document controls the content *and* design of a document—the content dictates what design is appropriate. By splitting up the two, SGML and HTML make it easier for the person *reading* the document to control how the document appears, while preserving the author's ability to split up the document into chapters, sections, lists, and so on.

Even with this explanation, you might still be asking why you would want to split up appearance and content. Imagine that you've bought an electronic version of this book for your family. Here are the browsers your family might use:

✿ While at home, you and your spouse use a 17-inch monitor running at 1024×768 in 16-bit color. Most of the time, you leave image loading enabled, but sometimes when you're in a hurry you turn images off.

- While you're using the computer, your kids are using your WebTV box downstairs, with an effective resolution of around 640×480 in 8-bit color: 39% as big as your monitor upstairs.

- You also want to read the book while on the subway, so you put it on your Newton MessagePad 2000. It's a great palmtop, but its screen is only 320×480 with 16 shades of gray—only 19% as big as your desktop.

- Your mom wants to work on a Web page, but her eyesight's failing, so you set her up with a copy of the Lynx text-only browser and a screen reader that converts screen text to speech. Figure 1.2 shows what a page displayed by Lynx looks like.

Each of these display devices has different capabilities: the beautiful full-color illustrations that look so good on your monitor upstairs look funny on the WebTV, huge on the Newton, and invisible on the speech-enabled browser. Furthermore, each of these browsers uses different fonts and sizes for headings, navigation bars, and so on; and the speech-enabled browser can read these elements with differing pitches or even with different voices!

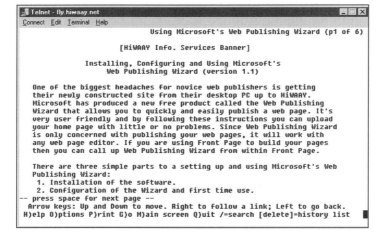

Figure 1.2

Lynx is a text-only browser often used by people at public access terminals and libraries.

Even though HTML may not give you the exact pixel-level control you would get when designing a printed PageMaker, Photoshop, or Word document, you can simulate page layout tools, as you'll see in the Saturday morning session. When designing your pages, though, always bear in mind that not everyone will be using the same kind of browser that you use and that you need to preserve the structure of your pages even as you build in sizzle with the tricks you learn in this book.

FIND IT ON ▶
THE WEB

The University of Wisconsin's TRACE project maintains a terrific page at **http://www.trace.wisc.edu/world/web/**; it explains how to design your pages to make them most accessible to people with visual handicaps.

Browser-Specific Additions to HTML

In the beginning, there was Mosaic. Even though other browsers existed, like Lynx and Cello, most Web page authors stuck with the tags supported by the Windows, Mac, and Unix versions of Mosaic. This was easy because all the different versions of Mosaic supported the same tags, as did many of the non-Mosaic browsers.

When Netscape began to develop its browser software, it took the risky move of supporting new tags that weren't part of the HTML standard. Some, like <CENTER> and <BLINK>, were total Netscapeisms; others, like the <WIDTH> and <HEIGHT> tags for images, were part of the proposed HTML standard but hadn't been formally approved. These new tags made it possible to design pages that looked great with Netscape but odd with Mosaic; however, Netscape viewed its proprietary tags as a competitive weapon.

Enter Microsoft. As is Microsoft's habit, it added its *own* set of proprietary tags in Internet Explorer. To further muddy the waters, some of the tags Microsoft added were Netscape's; others were Microsoft-only. Authors were stuck with the task of trying to figure out which extensions to use on which pages. As the browser market has settled, most PC and Mac users have settled on either Netscape or Microsoft browsers. As mentioned earlier, though, many other browser types are out there. Some support the Netscape and Microsoft extensions; some don't.

Netscape HTML Extensions

Early versions of Navigator started the trend towards browser-specific extensions. Netscape was the first vendor to support HTML tables (even though its initial tags didn't match the proposed standard for table layout), and it has been aggressive about adding support for proposed HTML standard features.

Navigator 3.0 added support for HTML frames, embedded Java applets (programs that run in a Web page; you'll see them again in Sunday morning's session), the tags required for embedding JavaScripts (other small programs that run on Web pages; they do things like change the color of text when your mouse moves over an image) in Web pages, and tags for increasing or decreasing the font size used to display text.

To that list, Navigator 4.0 adds support for the *Cascading Style Sheet* (CSS) specification. CSS allows designers to use style sheets to apply a consistent format to their pages. In addition, CSS styles provide more precise control over the position, appearance, and behavior of items on a page. CSS is a powerful design tool, but it's beyond the scope of this book. In addition, it adds two new tags, <LAYER> and <ILAYER>, for dividing page contents into layers that can be independently hidden, moved, or changed under control of JavaScripts.

Microsoft HTML Extensions

Microsoft had an advantage in the HTML extension war. Because Netscape had already proposed many of its 2.0 and 3.0 extensions as HTML standards, Microsoft could—and did—incorporate the most popular Netscape extensions into Internet Explorer 3.0. In addition to tags for supporting JavaScript, Java, frames, and font size changes, Microsoft upped the ante by adding its own new tags for playing background music on a page, marquees that automatically scroll text from left to right, and tags for specifying which fonts were used to display a page, among others.

Microsoft also improved on some of Netscape's original proposals. For example, Microsoft extended the <EMBED> tag to allow embedding of ActiveX controls, made it possible to make frames without ugly borders, and allowed frames to contain ordinary Web pages (these *floating frames* are discussed more in Saturday morning's session on frames).

Microsoft also supports CSS, but the precise list of CSS elements, and how they're interpreted, varies between Netscape Communicator, Internet Explorer 3.0, and Internet Explorer 4.0.

Depending on Browser Behavior

Designing your pages to work well with a single browser has advantages and disadvantages. On the upside, you can take maximum advantage of features like JavaScript, ActiveX, or floating frames to make your pages look dynamite. The downside is that people who aren't using your preferred browser will be stuck with pages that either look funny or don't work properly, if at all.

One alternative is to use a Web server such as NetCloak (for WebSTAR) or Microsoft's IIS, which allows you to serve different pages to different browsers. With this approach, you have some extra work to do because you have to individually maintain several versions of the same page. The benefit is that you can tweak the pages to look great in each individual browser.

A more popular, and overall better, alternative is to avoid extensions implemented in only one browser. Netscape and Microsoft both have promised to be better Internet citizens and work within the HTML standard process to make their tags widely supported; until they deliver, "just say no" is a good watchword. Staying away from vendor-specific extensions makes it easier for you to preview and edit your pages with whatever tools you have available, and it maximizes the number of people who can view your pages without difficulty.

NOTE Of course, if you're using Microsoft FrontPage, Netscape Navigator Gold, or Netscape Composer (among others!), you may find that the editor's putting in browser-specific tags all by itself. You can guard against problems by previewing your pages in more than one browser, as discussed in "Tool Tips" at the end of this session.

What Makes an Effective Web Page?

Basically, this book is about making your Web pages more attractive and effective. An effective Web page gets your message or information across to visitors with a minimum of effort on their part; this means that you have to spend some time up front asking yourself some questions and planning based on the results.

There aren't any wrong answers; these questions are just to get you thinking about your pages and their contents as you design and create them. Don't be afraid to experiment. After all, one constant of Web page design is that page designs evolve and change as the designers become more skilled and as they have new material to put up for display.

NOTE This session requires a lot of thinking and pondering but not much action. All these questions and decisions may seem sort of stifling. Don't be afraid to read ahead and learn some new tricks, and then come back and think about how you can apply your new skills to your pages.

Do I Have Useful Content?

In the early life of the Web, there weren't many pages, but there were many excited, curious surfers. You could take almost anything—pictures of your cat, obscure inside jokes about your college, data from arcane research projects—and slap it on the Web, and people would visit it just for the novelty. For better or worse, most surfers are now much more selective. This newfound pickiness comes from four primary sources:

- The number of Web sites has skyrocketed. With tens of thousands of sites for people to visit, they're not as likely to browse a site they're not interested in.

- The proliferation of fast search engines such as AltaVista (**http://altavista.digital.com**) and Infoseek (**http://www.infoseek.com**) means that even a simple query for "roses" can return thousands of pages that match the query for a surfer to wander through. If your site's not listed, or is listed as item #925 on the list of 11,277 found pages, how many people will find it?

- The "TV-ization" of the Web—large, well-designed, content-rich sites (**http://cnn.com** and **http://www.weather.com** are two well-known examples)—has raised the standard for what makes a site "good."

- As more and more people become familiar with basic HTML, they become more aware of the difference between well-designed sites and those thrown together by beginners.

Supply Interesting Content

This is not to say that you shouldn't build a page unless you can rival *The New York Times* and CNN; rather, you have to decide who your audience is and what content will be useful or interesting to them. For example, if you're building a site detailing your family genealogy, other family history researchers might be interested in your pages—so plan accordingly and include family trees, biographical sketches of famous ancestors, and so on.

Use Links Judiciously

Links make the Web go 'round, and you should use them whenever possible—as long as they make sense! If your pages are about baseball, then use links to other baseball-oriented sites in your text. Links to pages about hockey, gardening, or auto repair likely won't interest your visitors.

Serve Fresh Content

If you're building a site for people interested in growing roses, don't stop with just pictures of your roses; include a list of rose resource links, or maybe a periodically updated list of rose news (What's the 1997 rose of the year? Can lemon juice stop black-spot disease?) to draw people in to your site. Update your site regularly to keep visitors coming back. You don't have to update the site daily, but adding new links or revising material every few weeks gives your site a cared-for look and feel.

Are My Pages Easy to Use?

Some devices are more difficult to use than others. For example, a toaster is pretty simple: put in bread, press lever, wait for toast. A washing machine is a little more complicated, as is a blender. Eventually, as you move up the complexity scale, you reach VCRs, computers, and so on.

Web pages can be easy or difficult to use too. A well-designed Web page gives you cues to tell you where you are in relation to the rest of the site, as well as making it easy to figure out how to get where you want to go. Figure 1.3 shows an example of a site that's hard to navigate, whereas the Web page in Figure 1.4 makes it clear what other pages you can jump to from the current page. Here are some tips to guide you in making your pages easy to use.

Use Chunks

You may have heard the famous factoid that humans can deal with a maximum of seven to nine items at a time. These groups are called chunks. Chunks are why local phone numbers are seven digits, and they also explain why most states use six- or seven-digit license plates—longer ones are too hard to remember. If your page presents more than about seven items at a time, that's too many; users can't hold all of them in their minds at once.

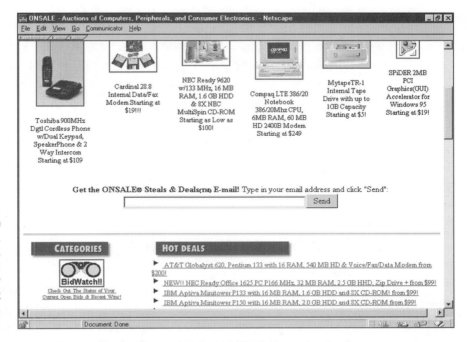

Figure 1.3

Navigating this Web page is confusing; there are too many things to click and not enough consistency.

Figure 1.4

This site clearly shows where you are and provides an easy way to jump to other areas.

Be Consistent

When talking about your home page, call it whatever you want—but don't call it a home page on one link and an index on another! Remember that not everyone uses the same words you do; try always to use the same word to refer to a particular part of your site.

Use Consistent Graphics

If you're going to use icons on your pages, repeat them where necessary. This repetition makes it easy for visitors to recognize the connections between the link they clicked and the page they got.

Offer Navigational Aids

Navigating an unfamiliar Web site can be tricky. Easy-to-use sites offer a bar, like the one at the top of Figure 1.5, that you can use to quickly jump

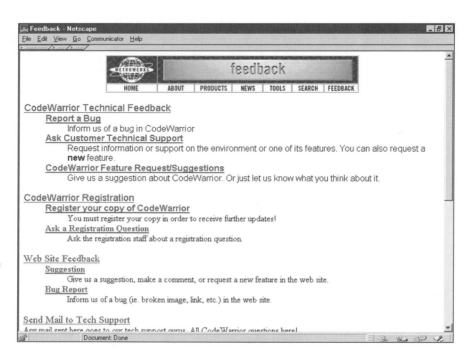

Figure 1.5

The navigation bar for this site offers an easy way to jump to other pages.

to other parts of the site. Your bar can be a simple text-based bar, an exotic set of icons, or anything in between; it can be horizontal or vertical.

You should also consider adding some way to show visitors where they are on your site. This can be as simple as a line of text that says "Page 1 of 5," or it can be a compact graphic. In addition, you can use text highlights, like the ones shown in Figure 1.6; Figure 1.4 shows yet another presentation—the page contents appear in the text box above the navigation bar.

In Sunday morning's session, I'll show you how to build a good navigation bar; for now, just think about what kind would make sense for your site.

Help Visitors Search Your Site

If you have a very simple site, people won't have any trouble finding the information they're looking for. After you get past a few pages, though,

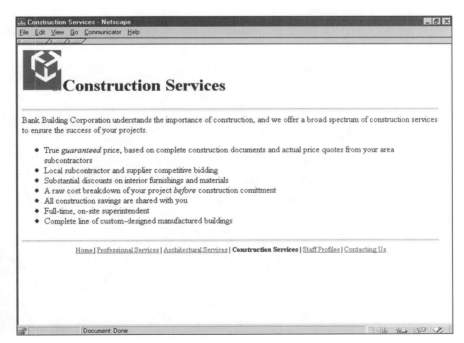

Figure 1.6

The bold text in the navigation bar indicates that you're already on that page.

visitors will benefit from having a way to quickly scan your site to find what they're looking for.

One way to do this is to build search engine support into your site, which we'll do on Sunday morning. Another is to use a search engine on your site, but this usually requires help from your Internet service provider. A third alternative is to provide an index or catalog page that lists all the pages on your site. Books like this have indexes for a good reason: they're the fastest way to find something when you know what you're looking for.

Another example: if you've ever used a Rand-McNally road atlas, you know that in the back is an alphabetical list of all the counties, cities, and towns in the U.S. If you want to find Limestone County, or Houma, or even Hell, the index will tell you where they are (Alabama, Louisiana, and Michigan, respectively). In the same vein, an index page like the one shown in Figure 1.7 can help visitors zero in on what they're looking for

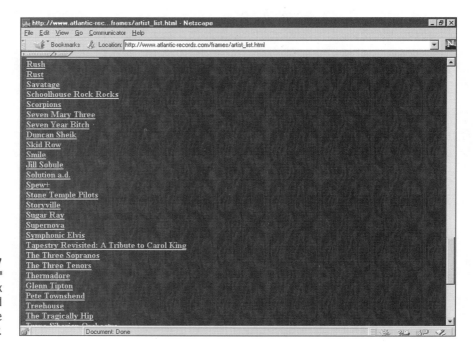

Figure 1.7

An A-to-Z index helps visitors find what they're looking for.

without a lot of aimless clicking. (Of course, you have to put a link to your index somewhere that visitors can easily find it!)

Is My Design Attractive?

Beauty is in the eye of the beholder, even on the Web. As with any other visual medium, the way you color and arrange your work affects how people will view it. Unfortunately, HTML doesn't yet give you the same degree of control that graphic artists, painters, or sculptors enjoy, but you can achieve a lot with the available tools if you're careful.

Don't worry if you feel like your artistic skills maxed out with finger-painting in kindergarten; even without being a Certified Artiste, you can still make pages that look good and work well.

Are My Colors Reasonable?

Navigator and Internet Explorer both give you control over what colors appear on your pages' backgrounds and links. In addition, you can use any colors you want in the images on your pages. However, some pitfalls may make your pages hard to read or funny looking on visitors' computers:

- *Some color combinations are just plain hard to read.* Human eyes need to sense contrast to distinguish letter shapes; when there's little contrast between text and background (say, yellow text on a white background) it's difficult for your eyes to make out the fine details needed for reading.

- *Some computers can display more colors than others.* On computers set to display 256 colors at a time—still the most common setting— the browser only has about 216 colors to choose from; the remaining colors are reserved for the system to draw its windows, icons, and desktop. This range has to cover the gamut of colors you use on your pages and images. If you create your pages and images with 16-bit color, you can easily create combinations that take more than 216 colors to show, so the visitor's browser will have to fake colors to keep up—resulting in unsightly splotches and patches.

✿ *The contrast settings on the visitor's display might be different from yours.* A page that looks just right on your screen might be too dark or too light on theirs. In particular, some laptop screens have a limited contrast range.

There aren't any hard-and-fast rules for color selection; the theme of your site might dictate the use of particular colors, or you might just choose some colors you like and use them. What's important is that your colors shouldn't distract visitors or make it hard for them to read what you have to say.

Are My Pages Overstuffed?

If you've ever seen footage of people boarding a Tokyo subway, you know how a good idea (mass transportation, in this case) can be carried to an extreme. So it is with Web pages—except that you won't have any *eki-jin*, the people who stand on the platform and help passengers stuff themselves into the cars!

Reading long passages of text on the computer can be an eye-straining experience, even if you have a large, clear monitor and a well-lit reading area. Scrolling a long page requires the visitor to take her attention away from what she's reading and focus it on the PgDn key or the scrollbar.

Instead of presenting long, monotonous flows of text, break them up into several smaller pages, with "next page" and "previous page" links at the bottom of each page. How do you know when to split pages? Because you never know how tall the reader's browser window is, you can't easily tell the "right" amount of text to put on a page. You can use your own monitor as a guide, though (unless you have a monster 27-inch). As a general rule, any page that takes up more than about two screens' worth of your monitor is worth splitting.

There's another kind of overstuffing, too—see the page shown in Figure 1.8 for an example. Pages like this just offer a visitor too many choices

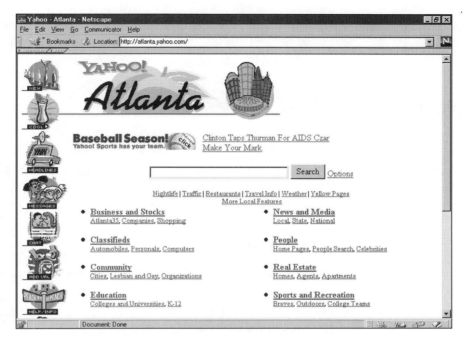

Figure 1.8

This page has lots and lots of icons, hotspots, and things to click on; it's a bit overwhelming.

in one bundle. It should always be easy for a reader to figure out where she can go from a particular page; if you festoon your pages with all kinds of gadgets and links, the result might be that your message gets lost in the noise.

Making Your Web Pages Effective

Now that you know some techniques and questions for deciding how effective your pages are, it's time to apply the answers and make your pages more effective. You can accomplish this by making three sets of decisions about what you're trying to do. The results of these decisions will guide you in focusing the content and design of your site on the people you want to stop by and visit.

Each set of answers can be phrased with "I want. . . ." Although this may seem terribly selfish, it helps you to set a visible goal; feel free to reword your goals in whatever way you find most motivating.

Decide Who Your Pages Are For

The first, and often hardest, decision is to figure out who your site is for: who do you hope will come by to visit? Your answer might be very narrow: "I want visitors who are interested in the value of different pieces of 19th century antique American glass." Or it might be broad: "I want visitors who like flowers."

Who's Visiting?

You might not have a well-defined target audience in mind when you start on your site. Of course, your site may seem like it wouldn't appeal to any group in particular. Perhaps you're putting up a family home page with subpages for each family member's interests. In this case, your audience is people interested in your family!

Of course, if you're setting up pages for a business, hobby, or nonprofit organization, your audience will be people involved in, or interested in, whatever the site's about. The more specific you can be, the better you'll be able to answer the remaining questions in this section. Here are some example statements that might help you get started:

✪ "I want visitors who are interested in the city soccer league schedule for this summer."

✪ "I want visitors who want to know more about growing hybrid tea roses."

✪ "I want visitors who are professional engineers interested in taking continuing education classes."

✪ "I want visitors who need information about programs for helping victims of domestic abuse."

Why Are They Visiting?

You probably want people to visit your site because they're interested in whatever it's about—not just because they're bored or end up there accidentally. If you can think of specific reasons why someone might visit your site, write them down too.

Random browsing is one of the things that makes the Web so cool, so not everyone who reaches your page may be searching for a particular fact. In general, though, visitors go places looking for information. You still have to decide *what* they'll be looking for. If you can, combine your knowledge (or intuition) about what visitors want to know with the "I want visitors who . . ." from the previous section—that way, you can sum up who's coming and what they're looking for in one convenient form. Your statement becomes "I want visitors who are *whatever* and are looking for *whatever*."

Decide What Content to Include

Now that you know who's visiting and why, the next step is simple: decide what content you want to offer. Your content should be attractive to your target audience, and it should fit into the bandwidth you and your visitors have available. It's not important to decide *how* you'll present your information yet; instead, concentrate on figuring out what you want to share with the world. The more specific you can be, the better.

What Do You Have to Say for Yourself?

If you've made it this far, you must have some idea of what you want to put on your pages. Try phrasing this decision with "I can offer . . ."; this phrasing helps you concentrate on what kind of material you want your pages to show, and it gives you a way to tie your audience and content together. Here are some examples:

- "I can offer detailed statistics for the local minor league baseball team."

⚙ "I can offer portions of the history of the 5th Marine Regiment's campaigns in the Korean War."

⚙ "I can offer cartoons I drew for our garden club's newsletter."

⚙ "I can offer a list of other sites and pages with information about low-fat cooking."

How Much Bandwidth Do Visitors Have?

Unless you take a survey (and maybe not even then!), there's no way for you to know how much bandwidth each individual surfer who comes to your pages has. However, you can make a decision about how much bandwidth you're going to require them to have.

This means that if you design a site with many big, heavy graphics, you'll probably turn off some visitors who have slow modem links. This may be unavoidable. If your site is dedicated to pictures of World War II aircraft nose art, you're going to have large images. By contrast, if your site's targeted at high-school students, America Online users, or others who you know will have slow links, try to keep them in mind as you decide how many images, graphics, animations, and video or sound clips you put on your pages.

How Much Bandwidth Do You Have?

Bandwidth is a two-way street. It doesn't matter how much bandwidth your visitors have if your content is stuck on a slow server or behind a slow link to the Internet. Your Internet service provider should be able to tell you how fast its Internet link is; from your own testing, you can gain a feel for how fast the server you're using is.

NOTE Some service providers charge for Web site service according to how much bandwidth you use! If you're using such a provider, make sure that you can get a trial period to see how much bandwidth your site's going to use. If you have big pages or many visitors, bandwidth-based pricing can bring a nasty surprise when the bill arrives.

Decide on an Attractive Layout

After you've determined who's going to visit your pages and what information you're going to present, it's time to think about how you'll actually lay out the pages. (You'll start learning *how* to lay them out in Saturday morning's session.) It's often helpful to sit down and sketch out some rough layouts with pencil and paper or your favorite drawing software. This can help you get a concrete idea of what your designs will look like.

One source for good layouts is other Web page authors. If you see a page whose design you find particularly pleasing, send the author some e-mail and ask her why she designed the page as she did. You may get some valuable advice or even specific suggestions that you can use in your own project.

The design you choose will end up being a matter of personal preference—after all, the pages are yours to design and should reflect what *you* think they should look like. If you ask yourself the questions listed earlier in "What Makes an Effective Web Page?," let the answers guide you to a design that you like.

Finally, let me close this section by offering an encouragement: feel free to experiment with your layout and design. No one, not even an experienced designer, produces perfect pages the first time—so don't be afraid to refine, tweak, and edit your pages until you're truly satisfied with their appearance.

Tool Tips

Even though I promised this would be a mostly theoretical session, now I get to sneak some technical tool tips in here at the end. Each session in the rest of the book will close with a set of tips for getting the most out of whatever tools you use. Even though we didn't *use* any tools tonight, there are still some tips you can follow to take best advantage of the tools you use later.

Use Several Browsers to Preview Your Work

If you read the previous discussion about HTML's intended use as a document structuring language, you'll probably remember the suggestion that you should look at your pages with more than one browser to make sure that nothing looks out of place. For example, the same site can appear quite differently in three differently configured browsers (see Figure 1.9, Figure 1.10, and Figure 1.11 to see exactly what I mean.)

Most users will stick with a single browser after they find one that meets their needs and can comfortably run on their systems. Even if you have a strong preference for one browser or another, the time it takes to review

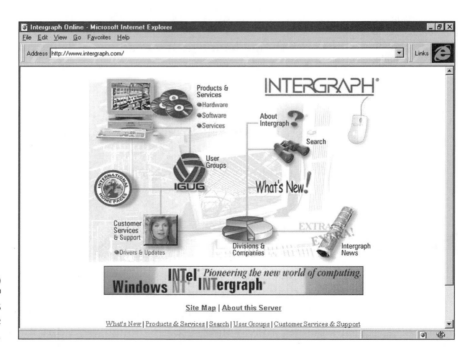

Figure 1.9

This page looks terrific when image loading is enabled.

Figure 1.10

The same site with image loading off; it's a little harder to figure out how to navigate.

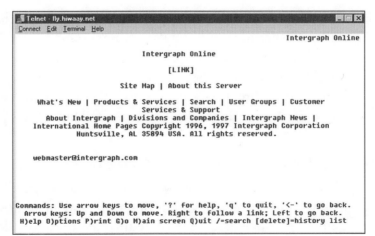

Figure 1.11

Finally, the same site when viewed with a text-only browser; it's still usable thanks to careful design.

your pages in other browsers—which your audience may actually prefer—is time well spent.

FIND IT ON ▶ BrowserWatch, at **http://browserwatch.iworld.com**, is a great place to keep track of
THE WEB the latest changes in the browser wars.

Get a Good Image Editor

Earlier in this session, I brushed off the question of HTML editors by
assuming that you'll be using one but leaving the details of exactly how it
works to you. The same is true for image editors; there are many good
ones, ranging from expensive professional tools such as Adobe Photoshop
and HSC's DeBabelizer to inexpensive but polished shareware tools such
as Thorsten Lemke's GraphicConverter and JASC's PaintShop Pro.

ON THE

CD

The CD includes a crop of image editing tools, including Animagic (you'll see it again in
Saturday evening's session), LiquidFX, WebPainter, and WebImage for Windows, plus
GIFmation, PhotoGIF, and the truly cool LightningDraw/Web for the Mac.

The one you choose is up to you; choose the one that best matches your
skills, background, and budget. It's important to *have* an image editor,
though, because image size and composition have such a strong influence
on the appearance and download time of your pages. Don't worry,
though; in Saturday evening's session, I'll talk about the specialized tools
you can use to create animated images and video clips.

Pick a Volunteer from the Audience

Writing books, designing Web pages, or any other creative endeavor
involves two parties: an author or creator and an audience. Don't underestimate the practical value of getting advice, feedback, and comments
from your audience.

As I wrote this book, I frequently showed draft versions of sessions to
people I thought would be interested in learning how to jazz up their

pages. By doing this, I got valuable feedback on what I had written, and I knew how to adjust it to make it more useful for my target audience.

You can do the same with your Web pages. No matter who your target audience is, you can find people who fit into it and who can tell you what's right—and wrong—with your pages. In fact, when you put pages on the Web, you're likely to get comments from visitors anyway, so why not start early and get some input as you get started?

Wrap It Up!

You should now have a working knowledge of the basic concepts behind designing attractive, effective Web pages. Professional site designers use these concepts, and others, every time they build a new site; now you can too!

In the next session, you'll learn how to start using HTML tables to lay out your pages with precision and finesse. In the meantime, get a good night's sleep!

Designing Pages with Tables

- ✿ All About HTML Tables
- ✿ Designing Pages with Tables
- ✿ A Table Layout Sampler

In Friday evening's session, you learned how to think about your design and content. Now it's time to plunge in and get started! This session will teach you all about HTML tables. If you're used to thinking about tables as things you use to hold food or as the backbone of spreadsheet programs, you're in for a pleasant surprise. HTML tables are extremely versatile, and you can use them to give your pages exactly the look you want.

All About HTML Tables

Tables have been in the HTML language standard for a long time, but they really started to take off after Netscape implemented them in its original browser. Netscape's achievement spurred NCSA to include table support in its Mosaic browser, which provided the original core for Microsoft's Internet Explorer. At first, not all browsers supported the same table tags; as time has passed, Netscape, Microsoft, and the HTML standard are more or less in agreement on how tables should be built and how the browser should display them.

Printers have been using tables for hundreds of years—a lot longer than Web designers—so there are already many specialized terms for talking about how tables are built and how they look on the page. Many of these special words apply to HTML tables, too; so let's start off with a quick vocabulary session. You can use Figure 2.1 as a visual guide when you read the following sections.

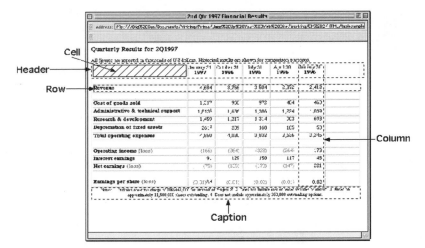

Figure 2.1

Some parts
of a table have
special names.

If you're used to using tables in a word processor or spreadsheet, you already understand the basic concept: a table is a group of items arranged in a rectangle. Each item lives in its own *cell*, not unlike federal prisoners. These cells are arranged in *rows* and *columns*. Columns are vertical, and rows are horizontal. People often describe tables by the number of rows and columns they have, rows first. When someone tells you a tic-tac-toe board is a "3×3 table," they're telling you that it has three rows and three columns.

The *header* of a table is its topmost row. For example, in an Excel spreadsheet, the labels at the top of each column (A, B, and so on) make up the spreadsheet's header. HTML has special tags for designating header cells.

Individual cells can *span*, or stretch, to cover more than one row or column. (You may also hear spans called *straddles*.) Spans are useful when you have an image or text that applies or belongs to more than one adjacent item.

Gutter isn't just where your bowling ball goes; it's also the white space between table columns. Adjusting the amount of gutter in a table lets you emphasize how the table's contents are organized; you can also use a single HTML table with the right gutter size to simulate two adjacent tables.

Tables can also have labels to tell you what's in them. These *captions* can ride above or below the table, and you can apply whatever font, size, style, and alignment you want the caption text to have.

Why Tables Are Important

If you ask any working Web site designer about the most useful tool in her toolbox, you're likely to hear "tables" as the answer. Why? Because tables are so versatile. They can display information in conventional tables, like you might see in a company's annual report (see Figure 2.2 for an example), but they can also be used to lay out complicated pages using some of the same page layout features that graphic artists and designers depend on. Figure 2.3 shows the web edition of *InfoWorld*, a paper publication that's successfully moved its print edition's look and design to the Web.

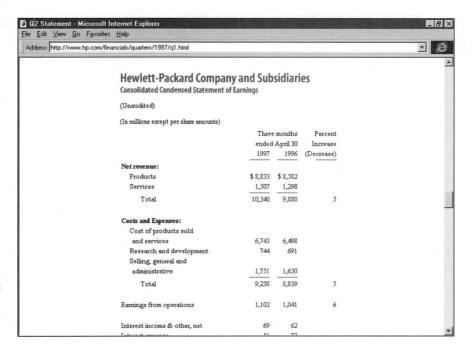

Figure 2.2

Tables can display ordinary tabular data.

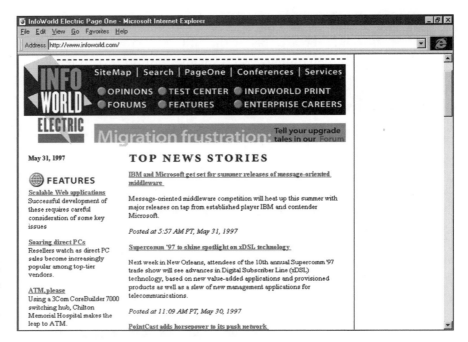

Figure 2.3

You can use tables to control where elements go on a page.

Tables get their flexibility from some key features. First, you can set table widths and heights yourself, or you can leave them up to the browser, which can adjust them to make the table fit properly in the browser window, no matter what size it is. In addition, each element within the table can have its own horizontal and vertical alignment, and a single cell can expand to cover more than one horizontal or vertical space on the table.

As an added capability, tables can act like the famous nesting *matroshyka* dolls from Russia, where you only see the outermost doll until you open it up and delve into its contents. In the same vein, table cells can contain any other kind of HTML content. The combination of tables' flexibility and the capability to put anything you want into a cell gives you a powerful way to design your pages so that they look like you want them to. In fact, in later sessions you'll learn how to use forms, graphics, and multimedia content together with tables to give you maximum layout power.

CAUTION   ◆

Using tables for page layout makes it difficult for non-graphic browsers to display anything intelligible. Text-only browsers and browsers that read pages to visually impaired
users may not pay attention to your table data, so be forewarned.

◆ ◆

How Tables Work

Tables are made up of ordinary HTML, so they arrive at your browser in
the ordinary way. After the browser has finished loading the page, it scans
the table definition to see how many rows and columns are in the table.
Along the way, it remembers any width or height settings you've applied
to individual cells. If any cells contain tables themselves, the browser will
scan them too.

The browser's goal is to figure out how big each cell in the table needs to
be so that it can decide how to display the table. After it calculates the size
of each cell, it starts drawing each cell's contents. If any cell contains
images, plug-in data, Java applets, or other non-text content, the browser will fetch the content and keep on drawing the remaining cells while
it waits for the needed data to arrive.

Finally, after all the cell contents are drawn, the browser will apply any
background colors or images that you've specified for individual cells,
entire tables, or the page itself. The page will then be completely drawn
and ready for the visitor's use. (Of course, many visitors will see what
they're looking for and move on before the page has completely loaded,
so not everyone will see the finalized version.)

How Tables Are Defined

NOTE   •

Throughout this section, I'll show examples of tables along with the HTML that generated them. In figures, I'll turn the table borders on so that you can see where the tables
are. Normally, you'll leave borders off because they can spoil the look of your creations.

• •

Tables use some fairly simple HTML tags; the trick to using them is knowing what attributes each tag can handle, and how to combine the tags to get the effect you're looking for. Most of the time, you'll be using an HTML editor to build tables for you; it's still important to know how table tags work so that you can see—and change—their output.

ON THE

CD

Claris Home Page is a solid visual HTML editor. Its table editor is particularly good; it's easy to use and has intuitive controls for building complex tables. A 60-day trial version is included on the CD.

Building Tables

The `<TABLE>` tag is the foundation of all tables. It's a container, so you'll always enclose your table content in a `<TABLE>` . . . `</TABLE>` pair. When you create a table, you can specify a number of settings that govern what the table looks like:

- ✪ The `ALIGN` parameter controls how the table is aligned with the left and right edges of the browser window. You can align a table to the left, right, or center of the page by using `ALIGN="LEFT"`, `ALIGN="RIGHT"`, or `ALIGN="CENTER"`, respectively. The default is to place the table along the left margin of the page.

- ✪ The `WIDTH` parameter can specify the table's width in two ways: as a percentage of the total area (`WIDTH="80%"` will make the table 80% as wide as the browser window), or as a fixed number of pixels (`WIDTH="512"` will make the table 512 pixels wide, no matter how wide the window is). If you don't include a `WIDTH` attribute, the browser will make the table as wide as necessary to display all its contents.

- ✪ Unless you say otherwise, browsers won't display a border around the table or its cells. Many table editors, though, will turn on the border unless you override their setting. If you want a border, use the `BORDER` attribute to specify a width in pixels.

After you build a table, the browser won't display anything until you put some rows and columns into it so let's see how you can do that.

Building Table Rows and Columns

Every table has to have at least one row and one column. A 1×1 table would only have a single cell, so it might not be very useful—but it would be legal HTML! Before we go any further, it's time for me to confess: throughout this session, I've been talking about rows and columns, but HTML only knows about rows and *cells*. Each row in your table has to have at least one cell in it, but not all rows will have the same number of cells. When I talk about a column, I mean all the cells, from top to bottom, aligned in a single vertical section of the table; an individual cell still stands on its own.

Because of the way browsers interpret table tags, you have to start your table by defining a row. The <TR> container (*TR* stands for "table row") creates a row with no cells in it.

For each row, you can specify the horizontal and vertical alignment to use for all columns in the row. These alignment settings control how each column's data is aligned, but individual cells in the row can use their own alignment settings, which override the row's alignment.

⚙ The ALIGN attribute controls the horizontal alignment; as with the <TABLE> tag, you can use the LEFT, RIGHT, or CENTER keywords to control where the row goes in relation to the table itself.

⚙ The VALIGN attribute controls the row's vertical position. VALIGN="TOP" (the default) forces cell contents to "stick" to the top of the cell; VALIGN="MIDDLE" centers cell contents vertically, and VALIGN="BOTTOM" makes the contents stick to the bottom edge of the cell.

TIP ALIGN and VALIGN apply to more than just rows—you can use them with table cells, images, forms, and plain paragraphs. You'll see them used again in later sessions.

You can use both ALIGN and VALIGN in a row definition to position its cells' contents exactly where you want them while still keeping the flexibility of being able to set special alignments for cells that need them.

Inside a row, you should create a cell for each column you want to use *in that row.* To do this, you use the <TD> tag (which stands for "table data"), which creates a single cell. The cell's contents determine what the browser will display in the cell, and its attributes determine how the content is aligned and positioned.

You'll usually have the same number of cells in each row (though you won't if you're using spans, as discussed a bit later). If you accidentally add extra cells, or leave some out, in one row, how the table looks is up to the browser. Some browsers will add or remove space to all rows, whereas others will display funny-looking "blank cells" in some rows. (See "The Gray Blotch Disease Trap" later in the session to learn how to handle this problem.)

Almost any HTML is legal in a cell; you can use text, hyperlinks, images, or form elements like text fields and buttons. In fact, many of the most useful applications of tables require you to mix several types of HTML tags within a single table—but more on that later.

Remember my earlier mention of headers? As an alternative to <TD>, you can designate header cells with <TH> instead of <TD>. Some browsers will mark the difference by using different fonts, styles, or even voices to display or read the header cells, whereas others treat header cells just like every other cell.

NOTE   It's perfectly legal to use the <TR> or <TD> tags without their end tags. Some browsers get confused when the end tags are missing, though; so I recommend using them— they also help you pick out where one row ends and the next begins.

Specifying Cell Width and Height

When you build a page, you don't know how big the visitor's browser window will be, so it's hard to tell how big to make individual cells. Ordi-

narily, the browser will size each cell according to how much space its content needs; you might sometimes need to override this automatic sizing by giving cells an explicit width, height, or both.

The WIDTH and HEIGHT attributes let you specify a cell's size, in pixels or percent. You can use them together, or not, depending on which dimensions are important to you. They're useful for building cells that are exactly the same size as images that fit inside the cells; for example,

```
<TD WIDTH="180" HEIGHT="32"><IMG SRC="http://www.ljl.com/graphics/
    ➥welcome.gif"
    ALT="Welcome" WIDTH="180" HEIGHT="32"></TD>
```

creates a cell that is just big enough for the welcome.gif image, and no bigger. This effect is handy when building tables of images, which you might do when building a toolbar or image mosaic.

If you accidentally give your cells widths that add up to more than 100% of the table width, the browser might ignore your cell widths so that it can fit all the cells in the allotted space, or it might ignore your table width and make the table wide enough to hold all the cells

WIDTH and HEIGHT can be used with other HTML elements, too, including images— you'll see them again in future sessions.

Making Cells Span Rows and Columns

Sometimes you want one cell to flow across adjacent rows or columns. For example, you might want a graphic to stretch across the full width of a table, or you might want to label several rows together These *spans* are easy to do with conventional desktop publishing software, and HTML includes a way for you to use spans in your Web page tables. Figure 2.4 shows a table of financial results that uses row and column spans to group categories of data together. This type of grouping is common in printed tables, and it can be of great use to your Web pages too.

Any cell can span any number of rows or columns. In fact, a single cell can span both rows and columns if you need it to! You specify spans with the ROWSPAN and COLSPAN attributes, which attach to the <TD> tag. The topmost row of the table in Figure 2.4 has six cells, but two of them—"Operating Expenses" and "Earnings"—span multiple columns (also notice that these two cells are defined with <TH> for those browsers that distinguish between <TH> and <TD>). Other rows have 11 cells total, but without the spans each of those cells is individually accessible. The HTML for the row looks like this:

```
<TR>
<TD WIDTH="2%"> </TD>
    <TD WIDTH="17%"> </TD>
    <TH VALIGN="TOP" COLSPAN="4" BGCOLOR="#CC9900">Operating
    ➥Expenses</TH>
    <TD WIDTH="16%"> </TD>
    <TH COLSPAN="3" BGCOLOR="#CC9900">Earnings</TH>
    <TD WIDTH="58%"> </TD>
</TR>
```

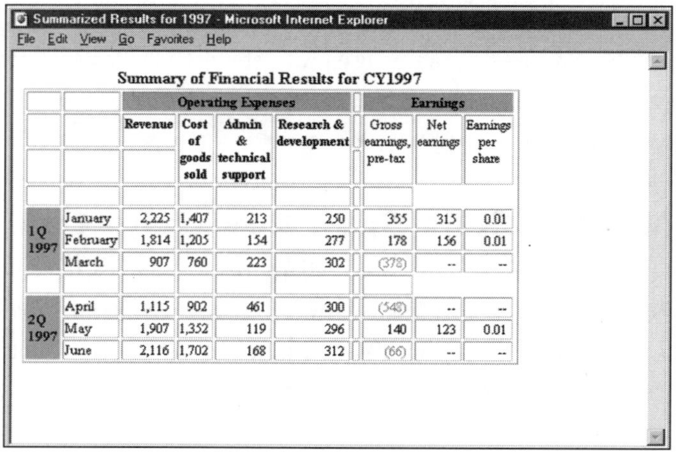

Figure 2.4

This table uses column and row spans to group related items.

Summary of Financial Results for CY1997

| | | Operating Expenses | | | | | Earnings | | |
		Revenue	Cost of goods sold	Admin & technical support	Research & development		Gross earnings, pre-tax	Net earnings	Earnings per share
1Q 1997	January	2,225	1,407	213	250		355	315	0.01
	February	1,814	1,205	154	277		178	156	0.01
	March	907	760	223	302		(378)	--	--
2Q 1997	April	1,115	902	461	300		(548)	--	--
	May	1,907	1,352	119	296		140	123	0.01
	June	2,116	1,702	168	312		(66)	--	--

Spans start from the cell they're defined in. This means that if you add COLSPAN=3 to the second cell in a row, its span will take up columns 2, 3, and 4. If you want it to span "backwards" into column 1, you'll have to move column 2's contents into column 1.

Coloring Cells and Tables

Graphic designers often use color to add emphasis to a paper document, and you can do the same with your tables. You can select colors for an entire table or individual cells—or both! The colors you put on individual cells override any colors you've applied to the entire table; in general, cell settings usually override table settings.

You specify the background color of tables and cells the same way: with the BGCOLOR attribute, which takes as its argument a string that indicates the color values to use. The string specifies individual values from 0-255 for the amount of red, green, and blue in the color. To complicate things, though, the 0-255 values are written in *hexidecimal*, a special numbering system used by programmers (and now Web designers). It uses the digits 0-9 and the letters A-F to represent values from zero to 16.

These so-called *RGB colors* are always preceded by a # character, so that the browser knows what it is. As a simple example, #000000 is black: it has no red, green, or blue. #FFFFFF is white: it has the maximum possible red, green, and blue values. #FF0000 is pure red, #00FF00 is pure green, and #0000FF is pure blue.

RGB colors can be confusing until you're used to them. The section titled "Setting Colors" in Appendix B has a number of useful places where you can learn, and practice, as much as you need to feel comfortable.

In most cases, you'll choose the background color from a color picker; so you don't need to memorize the codes, but you do need to recognize them when you see them because the BGCOLOR attribute uses these RGB colors. For example, to make your table a pleasing shade of purple, try this:

```
<TABLE BORDER="0" CELLSPACING="0" WIDTH="100%" BGCOLOR="#CC33CC">
```

You can use BGCOLOR with tables and cells, and you can freely combine the two.

If you want to experiment with more coloring effects, you can also control the color of table borders with the BORDERCOLOR attribute. Normally the borders will be gray, if they appear at all—you'll have to use BORDER=1 or bigger to get a border, then BORDERCOLOR= to set the color, like this:

```
<TABLE BORDER="0" CELLSPACING="0" BGCOLOR="#CC33CC"
    ➥BORDERCOLOR="#FFFFFF">
```

Controlling Cell Padding and Spacing

After you have a table full of data, you can still tweak how much space the table takes up by adjusting the *cell padding* and *cell spacing* used to draw the table. Although they may sound like the same thing—filler space—they're not; but they are confusingly similar.

Let's start with cell padding. It is just what its name says: extra padding between the cell's contents and its border. This padding is applied equally to all cells, regardless of whether they have spans. Its effect is to add some extra white space between the cell and its enclosing border, even when the border is not displayed. You apply padding with the <TABLE> tag's CELLPADDING attribute; there's no way to put padding onto an individual cell. The value of CELLPADDING is the number of pixels worth of padding that the browser should apply.

Cell spacing is another holdover from the world of paper documents. Normally, when you have a printed table (or even a table in spreadsheet form, like in Excel or Mesa), two adjacent cells have a single, shared border. There's no way to have different settings for that border; both cells have to share it as it is.

HTML tables support the concept of per-cell borders, and cell spacing is a result of that support. Each cell can specify how much space to leave between the cell's contents and its border. Because the distance between cells is fixed by the size of the cell contents, changing the cell spacing actually changes the amount of blank space between the cells. This has the effect of making the browser-supplied cell border get "puffier" (if the

table has a border) or of making the cells float farther apart. You specify cell spacing in pixels with the <TABLE> tag's CELLSPACING attribute.

If you still find padding and spacing confusing, check out Figure 2.5, which shows the same table with a variety of padding and spacing combinations. You can see how each combination affects not only the cell data but the cells' interrelationships—*and* how much space the table takes up on-screen.

Displaying Table Captions

When you see a table on paper, it's common to also see an accompanying caption that tells you what's in the table. In fact, the tables in this book all have captions! You can achieve the same effect in two ways. The first, and easiest, way is to use the <CAPTION> container as part of your table definition. Whatever HTML you put between the <CAPTION> tags will be displayed at the top or bottom of your table. You control where the caption goes with the ALIGN="TOP" and ALIGN="BOTTOM" parameters; by default, captions will go on top of the table. The browser will create an extra table cell, at the top or bottom, that spans the full width of the table,

```
┌──────────────────────────────────────────────────────────────────────────────────┐
│ □                                  Padding & Spacing                          回回 │
├──────────────────────────────────────────────────────────────────────────────────┤
│ Address: │ file:///Big%200un/Documents/Writing/Prima/Jazz%20Up%20Your%20Web%20Site/Submitted/Ch%202/HTML/padspace.html │
│                                                                                    │
│   ┌─────────┬─────────┬─────────┐      This table has CELLPADDING                  │
│   │ Cell 1  │ Cell 2  │ Cell 3  │      and CELLSPACING both set to                 │
│   │ Cell 4  │ Cell 5  │ Cell 6  │      0. Each cell's text butts up                │
│   │ Cell 7  │ Cell 8  │ Cell 9  │      against the cell's borders.                 │
│   └─────────┴─────────┴─────────┘                                                  │
│                                        This table has CELLPADDING=2                 │
│                                        and CELLSPACING=0.Notice                     │
│   ┌─────────┬─────────┬─────────┐      how the cells' vertical size                │
│   │ Cell 1  │ Cell 2  │ Cell 3  │      has changed to                              │
│   │ Cell 4  │ Cell 5  │ Cell 6  │      accommodate the extra                        │
│   │ Cell 7  │ Cell 8  │ Cell 9  │      padding.                                    │
│   └─────────┴─────────┴─────────┘                                                  │
│                                        This table has CELLPADDING=0                 │
│                                        and CELLSPACING=4.The                        │
│   ┌─────────┬─────────┬─────────┐      borders between cells have                  │
│   │ Cell 1  │ Cell 2  │ Cell 3  │      expanded to absorb the extra                │
│   │ Cell 4  │ Cell 5  │ Cell 6  │      space.                                      │
│   │ Cell 7  │ Cell 8  │ Cell 9  │                                                  │
│   └─────────┴─────────┴─────────┘                                                  │
└──────────────────────────────────────────────────────────────────────────────────┘
```

Figure 2.5

Changing the cell padding and spacing can make the same table look very different.

and it'll put your caption in it. Captions can be images, hyperlinks, or formatted text. You can't use tables or form elements in a caption, though.

Sometimes the ordinary <CAPTION> tag won't help you; for example, if you want to display a caption on the left or right side of a table, you'll have to do it yourself. The good news is that this is easy to do: just create a table cell for the caption and give it a span that covers as many rows as you want to use. Figure 2.4 (shown earlier) shows a complex table that uses captions on the top (built with <CAPTION>) and multiple captions on the left-hand side, each of which spans more than one row.

Picking Apart a Sample Table

Now that you know how tables *can* be put together, let's pick apart an example table to see how it was built. This technique—examining a page that someone else has already created—can teach you more about page design than you could ever learn on your own. In this case, Figure 2.6

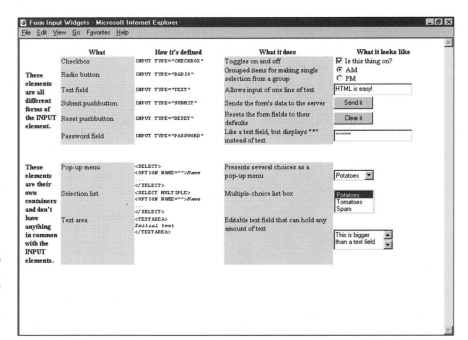

Figure 2.6

This table is the Web equivalent of two paper tables in Saturday morning's session on forms.

shows a Web table that combines material from two tables in this morning's session on Web forms. As you can see, the table mixes text and form elements, and it has some background cell colors to emphasize relationships between items.

ON THE

CD

The actual HTML for this table in all its glory is on the CD in IBM\SatMorn\Tables\ form-widget.html.

The table definition itself is pretty straightforward because the special formatting is all applied at the cell level. The WIDTH="100%" isn't strictly necessary because most browsers will assume that's what I want, but I add it for those that don't.

```
<TABLE BORDER="0" CELLSPACING="0" WIDTH="100%">
...
</TABLE>
```

NOTE

• •

Throughout the book, when I want to show the differences between two pieces of HTML, I'll show the additions in bold, **like this.**

• •

The first row of the table sets out the columns that all following rows will use. There are five columns; the first one is exactly 68 pixels wide, and the others have varying shares of the remaining 100%. Remember, WIDTH specifies how much of the *remaining* width is assigned to an element. In this case, the browser needs to reserve 68 pixels for the first column, and the remaining width—whatever it is—is to be shared according to the percentages I specified:

```
<TABLE BORDER="0" CELLSPACING="0" WIDTH="100%">
    <TR>
        <TH WIDTH="68"> </TH>
        <TH WIDTH="20%">What</TH>
        <TH WIDTH="24%">How it's defined</TH>
        <TH WIDTH="30%">What it does</TH>
        <TH WIDTH="26%">What it looks like</TH>
    </TR>
...
</TABLE>
```

The top row is established, but the second row is where the real action starts. In this row, the first cell spans the next six rows; it serves as a caption to explain what those six rows have in common. In addition, this span cell and two of the remaining cells have background colors specified with the BGCOLOR attribute. The cell widths in the second row are the same as the ones for the first row, and they'll remain the same for the rest of the rows as well.

```
<TABLE BORDER="0" CELLSPACING="0" WIDTH="100%">
    <TR>
        <TH WIDTH="68"> </TH>
        <TH WIDTH="20%">What</TH>
        <TH WIDTH="24%">How it's defined</TH>
        <TH WIDTH="30%">What it does</TH>
        <TH WIDTH="26%">What it looks like</TH>
    </TR>
    <TR>
        <TD WIDTH="68" VALIGN="MIDDLE" ROWSPAN="6"
        ➥BGCOLOR="#FFFFCC">
            <B>These elements are all different forms of the INPUT
            ➥element.</B></TD>
        <TD WIDTH="20%" BGCOLOR="#DDDDDD">Checkbox</TD>
        <TD WIDTH="24%"><FONT SIZE="2"><TT>INPUT TYPE=&quot;
        ➥CHECKBOX&quot;</TT>
            </FONT></TD>
        <TD WIDTH="30%" BGCOLOR="#DDDDDD">Toggles on and off</TD>
        <TD WIDTH="26%"><INPUT TYPE="CHECKBOX" NAME="CheckBox"
        ➥VALUE="CheckBox"
            CHECKED>Is this thing on?</TD>
    </TR>
</TABLE>
```

The remaining rows are all identical in design to one of the two already presented, so I won't cover them individually. You can see them on the CD if you're so inclined.

Designing Pages with Tables

Tables are a fundamental tool for Web page design. Not only do they give you a way to present actual tables of data (as you just learned!), they also

give you tools for getting precise control over where your text and graphics go. How you use tables depends largely on what you're trying to do; this section will show you how to use them to accomplish some common—but impressive-looking—design tricks.

TIP　When you're surfing the Web and see a well-laid-out page, take some time to view its HTML source—chances are excellent you'll find tables at the heart of the page design. You can learn a lot from perusing other people's pages; just be careful to respect their intellectual property.

Laying Out Pages with Tables

I don't know who first discovered that you could use tables to arrange page contents the way you wanted, but we owe whoever it was a debt of thanks. Even though HTML is primarily about information, not presentation, good presentation helps make your information clearer, more persuasive, more attractive, and more accessible to visitors.

Learning the art of graphic design can take years. Professional designers start off in school and then often apprentice themselves to master designers before becoming masters themselves. However, this art is not for everyone; some people, me included, want to design attractive, effective pages without spending years to learn how.

I can't turn you into a master designer in a few paragraphs; however, I can teach you some things to think about when designing your pages with tables. If you apply them when you're thinking about how to lay out your pages, you'll be rewarded with efficient, attractive pages with minimum effort on your part.

Breaking the Page into Horizontal Sections

The Web makes it easy to build pages that run on forever—there aren't any physical page boundaries like there are in books, and it's difficult to judge how big a page will be on your visitors' computers anyway. One way to resist the temptation is to build your pages by splitting them up into horizontal sections. Each section can contain text, graphics, or white space. By varying the number of sections, and their width, you can control the orientation and flow of your page contents.

I typically split up pages into three horizontal sections, as shown in Figure 2.7. You can think of these sections like layers in a wedding cake, blankets stacked on a bed, or geologic strata—whatever helps you remember that they break up the page into related-but-independent parts.

Any or all of the sections can be tables; in the example in Figure 2.7, you can see where the tables are because their borders are visible. The header section at the top of the page is a table with the page owner's logotype in it. There's also a footer at the bottom, but it doesn't use a table so that the horizontal rules can extend into the left margin.

Figure 2.7

This page is split into three distinct parts: a header, a footer, and a central content area.

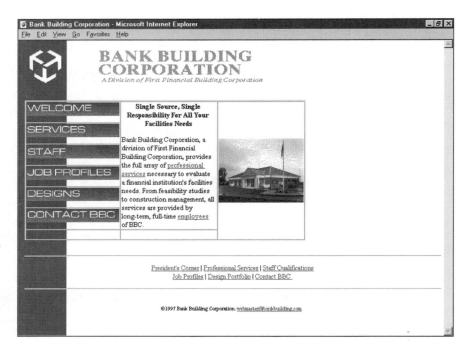

The "meat" of this page goes in the content frame in the middle of the page. Depending on what's in your pages, you might have more than one content area, or your content area might be itself split into several tables (you'll see a great example of this in the Webintosh pages, discussed in "A Table Layout Sampler" later in the session).

Breaking Sections into Vertical Chunks

First, you broke up your pages into horizontal sections. This gives you a convenient way to stack chunks of content together—but what goes in the chunks? Anything you want is the short answer; the long version is a bit more detailed because what you put in your chunks depends on what you're trying to do.

Many books on graphic design and typography recommend breaking the page area into a number of vertical columns. How many to use is a matter for some debate; in practice, anywhere from three to nine will do, depending on your content. Why so many? For the same reason that there are so many utensils surrounding your plate at a fancy dinner—each item has its special use.

Figure 2.8 shows a six-column layout—let's see what each zone is for.

ON THE

CD

The file that created this table is on the CD in IBM\SatMorn\tables\
6-zones.html.

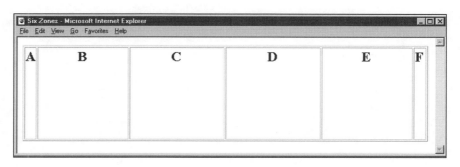

Figure 2.8

This page shows a sample six-column layout that you can easily adapt for your own use.

○ The outermost columns (A and F in the figure) are margins. Use them to provide a fixed-size buffer to separate your page content from the edge of the page. You can put decorative borders and graphics in the margin, but don't put anything that the user *has* to pay attention to in these zones.

○ The next layers inward (B and E) are where you can start putting content. For example, you can put navigational labels (as in Figure 2.7) in these zones, or you can add graphics that complement your text (as in the top part of Figure 2.9). Alternating opposite zones (B and E in the example again) is a good way to vary the layout of your pages to keep the visitor interested.

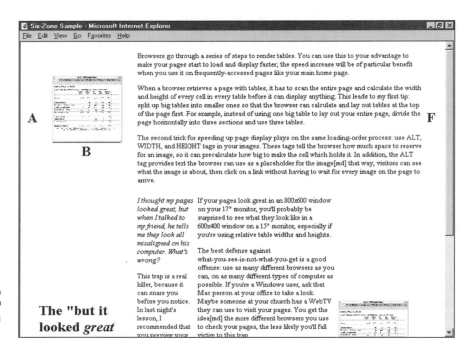

Figure 2.9

The six-column layout in action.

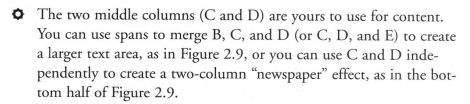

☼ The two middle columns (C and D) are yours to use for content. You can use spans to merge B, C, and D (or C, D, and E) to create a larger text area, as in Figure 2.9, or you can use C and D independently to create a two-column "newspaper" effect, as in the bottom half of Figure 2.9.

Tables give you extra flexibility when it comes time to break your page into columns. You can take the approach shown in Figure 2.9—making one table with however many columns you need—or you can group the columns into several tables. As you'll see in "A Table Layout Sampler," the latter approach can give you an almost limitless number of columns, on demand!

Using White Space

Blank space—especially white space—draws the human eye. Designers know this and use it to their advantage. That's why printed pages have margins and gutters, and why some of the most effective print advertising pieces of all time (Absolut vodka ads and the early-1970s VW Beetle ads, to name just two) have had lots of space surrounding a central symbol, with minimal text to clutter things up. Saturn and Hewlett-Packard have both adopted this same minimalist approach in their current print advertising.

Of course, your pages are likely to contain a lot of text, but you can still use space to draw the visitor's eye to what you want to be the center of attention. For an example, take the page in Figure 2.10. Notice how the white space around the page's center draws your eye towards it?

To get the same effect in your pages, break up your pages as described in the two preceding sections. Use indents and outdents to draw attention to key pieces of text. You can also use graphic elements like pull quotes and drop caps (each of which has its own section later in this session) to provide "eye anchors" that give a wandering eyeball a place to alight.

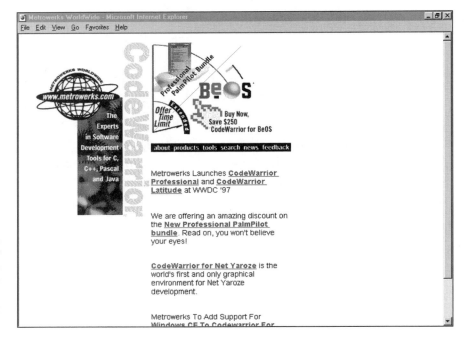

Figure 2.10

This page makes great use of white space to draw the visitor's eye to the central content.

Aligning Images and Text

As you learned in "Building Table Rows and Columns" earlier in the session, you can specify the horizontal and vertical alignment for every cell in a table. When you mix images and text in a table, you'll need to use this capability to control how they align with each other. Every browser (and most HTML editors) has a default alignment for table cells, but sometimes that default might not work well for your pages.

Aligning Table Cells

It's easy to align images in table cells using the ALIGN and VALIGN tags described in "Building Table Rows and Columns." In general, cells that are next to each other will use the same vertical alignment; sometimes you may find it useful to vertically center one cell while leaving the other aligned to the top or bottom, though. You'll have to let your good judg-

ment be your guide here. In some tables, it makes sense to stick the cells' data to the top edge of the cells, but your pages may benefit from a different alignment.

Aligning Text and Graphics

Back in the Middle Ages, monks used to produce what we now call illuminated manuscripts. These books featured fantastically detailed illustrations and beautifully calligraphed text. One distinctive feature that survives to this day is the *drop cap*, the large capital letter used to start a paragraph of text.

What do illuminated monks have to do with alignment? Sometimes you'll need to align text and graphics in the same cell, as when you want to build a drop cap. You already know how to set alignments for an entire table cell, but did you know that you can put alignment on images too? To build drop caps, all you need to do is put your image next to the text you want to use and then apply an ALIGN="LEFT" to the image. The browser will magically float the text next to the image.

You can also make text wrap around graphics, and there are many other ways to toy with alignments. Experiment with your image editor and HTML tools to get the right mix of text and graphics for your pages.

Building Pull Quotes with Tables

Print publications often use *pull quotes* to dress up the appearance of a long stretch of text. A pull quote (shown in Figure 2.11) is an excerpt from the text split out into its own area. Pull quotes often use different fonts, styles, or colors to distinguish them from the text; in addition, it's not uncommon to see them bracketed between horizontal rules that provide a further cue to their separateness.

Pull quotes come in three basic varieties: they can be inserted on the left margin, the right margin, or in the center of the surrounding text. Which type you use is entirely up to you, but they're all easy to implement using tables.

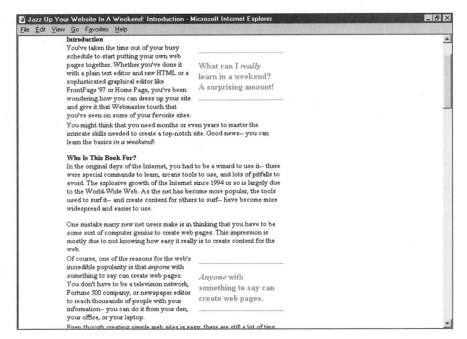

Figure 2.11

Pull quotes dress
up the appearance
of plain text.

The basic trick behind building a left- or right-margin pull quote is to use a 1×2 table all by itself. Even if your page design has six columns, you can make a 1×2 table from one row's cells—leave the leftmost cell alone and use the next two, with the second used as a span. The borders in Figure 2.11 show you what I'm talking about. The cell where you want the quote to go is the *quote cell*, and the other is the *text cell*.

After you've built the table, take a short section of your text and put it in the text cell. Use the VALIGN attribute to give it a vertical alignment of TOP so that it will start at the top of the cell; that way, you can judge how much space the cell will take up.

When that's done, you can pick out a quote to use in the quote cell. The quote should be short enough to fit well into the same amount of verti-

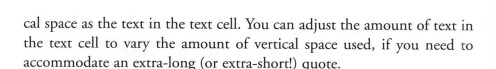

cal space as the text in the text cell. You can adjust the amount of text in the text cell to vary the amount of vertical space used, if you need to accommodate an extra-long (or extra-short!) quote.

TIP Your pull quotes don't have to be text—you can use hyperlinks, icons, symbols, or any other kind of graphics instead of plain text. Many media Web sites use graphics that contain text because it's easier to make the text distinctive.

It's a little harder to put a pull quote in the middle of a text run because of the left-to-right flow of English text. If you aren't careful, words will get out of order between the left and the right halves. If you want to add emphasis to the middle of your text, I suggest using an image with the alignment settings given earlier on—no worries about mismatched sentences!

As yet another alternative, you can use *sidebars*. If you read *Time, Newsweek, People, Scientific American*, or other print magazines, you've probably noticed that some articles have mini-articles (usually in a colored box at the bottom or side of the page) embedded within them. These mini-articles are properly known as *sidebars*, and you can use them on your Web site just as print designers use them on paper. Because you can color cell backgrounds, you can even imitate the look of a paper magazine!

A Table Layout Sampler

The best way to learn how to really make tables a part of your design toolkit is to see how other designers have put them to use. In that spirit, throughout the book I'll take time to dissect other designers' pages so that you can see how real-world Web authors are using the tips and tricks from this book. To start with, let's look at two sites that make heavy use of tables for layout control.

Webintosh

Webintosh (**http://www.webintosh.com**) is a free Macintosh-oriented Web site that carries news, software reviews, and commentary of interest to Mac users. Designed and maintained by Dan Hughes and a team from FriscoSoon Productions, the site garners several thousand hits per day. One key to the site's popularity is its friendly, well-laid-out main page, shown in Figure 2.12. (I turned on the borders; normally, the Webintosh team keeps them turned off.)

As you can see, the page is made up of several independent tables. The masthead and credits sections are in their own tables, and the bulk of the page is taken up by a single large 1×4 table that contains the news, reviews, and information that people come to see. The rightmost column of that table in turn contains several 1×1 tables, each of which has some

Figure 2.12

The Webintosh main page makes heavy use of tables.

featured content. Let's start by disassembling the masthead because it's at the top of the page.

ON THE

CD

The Webintosh examples are on the CD in the IBM\SatMorn\tables\Webintosh folder.

Dissecting the Masthead and Footer

Figure 2.13 shows the Webintosh page with everything except the masthead and footer stripped out, the better for you to see them. The first thing you'll probably notice is that there are actually three tables, all the same width (606 pixels). The first cell is used as a spacer, and it's slightly wider than the green stripe that serves as the background. The masthead itself is a three-column, one-row table. Each of the columns has a fixed pixel width to keep them from moving, and they total the table width—

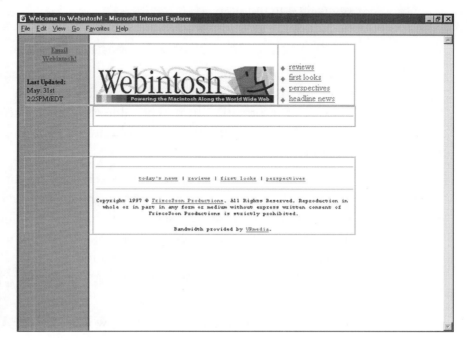

Figure 2.13

The masthead and footer tables are fairly simple.

no more, no less. The bulleted list in the masthead's rightmost cell uses `ALIGN=BOTTOM` to force the bullets to line up with the text.

TIP ■

In Saturday afternoon's session, "Adding Graphics, Backgrounds, and Accents," you'll learn how to use those cool background stripes.

■ ■

The second table is a spacer; its only purpose is to hold the horizontal rule that underscores the masthead and separates it from the main content table. Finally, the footer table is the same width as its two predecessors, but it's a 1×2 table. The leftmost cell is a spacer (and it's the same width as the other tables' leftmost cells), and the content is in the right-hand cell.

The consistent widths of these tables lends the page a nice, balanced look from top to bottom; the real action, though, is in the middle table, where the real content goes.

Dissecting the Main Content Table

The main table, shown in Figure 2.14, has four columns but only one row; this allows the table to grow or shrink vertically according to the amount of information in it. The table itself has a fixed width, like the masthead tables; in addition, each column has a fixed width to prevent it from moving.

The leftmost column serves as a quick reference to groups of pages; for example, the reviews section collects several current reviews in one convenient place. Each section starts with a header graphic, followed by a list of links. (Interestingly, each link is preceded by a non-breaking space, which you'll meet later in "The Gray Blotch Disease Trap." This provides a small, but noticeable, indentation to visually group the links below their banner.

When I first saw the table layout, I wondered why the page groups (reviews, First Looks, and so on) weren't in their own cells. The answer is

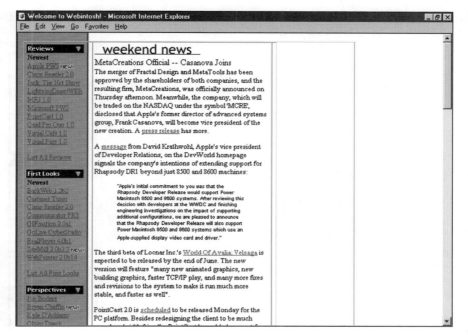

Figure 2.14

The main content table holds most of Webintosh's key content.

that adding cells to the left column would require making the center and right columns use spans. To keep everything simple and easy to update, the Webintosh designers decided to let the browser take care of sizing the entire table as a unit instead of adding an ever-changing set of extra cells.

The center column is the centerpiece of the page: it presents the key news, information, and analysis that people come to Webintosh to see. It's actually pretty unremarkable: just a single table cell, with a fixed width. The browser scales the cell's height as necessary. The designers use rules, banners, and other visual elements within the center column to break up separate sections—and you should too.

Dissecting the Right-Hand Column

The right-hand column of the main table is worth its own section; it's shown in Figure 2.15. (I widened the borders to make it clear where the

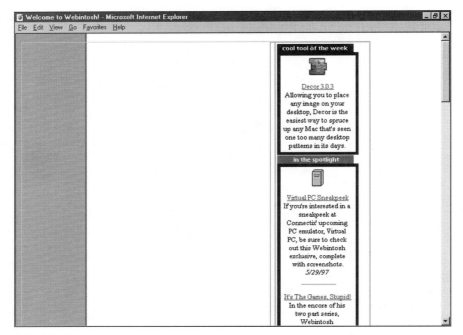

Figure 2.15

The right-hand column of the main table uses several 1×1 nested tables.

nested tables are; they don't look like that at the original site.) Each section of the table has its own graphic header, with colors to distinguish them from one another. In addition, each section is contained in a 1×1 table, with a distinctive background color to differentiate its contents. Both sections use ALIGN="MIDDLE" for text alignment; this keeps the horizontal rules, text, and icons neatly aligned.

www.crypto.com

I've had a long-running interest in cryptography, at first because I thought it was cool spy-type stuff and then because I realized how easy it is for anyone to protect his personal data with practically unbreakable encryption. I personally think it's important that you—and every other law-abiding citizen—have the capability to make unrestricted use of cryptographic tools for ensuring business and personal privacy.

Whew! Now that I'm off my soapbox, let me call your attention to Figure 2.16, the home page from **http://www.crypto.com**. It's not as fancy as the Webintosh page, but it's not designed to be. It has some solidly interesting content, but without as much jazz as the Webintosh site; it's a good model for information-oriented sites.

ON THE

CD

The `www.crypto.com` examples are on the CD in the `IBM\SatMorn\ tables\crypto` folder.

The table in the center of the page takes up most of the page—only fitting because it has most of the page's information. Although I turned on borders for the screen shot, the page designers used `CELLSPACING=10` to provide a ready-made gutter between the left and right columns. With `BORDER=0`, the spacing would be plain white space.

The left-hand column contains a list of links to other pages on the site, whereas the right-hand column has cryptography-related news and a

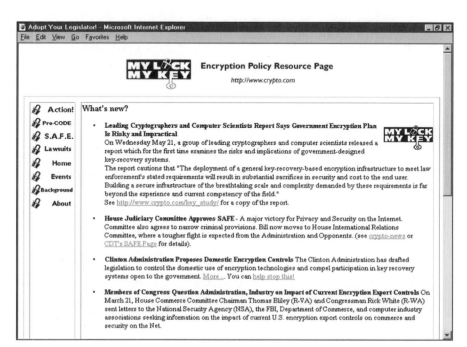

Figure 2.16

`www.crypto.com` is packed with juicy news tidbits.

form you can fill out to sign a pro-crypto petition. Putting the form right in the table keeps it with the related text and provides a neat, all-in-one appearance.

Tool Tips

Tables are a power tool. The problem with power tools, though, is that if you're not careful you might cut off your hand or ruin whatever you're trying to repair. Tables don't pose any risk to your life and limb, but there are some tricks—and traps—that you should know to make best use out of tables in your pages.

The Invisible Image Trick

I'm a perfectionist. How can I get pixel-by-pixel control over my table contents?

Back in the old days (that would be in 1994 or so in Web years), there was no way to put things where you wanted them on a page. Tables provided part of the solution, but they still didn't make it possible to precisely separate horizontal and vertical elements. However, there was a solution—David Siegel, one of the foremost Web designers in the world—realized that you could make a tiny invisible image and use the WIDTH and HEIGHT attributes to make it as large or as small as needed.

Siegel recommends a 1×1-pixel image, but you can safely use larger ones—but they shouldn't be any larger than 10×10 or so, or they'll be too big to use. How do you make them invisible? Remember that GIF images can have a transparent color that will fade into the background when used. So, when you create your "invisible friend," make it a solid block of one color; then use an image editor like PaintShop Pro or Graphic-Converter to make that one color transparent. Voila!

ON THE

CD

If you don't want to make your own invisible image, there's one on the CD: check out IBM\SatMorn\tables\10x10.gif.

Figure 2.17 shows an example of using this trick in practice. The table cell on the left uses a 10×10 picture that I've purposely colored green, so that you can see it. Notice how it's scaled to a 15×3 chunk to provide an indent for the paragraph; then scaled again to a 1×22 stiletto for use as a vertical spacer. The right-hand cell shows what the text looks like when you *can't* see the supposedly invisible image.

TIP David Siegel's *Designing Killer Web Sites* (Hayden; ISBN 1568302894) is an excellent technical guide to very advanced Web site design. It's not for the faint of heart, but it has some dynamite tricks and tips for real hard-core Web design.

The Computer-Paper Trick

My tables have a lot of repetitive data in them because they're for a catalog. How can I dress up the table without making it too confusing?

Regardless of whether you're a longtime computer user, you've probably run into that odd-looking striped computer paper that's a hybrid of pale green and white. It was originally designed like that to make it easier to produce formatted reports; the alternating stripes, in conjunction with the tiny line numbers along the left margin, made it possible for

Figure 2.17

The invisible image is visible here so that you can see how I used it.

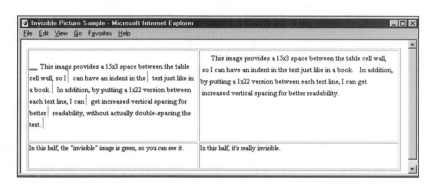

mainframe line printers (and later, PC printers) to spew out text that humans could read without getting instant eyestrain.

If you're producing a lot of information in a single table, as you might if you're producing a catalog, parts list, or other data-oriented page, try using alternating rows of color. Set your page background to white; then use a pale color (#FFFFCC, a very pale yellow, is my current favorite) on every other row. This will help visitors' eyes follow the lines across and adds a touch of variety to what might otherwise be a monotonous list.

The Fast-Loading Trick

I want my pages to load as fast as possible. How can I design tables for maximum speed?

Browsers go through a series of steps to render tables. You can use this to your advantage to make your pages start to load and display faster; the speed increase will be of particular benefit when you use it on frequently accessed pages like your main home page.

When a browser retrieves a page with tables, it has to scan the entire page and calculate the width and height of every cell in every table before it can display anything. This leads to my first tip: split up big tables into smaller ones so that the browser can calculate and lay out tables at the top of the page first. For example, instead of using one big table to lay out your entire page, divide the page horizontally into three sections and use three tables.

The second trick for speeding up page display plays on the same loading-order process: use ALT, WIDTH, and HEIGHT parameters in your images. These parameters tell the browser how much space to reserve for an image, so that it can precalculate how big to make the cell that holds it. In addition, the <ALT> tag provides text the browser can use as a placeholder for the image—that way, visitors can see what the image is about and then click on a link without having to wait for every image on the page to arrive.

The Jailhouse Rock Trap

You can see all the borders in my table, even the ones surrounding empty cells.

Every time I see a large table with borders turned on, it makes me think of barred prison windows. I'm not sure whether it's the regular horizontal and vertical patterns or the industrial gray color, but something about borders just makes me think "penitentiary."

More seriously, though, borders draw attention *away* from what's in the table. The eye tends to follow straight lines when it sees them, so long, narrow, straight borders tend to distract visitors when they're scanning your pages—the opposite of what you want. There's no way to use borders on just *some* cells, as you can in Microsoft Excel and most other spreadsheets and word processors—your table can either have borders everywhere or nowhere.

To avoid making your visitors feel like extras in the latest remake of *Escape From Alcatraz,* turn off borders for large tables. If you absolutely need to use borders to separate items in a table, use standard HTML horizontal rules (the <HR> tag) for horizontal separators and draw your own 1-pixel lines for vertical separators.

The Gray Blotch Disease Trap

Some of my empty table cells show up as funny gray blotches. What's going on?

As you can see in Figure 2.18, tables can indeed suddenly sprout odd-looking gray blotches—check out the rows between items 2–10 and 2–11. Don't worry, though—you won't need fungicides or antivirus software to fix them! These blotches appear when the browser thinks a cell is empty. Empty cells are usually drawn with a 3-D effect that results in the blotches you see in the figure.

To solve this problem, you have to get rid of the empty spaces. The easiest way to do this is to use a special HTML character, the *non-breaking space,* or NBSP. Browsers are free to ignore ordinary spaces when they

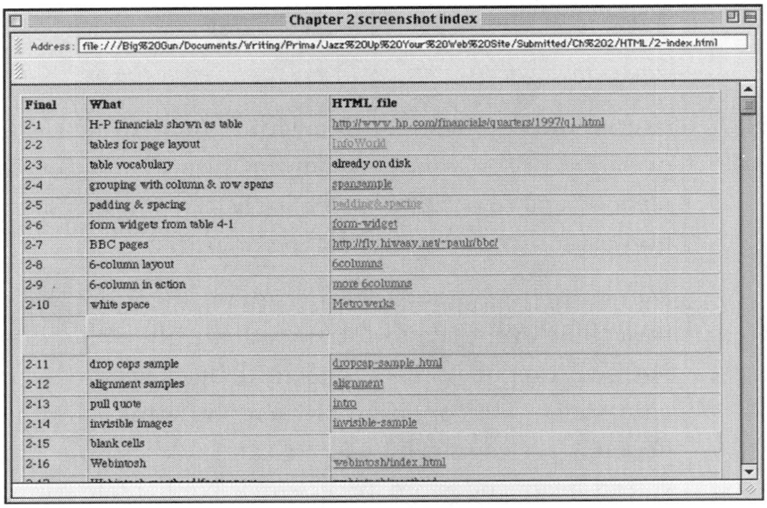

Figure 2.18

The top table has "blank" cells, whereas the bottom one doesn't.

need to wrap words in a table cell, but they're required to respect NBSPs. HTML defines the NBSP as , and you use it like this:

```
<td> </td>
<td>The cell to the left is blank!</td>
```

Some HTML editors are smart enough to automatically put NBSPs in empty cells; if yours isn't, you'll have to do it yourself.

The Moving Sidelines Trap

My table borders keep moving around on me. Are they possessed?

Fortunately, no—no need for an exorcist, just a little adjustment. When you specify table or cell widths as a percentage, you're telling the browser that it's okay for it to change the amount of screen space it uses to draw the table, depending on how big the browser window is. As soon as your browser window changes size, the browser will redraw everything accordingly—and all your carefully placed text and images start doing the Boogaloo.

So, should you specify all your widths and heights with pixel values? No! The browser *needs* to be able to resize table parts depending on the window size; otherwise, your pages might be difficult or impossible to read in small windows.

The best solution to this problem is to accept that table sidelines can move. If you have a table part that you absolutely don't want moved (say, if it contains a navigation element or something else that needs to stay in a fixed position along an edge of the page), specify its width as an absolute number of pixels, but leave the other elements alone. This keeps your stuff where you want it without tying the browser's hands behind its imaginary back.

The "It Looked Fine Yesterday" Trap

I thought my pages looked great, but when I talked to my friend, he tells me they look all misaligned on his computer. What's wrong?

This trap is a real killer, because it can snare you before you notice. In Friday evening's session, I recommended that you preview your pages with several different browsers, and tables are one of the biggest reasons why— a single layout can look very different in two different browsers.

The biggest difference is usually caused by great differences in browser window or monitor size. If your pages look great in an 800×600 window on your 17-inch monitor, you'll probably be surprised to see what they look like in a 600×400 window on a 15-inch monitor, especially if you're using relative table widths and heights.

The best defense against what-you-see-is-not-what-you-get is a good offense: use as many different browsers as you can, on as many different types of computers as possible. If you're a Windows user, ask that Mac person at your office to take a look. Maybe someone at your church has a WebTV they can use to visit your pages. You get the idea—the more different browsers you use to check your pages, the less likely you'll fall victim to this trap.

Wrap It Up!

Tables can be complicated, but I introduced them first for a reason: they're a key asset when you're designing pages, and they're easy to use after you get the hang of it. This session gave you the basics on how tables work and how they can work for *you*. I encourage you to experiment with table layouts to see what looks best for your pages. The odds are excellent that you'll find a new look that suits you and your content perfectly!

If all this seems a little overwhelming, relax and have a glass of orange juice (or whatever your favorite Saturday morning beverage is). In the next session, you'll learn how to use the often-misunderstood HTML frame to give new organization to your Web pages.

Designing Pages with Frames

- ✿ All About Frames
- ✿ Designing Pages with Frames
- ✿ Building Framed Pages with an HTML Editor
- ✿ A Frame Layout Sampler

In the previous session, you learned how to build hot-looking pages with HTML tables. Tables are powerful and flexible, but there are some things even they don't do well. Sometimes you need, or want, to split up a single web browser page into several independent content areas.

Often frames are used to provide a way to put banners or advertising in a constant location on a Web page. Although this is all right for occasional use, it's easy to over-design a site with frames so that visitors get completely lost.

In this session, you'll learn how to build sites and pages with frames so that the layout doesn't confuse business. You'll also learn when you shouldn't use frames.

All About Frames

Frames were the first real way to lay out a whole page with HTML. Without frames, you have no way to accurately position graphics or text in a given area. Of course, tables let you put things in the same position relative to each other, but frames let you easily change what's displayed in an area.

NOTE   You may remember cascading style sheets, which I mentioned in Friday evening's session. Style sheets provide much better control over where things go on a page. When Netscape introduced frames in 1994, style sheets were still just science fiction. Until major browsers can use style sheets, you can combine tables and frames to get some of the same effects.

Because they stay in the same place on a page, frames work well for pages with elements that stay the same. Many sites use frames for navigation bars, copyright banners, mastheads, and other elements that are reused in the same place on several pages.

Figure 3.1 shows a framed site that uses three frames: a logo frame across the top of the page, a navigation bar down the left side of the page, and a content area in the remainder of the page.

Frames also offer a great way to provide a running table of contents. For example, if you're putting a catalog on the Web, a frame on the left side

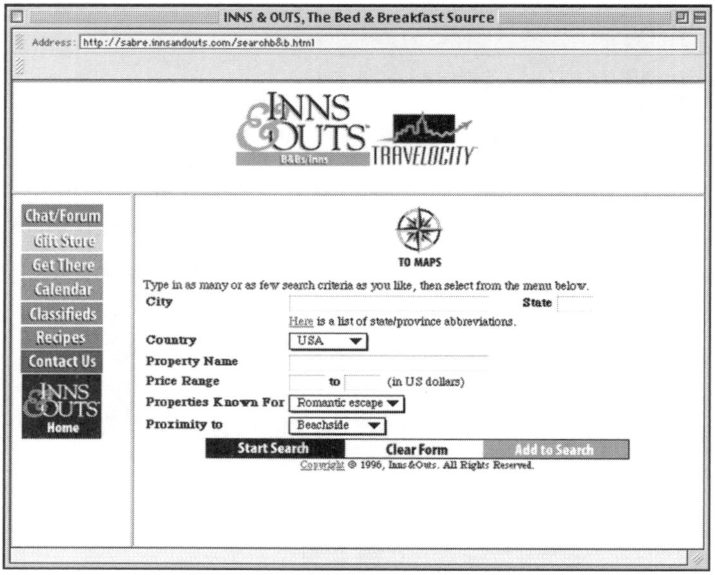

Figure 3.1

This page uses three frames; the bottom-right frame's contents change as you navigate around the site.

of your catalog pages can display an index of products, and the currently selected product can be shown on the rest of the page. (You'll see an example of a product catalog at the end of this chapter.)

Before we start designing pages with frames, let's see how frames work and how you build them in HTML.

How Frames Work

To use frames within a page, you begin by creating an HTML file, called a *frameset*, which contains links to the files that create the frames themselves. Each link in the frameset is shown in its own frame.

In addition to the link, you can specify whether the frame has a border, whether it's resizable, what colors the browser should use, and so on (you'll learn more about these attributes later in the session). The frameset can also provide an alternate block of HTML so that browsers that can't display frames can still show something meaningful.

After you create the frameset file, you then create one HTML file for each frame. When the browser loads the frameset, it will display each frame as an independent area in the browser window. If a frame's content is too big for the frame's area, the browser will display scroll bars so that the user can move around through the available content.

Figure 3.2 shows a page with two frames displayed. Each frames takes up half the page; the left-hand frame displays some text, whereas the right-hand frame displays the HTML used to generate the entire page.

Each frame shows its own content. Links in a frame can move to another frame, another page, or an anchor on any other Web page. You can specify where the link is displayed: it might be in the same frame, another frame in the current set, or even in a new browser window. You'll see examples of all these a bit later on.

You design a frameset by splitting up the page into as many frames as you want to use. Each frame can have a width and height associated with it; these can be expressed either as absolute or relative measures. If you

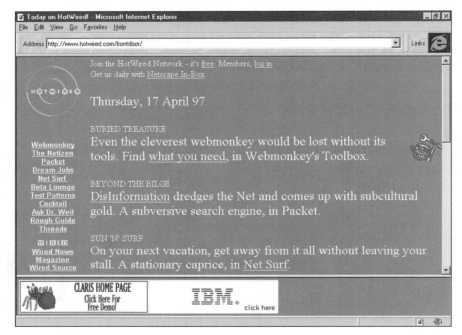

Figure 3.2

Each frame can
display its own
independent
content.

specify relative sizes, the browser will try to keep everything sized right
when the window size changes. You can also specify whether your visitors can resize your frames in their browser window; this setting is useful for making sure that your page elements don't get too far out of
whack when resized.

How Frames and Framesets Are Defined

You've probably guessed by now that you build framesets with the
<FRAMESET> tag; if so, you're right! <FRAMESET> is used a bit differently
from the normal HTML tags you're used to seeing. In addition, when
building frames, there are some other tags and parameters that give you
complete control over how your finished frameset appears. Let's start with
a simple page with two frames, as shown in Figure 3.3. The HTML that
generates this frameset is shown in Listing 3.1.

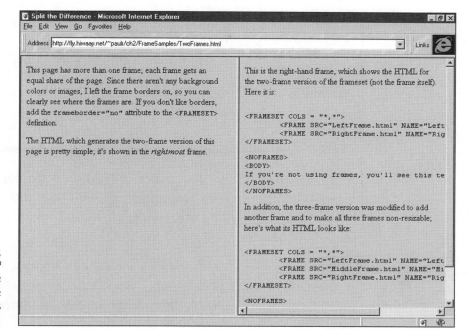

Figure 3.3

A two-frame frameset where each frame has half the page.

Listing 3.1 TWOFRAMES.HTML

Framesets don't go in the <body> section like you might expect.

```
<!DOCTYPE HTML PUBLIC "-//W3C//DTD HTML 3.2//EN">
<HTML>


<HEAD>
    <META HTTP-EQUIV="Content-Type" CONTENT="text/html;CHARSET
    ➥=iso-8859-1">
    <TITLE>Split the Difference</TITLE>
</HEAD>


<FRAMESET   COLS = "50%,50% "   >
    <FRAME SRC="LeftFrame.html" NAME="LeftFrame" RESIZE>
    <FRAME SRC="RightFrame.html" NAME="RightFrame" RESIZE>
</FRAMESET>
```

```
<NOFRAMES>
<BODY>
If you're not using frames, you'll see this text.<P>
</BODY>
</NOFRAMES>


</HTML>
```

A browser that can't display frames can still show the content defined in the <NOFRAMES> tag. It's important to include a <NOFRAMES> section, because visitors may be using a browser (like a Newton or WebTV) that can't show frames.

NOTE In case you're wondering, the <FRAME>, <FRAMESET>, and <NOFRAMES> tags aren't part of the HTML 3.2 standard. Microsoft and Netscape both support frames in their browsers, so it will probably be added to the standard soon.

Setting Up the Frameset

As with any other properly formatted HTML document, the frameset document has a <HEAD> section. Instead of a <BODY>, though, the <FRAME-SET> tag comes next. Like <BODY>, <FRAMESET> is a *container*—it holds other elements inside it. Containers always are *balanced* with a closing tag at the end—thus the </FRAMESET> at the end of the frameset definition.

Within a frameset container, you can only use the <FRAMESET>, <FRAME>, and <NOFRAMES> tags. Any other tags will be ignored.

NOTE If you're not familiar with what the <HEAD> and <BODY> containers are for, a quick HTML review can bring you up to speed. Friday evening's session has a quick HTML primer in it, or you can see Appendix C for a list of suggested references.

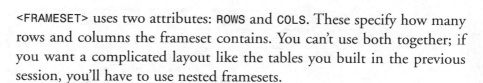

<FRAMESET> uses two attributes: ROWS and COLS. These specify how many rows and columns the frameset contains. You can't use both together; if you want a complicated layout like the tables you built in the previous session, you'll have to use nested framesets.

You can specify the value of either tag in several ways. The width or height of a frame can be given as a percentage of the screen size or as a number of pixels. You can also tell the browser to use whatever space is left for a frame.

The simplest way to specify a frame's size is as a number of pixels. To specify a fixed-size frame, just use its size. For example, <FRAMESET ROWS="220, 150"> will build two horizontal frames: one 220 pixels high, and the other 150 pixels high. Use fixed widths carefully—you never know how big the viewer's window is, and browsers will enlarge or shrink fixed-size frames to fill the user's window.

You can also specify frame sizes as a percentage of the total by using a percentage. <FRAMESET COLS="25%, 45%, 30%"> will create three vertical frames, each using the specified amount of the window's width. If the percentages total more than 100%, the browser will scale all frames down by the same amount; if it's less than 100%, the browser will scale the frames up.

The * character has a special meaning in frame sizing: it tells the browser to assign whatever space is left to the remaining frames. For example, <FRAMESET COLS="20%, 35%, *"> will create three vertical frames. The first two frames will use the specified percentages for their widths, and the third frame will use whatever is left.

Finally, * can also divide a window evenly. <FRAMESET ROWS="*, *, *"> will build three evenly sized frames, no matter how big the window is. You can influence the frames' proportions by adding a number in front of any * in the frameset. This definition

```
<FRAMESET COLS="3*, *">
```

creates two frames, one of which is three times as wide as the other.

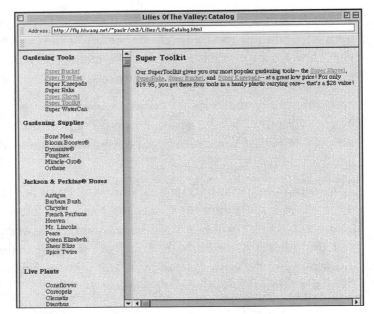

Figure 3.4

This page has two frames: one fixed-size and one that takes up whatever space is left.

You can combine these ways of setting sizes and mix them however you like. For example, you could create a layout with a single fixed index frame and a data frame (as shown in Figure 3.4) that fills the rest of the window like this:

```
<FRAMESET COLS="215, *">
```

Filling in the Frames

<FRAMESET> is a container, so you have to put something in it to make it useful. You fill the container with one or more <FRAME> tags; each <FRAME> will appear in a frame when the frameset is displayed. You can put as many frames into a frameset as you want, but remember that the browser will jam them all together in the browser window; if you have too many, the results may be ugly.

You have a surprising amount of control over how the frames appear. The <FRAME> tag has a total of nine attributes that you can specify (see Listing 3.1 for an example of these attributes in action). Let's start with the most

obvious—all your frames will probably have something in them! You specify what to put in a frame with the `<SRC>` tag, just like you do for images. `<FRAME SRC="LeftFrame.html">` specifies that the HTML for the first frame comes from the named file. If you don't specify a source, the frame will be left blank.

You can name frames with the `NAME` attribute. The name isn't displayed anywhere, but you can use the name as the target of a hyperlink to put data in a frame (more on that later in the section on "Putting Things in Frames").

If you want a margin between the frame's edges and its contents, use the `MARGINWIDTH` and `MARGINHEIGHT` attributes. Margins can be any size greater than zero, and they're specified in pixels, so that `MARGINWIDTH=5` tells the browser to leave a 5-pixel margin on the left and right of the frame. If you don't specify any margins, the browser will do its best to make things look good; note that this might make your pages look different in different browsers.

You may not want viewers to be able to change the frame's size. The `NORE-SIZE` attribute does this; when you use `NORESIZE`, the user can't resize your frame, even when they resize the window it's in. When you put `NORESIZE` on a frame, it affects all frames that touch that frame; Figure 3.5 shows a frameset where the middle, nonresizable frame "glues" its neighbors in place. By default, frames are resizable.

You can guesstimate how big your frames need to be because you know how big each frame's content is. You *can't* guess how big the visitor's browser windows are, though. If a frame's content is too big to fit in the frame when it's displayed, the browser will ordinarily add a scroll bar to the frame. You can override this behavior with the `SCROLLING` parameter. The normal setting, `SCROLLING="auto"`, tells the browser to show a scroll bar if one's needed. `SCROLLING="no"` will suppress the scroll bars, even when they're needed. `SCROLLING="yes"` will force them to appear, even when they're not needed.

The remaining attributes control the appearance, color, and width of frame borders; I'll talk about them in "Using and Coloring Frame Borders" later in the session.

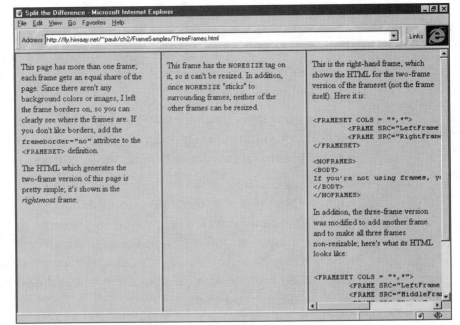

Figure 3.5

The middle frame has NORESIZE specified, so the left and right frames can't be resized either.

Using the <NOFRAMES> Tag

The final section of the frameset definition in "Setting Up the Frameset" earlier is the <NOFRAMES> tag. This balanced tag holds a normal HTML BODY section, which is displayed to browsers that can't display frames. Although it may seem odd that the body be inside <NOFRAMES>, there's a good reason for it. Browsers that don't understand frames will look for a body tag after they finish parsing the head section. They'll happily ignore the <FRAMESET> and <FRAME> tags and just display the body.

You can put anything inside the <NOFRAMES> body. If it's legal HTML, it's okay here too. Of course, if you duplicate your page contents in the <NOFRAMES> section, you'll have to keep up with and maintain two individual pages. There's no way to link the contents of a <NOFRAMES> body with another HTML file. Most sites just put a short paragraph that explains why they require frames. If you really want to be helpful, you can

include links so that visitors can get a browser that understands frames, like the latest Netscape or Microsoft browser.

When Frames Are Appropriate

Frames are best used to give a consistent look and feel to a site. Product catalogs, indexes, and other pages that benefit from having an index area are good candidates for framing. Figure 3.4 shows an example of a frame-using catalog; you'll learn how to build a site like this a bit later in the session.

Another good use for frames is to display a header or footer on a series of pages. Although there are other ways you can do this (as you'll see in Sunday afternoon's session), frames are convenient for you and your visitors.

What to Watch Out For

When combined with tables, frames offer a fairly precise way to lay out your pages. You might be tempted to use them *everywhere*. My recommendation: don't yield to temptation.

Why not? Well, for starters, frames can confuse novice browsers. The older 2.x versions of Netscape didn't quite know what to do when you pressed the Back button while viewing a page with frames; this bug is fixed in later versions, but visitors can still get disconcerted when they expect Back to move them one place, and they end up another.

Even worse, framed pages don't always print the way you expect. Say that you have a frameset with three frames. When the user prints the page, how do you know what frame gets printed? No current browser prints all three frames in the set; both Navigator and Internet Explorer print whichever frame the user clicked in *last*.

Jumping in and out of frames can be disorienting, too. It's okay to use a link in one frame that replaces the contents of another frame in the same set, but it can be confusing if the link replaces its frame's contents. In general, I recommend that you try to avoid having links in frames except for catalog and index pages. By keeping links off your framed pages, you turn them into "dead-end" pages. This helps keep your visitors from getting confused by links inside a frame that erase the frame's contents; you can still have a navigational frame (or links) that will clear out all the frames and return them to a normal page.

Designing Pages with Frames

Like tables, frames can look good or bad—it's hard to tell what you'll get until you've tried a layout. The best way to start working with frames is to plunge in. Visual editors like FrontPage 97, Claris HomePage, and Adobe PageMill ease the process by letting you see what your frames will look like. Don't be afraid to open your frame files up in a browser, too, because that's the ultimate test of how your frames will look and act.

NOTE Every Web page editor that supports frames gives you slightly different tools to design and draw them. Rather than going into the specific steps for any one tool, I'm going to focus on the design essentials you need to know about and let you experiment with whatever editor you're using to get results that please you.

Designing Framesets

You can think of a frameset as a Web page; that's really all it is. The only difference is that an ordinary Web page is made up of one HTML file. A frameset lives in a single HTML file too, but when displayed it's actually using one HTML file for each frame in the set.

The simplest frameset is one that just puts two frames on the page, as shown earlier in Figure 3.4. More complicated framesets, like the one shown in Figure 3.6, are built with multiple framesets, stacked one inside another like puzzle pieces.

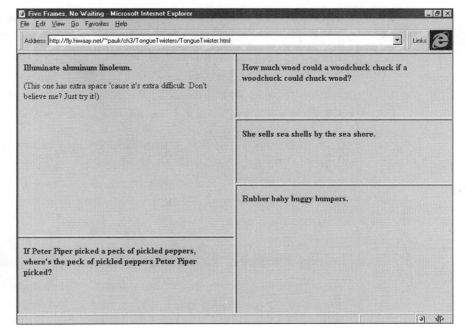

Figure 3.6

This page has five frames, split into two nested framesets.

Splitting the Page

The first step in deciding how to divvy up your page into frames is to visualize what you're going to put on the Web. This is easy if you're doing something like a Web version of an existing brochure, newsletter, or other paper document. It might not be as easy if you're creating something from scratch.

Try this: sit down with your favorite color of memo pad and a pencil. Sketch out some rough-draft layouts for your pages. (If you feel like cheating, you can use the wizards in Microsoft Word or another word processor to give you some ideas.) You can even sketch in headlines, frame borders, and other details to give you an idea of how things will look.

TIP

Don't be shy about using layouts you find pleasing, even if they come from magazines, newspapers, or other print media. Print designers tend to be much more experienced with page design than most Web designers, and it shows. (Of course, you shouldn't copy images or text without permission.)

The goal of this sketching is to figure out how many frames your page will need. You need to know this so that you can decide how best to nest your framesets. The simplest framed pages are those that have only horizontal *or* vertical frames. As soon as you want to mix them, you'll have to use nested framesets.

Using Nested Framesets

Take a look at the *ComputerGeek Magazine* page shown in Figure 3.7. (No, it's not a real magazine, but it should be—I know lots of potential subscribers!) It's pretty simple-looking. There's one horizontal frame for the logo, and two vertical frames: one for the top stories and one for this issue's advertisers.

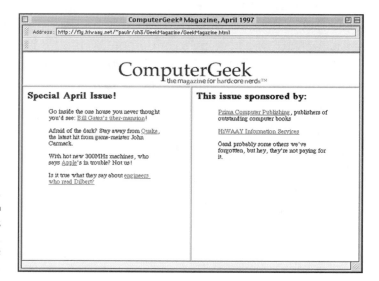

Figure 3.7

This page uses two framesets, one nested inside the other.

Now take a look at Listing 3.2, which shows the HTML that defines the framesets. (The frames' definitions themselves aren't shown, but they're on the CD.) There are two <FRAMESET> tags; we'll call the first one the *outer* frameset and the second one the *inner* frameset (because it's inside the outer frameset's container).

Listing 3.2 GEEKMAGAZINE.HTML

The frameset for the magazine's home page is actually a pair of framesets.

```
<!DOCTYPE HTML PUBLIC "-//W3C//DTD HTML 3.2//EN">
<HTML>


<HEAD>
    <META HTTP-EQUIV="Content-Type" CONTENT="text/html;CHARSET
    ➡=iso-8859-1">
    <TITLE>ComputerGeek&#170; Magazine, April 1997</TITLE>
</HEAD>


<FRAMESET  ROWS = "16%,84%">
    <FRAME SRC="LogoFrame.html" NAME="logoFrame" SCROLLING="NO"
    ➡NORESIZE>
    <FRAMESET   COLS = "50%,50% "  >
        <FRAME SRC="AprilTOC.html" NAME="Frame344067" RESIZE>
        <FRAME SRC="AprilSponsors.html" NAME="Frame345315" RESIZE>
    </FRAMESET>
</FRAMESET>


<NOFRAMES>
<BODY>
ComputerGeek&#170; Magazine requires a frame-capable browser. If you
    don't already have one you must not be much of a geek!
</BODY>
</NOFRAMES>
</HTML>
```

Figure 3.8 shows a map of how the framesets fit together; you might find it useful as you plunge into the frameset definitions in Listing 3.2. The outer frameset has two rows: the first gets 16% of the page, and the second takes the remaining 84% (though using "16%, *" would have worked too). The first row is filled with the file LogoFrame.html, has no scroll bar, and isn't resizable. The outer frameset's second row is filled with the inner frameset. It's pretty boring: it has two equally sized resizable columns, each of which displays an HTML file.

The complicated-looking page shown earlier in Figure 3.6 is actually made up of three nested framesets. The frameset definition is shown in Listing 3.3. It starts by splitting the entire page into two equally sized columns; the next frameset splits the left-hand column into two rows, one with 70% of the available space and the other with 30%. The last frameset splits the right-hand frame into three panes of varying sizes.

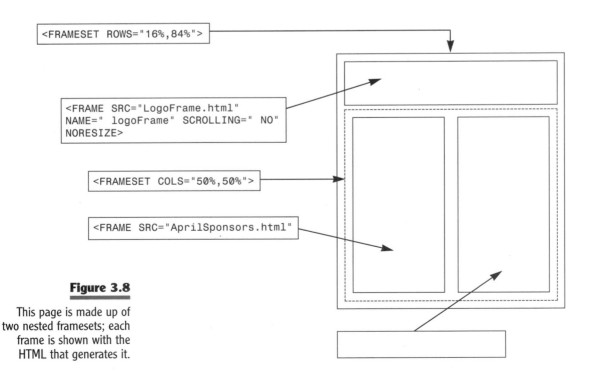

Figure 3.8

This page is made up of two nested framesets; each frame is shown with the HTML that generates it.

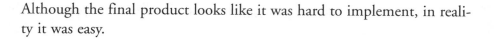
Although the final product looks like it was hard to implement, in reality it was easy.

Listing 3.3 TONGUETWISTERS.HTML

This page features five frames, split into three nested framesets.

```
<FRAMESET COLS = "50%,50%">
    <FRAMESET ROWS = "70%,30%">
        <FRAME SRC="linoleum.html">
        <FRAME SRC="piper.html">
    </FRAMESET>
    <FRAMESET ROWS = "25%,25%,50% ">
        <FRAME SRC="wood.html">
        <FRAME SRC="seashell.html">
        <FRAME SRC="rubber.html">
    </FRAMESET>
</FRAMESET>
```

Most HTML editors that support frames let you subdivide frames as much as you want. Every time you split an existing frame, the editor will create a new nested frameset for you. You still have to decide what to put in the frames, though.

◆◆

CAUTION   Remember that the browser will add scroll bars when it thinks they're needed unless you use SCROLLING="no" in your frame or frameset definitions. Unwanted scroll bars can spoil a page's look, so beware!

◆◆

Using and Coloring Frame Borders

In "Filling in the Frames" earlier, you learned how to use six of the nine attributes that can apply to the <FRAME> tag. I saved three of them for later, and now it's time to explain what they're for.

Frames usually have borders; these borders appear in light gray, even if the page or frame uses a background image or color that makes the gray look out of place. Check out Figure 3.9 to see what I mean. (The original page uses two shades of purple, which goes against my recommendations from Friday night—but I'm exaggerating to make a point.)

On the other hand, sometimes you might want to emphasize the borders by making them bigger or by changing their color. (Of course, you could also de-emphasize them by setting their color to the page's background color.) You control how borders look with the FRAMEBORDER, BORDER, and BORDERCOLOR attributes.

FRAMEBORDER is the simplest attribute to use; it controls whether borders appear at all. You can use it either on individual <FRAME> tags or as part of a <FRAMESET>. FRAMEBORDER=0 turns off borders, whereas providing a numeric value to FRAMEBORDER makes the borders that many pixels wide (the default is 3). There are two rules to remember when using FRAME-BORDER:

✿ If you use FRAMEBORDER with the <FRAME> tag, that setting overrides any setting in the <FRAMESET> tag.

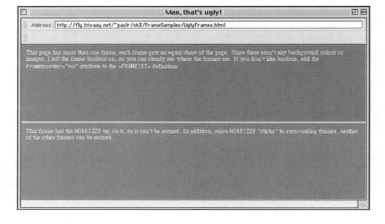

Figure 3.9

Frame borders look funny on this page.

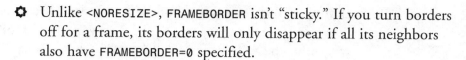

- Unlike <NORESIZE>, FRAMEBORDER isn't "sticky." If you turn borders off for a frame, its borders will only disappear if all its neighbors also have FRAMEBORDER=0 specified.

The BORDER attribute works just like it does for tables—it controls the width of the borders. You can only use BORDER in the <FRAMESET> tag; whatever you set there will apply to all frames in the frameset.

The BORDERCOLOR attribute lets you specify a color for borders. It works just like other color settings. You can provide an RGB color as a hex number (like #FF00FF for purple) or as a name ("aqua" or "white", for example), If you use BORDERCOLOR in a <FRAMESET> tag, it will apply to all frames that don't set their own colors. Frames that *do* have their own colors will override the colors set in their frameset. If two frames have different border colors, what color gets displayed depends on the browser.

Designing Frames

Of course, a frameset's nothing without frames to put in it. Your frameset design will control the spacing, size, and positioning of what appears on your page, whereas the frame design will control the actual content.

Choosing Frame Sizes

It's hard to know ahead of time how big your visitors' screens will be, but you *do* know how big the images and text you want to put in your frames will be. There's no one-size-fits-all rule for figuring out how to size your frames—just estimate what seems like a reasonable size and then look at it in Navigator and IE to see how it looks.

TIP

Leave frame scroll bars on until you can see whether your frame is big enough for its contents. When you're satisfied that the frame's not clipping anything off, you can turn scroll bars back off if you want.

If you're going to specify absolute frame sizes, keep them reasonable: a 300-pixel frame might look all right on your 1024×768 desktop, but it will either be resized or "scroll bar-ed" when displayed in a 480×320 browser window. In general, I recommend using fixed-size frames only when you're sure that they'll fit the majority of your visitors' screens, and that the content within them will fit in whatever size you specify.

Deciding What to Put in Your Frames

This is one of the easiest page design decisions you'll ever make: put what belongs. If you sketched out your page as suggested earlier, you already have an idea of where you want the graphic and text elements of your page to go. Ordinary frames can contain any legal HTML; floating frames, discussed later in the chapter in "Using Floating Frames," can display any Web page.

Choosing Frame Colors and Images

Sometimes designs that use a variety of colors can be very effective—think of a quilt, which uses different-colored squares to form an overall pattern. Depending on what you're trying to do, the quilt approach may or may not work well for your pages.

TIP

If you really want to achieve a seamless look, consider using tables with their cell borders turned off. See "The Jailhouse Rock Trap" in Saturday morning's session on tables for more details.

If you want to play down the fact that each frame has separate content—as you might want to do when designing a magazine, brochure, or other site where you don't want to distract from your content—you can do so by making all frames share the same background, text, and link colors.

You should also set the frame border size to a small value (1 is good) and the border color to the same as the background color, like this:

```
<FRAMESET ROWS="16%,84%" border=1 bordercolor="#ffffff">
```

Alternatively, you can turn off frames altogether by using the FRAMEBOR-DER attribute:

```
<FRAMESET ROWS="16%,84%" frameborder=0>
```

On the other hand, you might want to emphasize separate areas on your page. You can do this by making the frame(s) you want to accent have a different background or border color, or by setting their frame borders to be wider than the other frames. This kind of accent is easy to overdo, but it can still look good.

Frame Dos and Don'ts

By now you're probably sensing a pattern: first I'll tell you all the cool things you can do with a particular layout tool or feature; then I'll sternly lecture you not to use that feature. What gives? Well, the Web is littered (and I mean that literally) with poorly designed pages whose designers let their love of a particular feature get in the way of getting their message across. Frames are often abused, yielding pages with many independent little chunks of data that look like they don't belong together. Here are some rules to get you started:

- ✿ *The #1 rule—don't over-frame.* When you do, your page ends up looking like a ransom note, with text and graphics pasted onto a piece of construction paper. For an example of how you can design a complicated frame-based site without over-framing, stop by **http://www.olen.com/baby**, shown in Figure 3.10.

- ✿ *Rule #2—another "don't": don't use frames where they don't belong.* As you'll see in the "A Frame Layout Sampler" section, you can do

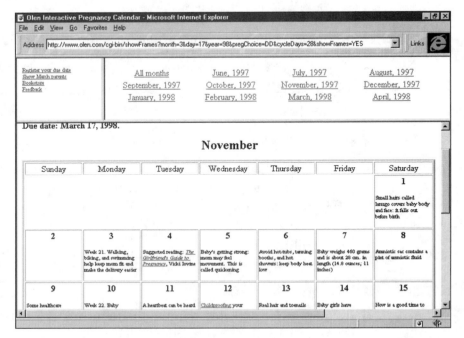

Figure 3.10

The Olen Publishing baby calendar uses frames unobtrusively but effectively.

many interesting and visually pleasing things with frames, but don't do them at the expense of readability or ease of use.

✿ *Rule #3—don't abuse your design powers by making ugly pages.* This ties in with Friday evening's discussion of good Web taste. You have control over the background and frame colors, the frame widths, and margins—in addition to control over the content that appears in the frame.

That concludes the "thou shalt not" section; let's move on to some more positive rules:

✿ *Do* use colors consistently, unless you're trying to accent a particular area or coordinate with adjacent frames.

✿ *Do* feel free to suppress borders, scroll bars, and resizing if you need to, but remember that the browser may override your settings.

✿ *Do* provide alternate content with the <NOFRAMES> container.
That lets people who don't, or can't, view frames know what's on
your page.

Building Framed Pages with an HTML Editor

Now that you've seen how frames work and how you can use them, it's
time to talk about the actual mechanics of designing pages with frames.
Because your HTML editor will handle most of the nuts and bolts, let's
focus on what you should tell the editor to do.

Building the Frameset

First, you must tell your HTML editor to create a frameset. The frameset defines the structure and layout of your framed pages. Your editor
takes care of nesting your framesets and frames.

Your task is to set margins, borders, and colors in the frameset using the
attributes discussed in the previous section. Depending on your editor,
you may be able to apply these changes directly in the editor, or you may
have to drop back and make them by hand, using Notepad, SimpleText,
or some other text editor to edit your HTML files.

Building the Frames

Next, instruct the editor to build each frame. You must supply any attributes (such as borders, margins, and colors) that vary from those you set
in the frameset. Building the frames is easy—because you've already built
the frameset, you know how much space each frame can occupy on the
page. Regardless of whether you set the borders, margins, and colors you
wanted in the frameset, you can change them on a frame-by-frame basis.
There are also a few other things you should consider, as you'll see in the
following paragraphs.

Naming Your Frames

You can name your frames with the NAME attribute, just like hypertext anchors. Some editors will prompt you for a name when you create a new frame; others will assign a meaningless name like Frame92563 and let you change it later.

No matter which tool you use, you should name your frames for two reasons: the name serves as a useful reference when you're poring over HTML, and you can use the name as the target of a link. Targeting allows you to fill your frames with new contents when the user clicks links on your pages.

Making New Links Appear in Frames

By default, most HTML editors will write HTML that tells the browser to use the entire window when opening a link. Most of the time, this is what you want—but when your pages use frames, a link that uses the whole window will destroy your frames. Sometimes that's what you want, and sometimes not.

Netscape added a new attribute to the standard <A HREF> . . . </A> tag. In addition to specifying a URL in a hyperlink, you can also specify a *target* that tells the browser where to display the window. For example,

```
<a href="http://www.geek-mag.com/april/toc.html" target="TOCframe">
```

tells the browser to display the HTML stored in **http://www.geek-mag.com/april/toc.html** in the frame named "TOCframe." When the user clicks that link, the contents of "TOCframe," whatever they are, will be replaced by the new file.

Targets allow you to design a page with frames whose contents change as the user clicks on links in the pages. Besides the names of your frames, there are some predefined targets you can use for special effects:

✿   top replaces the entire frameset in the current window with the link you specify. This makes all current frames disappear; it's a good way to leave a frameset and replace it with an ordinary page.

- ✿ blank opens a new, empty browser window on top of the current window and displays the new link in it. This is a good way to provide sidebars, annotations, or other supplementary material.

- ✿ self replaces the frame's contents with those of the new link. This target is useful for navigation buttons that appear within a single frame, perhaps as part of a slide show.

In general, it's a bad idea to tie frames together with links because the user may not be able to predict where new content will appear when she clicks a link. You'll see examples of each of these target types later on in "A Frame Layout Sampler."

Using Floating Frames

Floating frames are a cool Microsoft innovation that makes frames usable anywhere on your pages. Floating frames can live inside tables, frames, or plain pages—anywhere you would use an image, you can use a floating frame, with no need for framesets. This makes it easy to embed the contents of one page in another, as shown in Figure 3.11. The floating frame sits in the middle of an ordinary page; the frame's created with this HTML tag:

```
<iframe width="80%" height="75%" src="http://www.metrowerks.com">
```

The bad news is that they're only usable in Internet Explorer; Navigator and Communicator just ignore them.

NOTE If you've decided to make an Internet Explorer-only site, at least tell people on your first page so that they don't have to wonder why your page looks so odd in Navigator or Communicator.

You create floating frames with the <IFRAME> tag. Unlike their non-floating brethren, floating frames don't have to be inside a frameset. <IFRAME> can use several attributes:

Figure 3.11

The floating frame's
contents appear as
a separate area on
the page, but with-
out the ordinary
signs of a frame.

☼   The SRC attribute tells the browser where to get the frame's
    contents; it works the same way here as it does for ordinary frames
    or images.

☼   The WIDTH and HEIGHT attributes specify how much space the
    browser needs to allow for the floating frame. You can specify these
    as pixel counts or percentages of the total window size.

☼   The HSPACE and VSPACE attributes let you leave a margin between
    the frame's content and its border. Note that these work the same
    way as the plain frame's MARGINWIDTH and MARGINHEIGHT attributes.

In addition, you can use the <FRAMEBORDER> and <SCROLLING> tags just
like you can with ordinary frames.

FIND IT ON ▶
THE WEB

If you want some live examples of floating frames, point Internet Explorer at Microsoft's
floating frames reference page at **http://www.microsoft.com/workshop/
author/newfeat/ss_ffram.htm**.

A Frame Layout Sampler

Now that you've learned when, whether, and how to use frames in your pages, let's dissect some real-life examples to see how they were done. These pages reflect some of the ways you can use frames to design your pages.

Paging Dr. Weil . . .

Dr. Andrew Weil, a doctor whose specialty is unifying Western and alternative medicine, maintains a weekly column at *HotWired* (**http://www.hotwired.com/drweil/**). You can learn all sorts of interesting things, like how to make a healthy peanut-butter-and-jelly sandwich or whether migraine headaches disappear during pregnancy.

Figure 3.12 shows Dr. Weil's column home page. As you can see in the figure, the page is made up of three frames. The top frame carries an

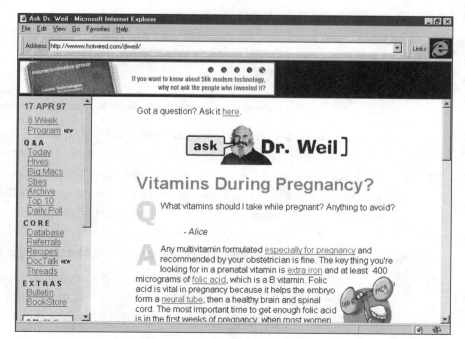

Figure 3.12

This page features a clearly marked table of contents in the left-hand frame (along with an annoying ad at the top!)

advertising banner; the left frame holds a navigational frame, and the right frame holds Dr. Weil's articles.

The frameset for this page is shown in Listing 3.4; it features two frame-sets. The outer frameset contains the ad frame and the inner frameset, which in turn contains two vertical columns.

Listing 3.4 HTTP://WWW.HOTWIRED.COM/DRWEIL/

The frameset for Dr. Weil's page is simple but effective.

```
<frameset frameborder="0" framespacing="0" border="0" rows="70,*">
    <frame src="/drweil/ad/ot_ad.html"name="adframe" marginwidth=0
        marginheight=0 noresize scrolling="no">

    <frameset frameborder="0" framespacing="0" border="0"
    ➥cols="135,*">
        <frame src="/drweil/97/15/nc_toc1a.html" marginwidth=0
            marginheight=0 scrolling="auto" name="toc" noresize>
        <frame marginwidth=0 marginheight=0 src
        ➥="/drweil/nc_qanda.html"
            Scrolling="auto" Name="right">
    </frameset>
</frameset>
```

Let's take a look at what makes this page so effective. First, note that all the frames have frame borders turned off with FRAMEBORDER=0. In addi-tion, their margins are set to zero with MARGINWIDTH and MARGINHEIGHT. Finally, the spacing between frames is set to zero (FRAMESPACING=0) so that the frames butt against one another, without any obtrusive borders.

Dissecting the Table of Contents Frame

Table-of-contents frames (also called *navigational* or *TOC* frames) clue you in on two key things: what other things you could be looking at, and how what you're looking at relates to the rest of what's available. You can sum

up these questions as "What's out there?" and "Where am I?" A well-designed TOC frame will show you what other pages you *could* be looking at and where they are in relation to what you *are* looking at.

Your eye is quickly drawn to the TOC frame on this page because its background is a different color from the other frames (it's a sort of lime green). This draws your attention to the fact that you can go other places. The font sizes and colors of the TOC frame are chosen to make them attention-getting without being unreadable.

The TOC frame has a fixed-pixel width, and it's not resizable. This means that the TOC won't change its size and that it stays fixed relative to the other frames. It's explicitly made scrollable with `SCROLLING="AUTO"`, which lets the browser decide when a scrollbar is needed. The TOC frame's purpose is to always be available, no matter what's displayed in the other frames, so these settings make sense.

Most of the TOC links put their new content in the article frame by specifying `TARGET="Right"`. However, a few, like the archive, use `TARGET="TOC"` to replace the current TOC with new contents. You could achieve the same effect with `TARGET="self"`.

Dissecting the Article Frame

At first blush, there doesn't seem to be anything noteworthy about the article frame. Like the TOC frame, it inherits its border and spacing attributes from its frameset, and it's scrollable. However, it's resizable, so when you resize the browser window, the article text wraps to the window width (minus the space reserved for the TOC frame). This keeps the article looking good no matter how wide the visitor's browser windows are.

More interestingly, the article frame's contents are designed to take subtle advantage of the frame layout. Listing 3.5 shows a sample paragraph from one of Dr. Weil's question-and-answer pages. Notice the first link shown in bold? It points to an outside Web site, and its target is set so that, if you click it, it'll replace Dr. Weil's page in your browser window. By contrast, the second bold link is to another one of Dr. Weil's Q&A pages; its target is set so that clicking it replaces the document in the article frame. This is a clever trick that reuses the article frame when it's appropriate and replaces it when it's not.

Listing 3.5 HTTP://WWW.HOTWIRED.COM/DRWEIL/97/12/ QANDA1A.HTML

The article text puts some links in the article frame and others in the top-level window.

```
<p>It's commonly held that pregnancy will protect against
    endometriosis, but recent studies have found
    <a href="http://www.endometriosis.org/endomyth.html"
    target="_top">no difference</a> in incidence between women
    who have been pregnant and those who have not. It is clear that
    the condition is strongly affected by hormones, and hormone
    therapies are the favored treatment. So I'd suggest minimizing
    your intake of estrogen from outside sources, such as<a href
    ="/drweil/96/35/qanda2a.html" target="right">commercially
    raised</a> animal foods.
```

Atlantic Records

Atlantic Records makes, well, records (although most of their business now is probably in compact discs). Its site, shown in Figure 3.13, serves as a jumping off point to pages for many Atlantic recording artists, as well as to other areas on its own site. The site is divided into four frames; the frameset is composed of a set of two vertical frames sandwiched between the skinny top and bottom frames.

One unusual thing about this page is that every link on it opens in a new browser window instead of replacing any of the frames' contents. There's good news and bad news about this. On the plus side, users can keep the main window open and quickly jump to as many other pages as they want. On the minus side, unless you have a big monitor, those extra windows become annoying pretty quickly.

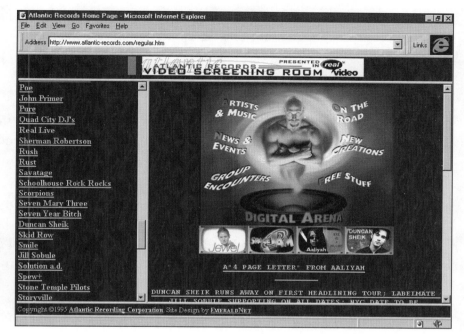

Figure 3.13

Atlantic Records'
main page has
four separate
frames, each
with a purpose.

Listing 3.6 HTTP://WWW.ATLANTIC-RECORDS.COM/ REGULAR.HTM

Atlantic Records' main page

```
<FRAMESET ROWS="47,*,24">
    <FRAME SCROLLING="no" NAME="alphebet_pick" MARGINWIDTH=1
➥MARGINHEIGHT=1
        NORESIZE SRC="icons/banners/js.html">
    <FRAMESET COLS="30%,70%">
        <FRAME SCROLLING="auto" NAME="artist_list" MARGINWIDTH=2
            MARGINHEIGHT=2 SRC="frames/artist_list.html" NORESIZE>
        <FRAME SCROLLING="auto" NAME="artist_home" MARGINWIDTH=2
            MARGINHEIGHT=2 SRC="main.htm">
    </FRAMESET>
```

```
<FRAME SCROLLING="no" NAME="copyright" NORESIZE MARGINWIDTH=2
    MARGINHEIGHT=2 SRC="frames/copyright.html">

...

</FRAMESET>
```

The top and bottom frames have small fixed heights; this preserves the maximum screen area for the content frames in the center. None of the frames are resizable, and the two center frames have autoscrolling turned on, whereas the other two have scrolling disabled.

The first frame, which spans the top of the page, provides an advertising banner; likewise, the bottom frame serves as a narrow ledge for a copyright statement and credits for the site designer. The real meat of the page is in the two middle frames: the *index* frame and an ordinary content frame.

Dissecting the Index Frame

The leftmost frame on this page is an *index* frame. Index frames usually run down the left-hand side of the page; they get their name from the fact that they provide a comprehensive list of whatever the site's contents are. When you select an item , the item's detail is displayed somewhere else— sometimes in the right-hand area on the same page, or perhaps (as in this case) in a new window.

Unlike TOC frames, index frames present *all* the contents of a site in some order: alphabetical, chronological, or whatever else makes sense. Think of the difference between this book's table of contents and its index—the index is a reference source, and the table of contents is a road map.

Like all the other frames on this page, Atlantic's index frame is nonresizable; its SCROLLING attribute is set to AUTO to give the browser control over the frame's scroll bar. The HTML for this frame is straightforward: it's

just a list of links, with an occasional graphic thrown in—but that's what index frames are for! Any visitor to the site can quickly find the entry for the artist they're looking for, from Aaliyah to the Zoo People, and get there without further ado.

Deal-Mac

Deal-Mac (**http://deal-mac.com**) is a nicely designed site that offers (you guessed it!) a central clearinghouse for good deals on Mac hardware and software. Its page, shown in Figure 3.14, uses two frames, each of which is filled with colorful tables. Listing 3.7 shows the frameset for the page.

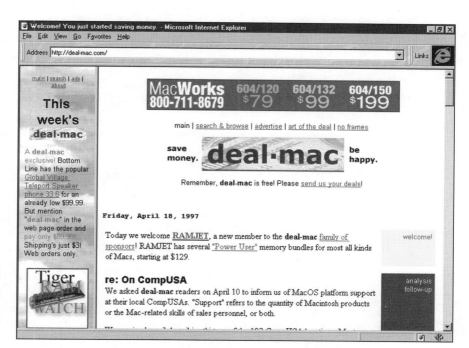

Figure 3.14

Deal-Mac uses only two frames, but they're effective ones.

Listing 3.7 HTTP://DEAL-MAC.COM

The frameset is simple but includes an automatic link to the non-frame version for non-frame-capable browsers.

```
<FRAMESET COLS="142,*" BORDER=2 BORDERCOLOR="">
    <FRAME SRC="nav.shtml" NAME="nav" SCROLLING=NO NORESIZE>
    <FRAME SRC="main.shtml" NAME="main">
    <NOFRAMES>
    <BODY>
        <P>Viewing this page requires a browser capable of
        displaying frames. But that doesn't mean that you can't
        visit DEAL Mac!
        Please <A HREF="index_noframes.shtml">click here</A>.</P>
        <P>If your browser supports it, you will go to our
        no-frames version of DEAL Mac automagically.</P>
        <META HTTP-EQUIV=REFRESH CONTENT="0; URL=index_noframes.
        shtml">
    </BODY>
    </NOFRAMES>
</FRAMESET>
```

TIP The `<META HTTP-EQUIV=REFRESH CONTENT="0; URL=index_noframes.shtml">` line tells the browser to automatically go to the specified page after displaying the `<NOFRAMES>` text. You can vary the time by putting your own value in place of the zero.

The right-hand frame is a content area that displays whatever deals are current. The left-hand frame serves as a combination ad banner, navigation frame, and content area. The links in the small navigation bar at the top all use the right-hand frame as a target, so you can bounce between

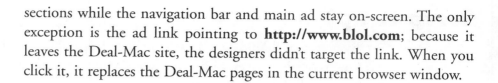

sections while the navigation bar and main ad stay on-screen. The only exception is the ad link pointing to **http://www.blol.com**; because it leaves the Deal-Mac site, the designers didn't target the link. When you click it, it replaces the Deal-Mac pages in the current browser window.

Tool Tips

Frames aren't hard to use, but there are some logistical tips that you can use to make them even easier to put on your pages.

Start with the Frameset

The frameset is really where the bulk of your frame work will go because it specifies which frames are in a document, how much space they take up, and where their content comes from. Always start your framed pages by building the frameset; when you open the frameset in a browser, you'll get immediate visual feedback on how the page looks and balances. You can adjust frame sizes, colors, and positions until everything is just right; then add links to your actual content and tweak the frames more, if necessary.

Name Your Frames

The TARGET attribute is a great way to put frame content exactly where you want it—provided that you can remember the name of the frame where you want it to go! Try to use a consistent naming system for your frames; for example, I start all my content frames' names with "content-" and then a word that reminds me where they are on the page: "content-right", "content-bottom", and so on. Logo frames start with "logo-", and navigation tool frames start with "nav-".

You can adopt whatever scheme makes sense to you, and if you stick to it you'll find using TARGET becomes second nature.

Wrap It Up!

By now, you should have a working knowledge of frames: how they work, how to design pages with them, and—most important—how to make them look the way you want!

In the next chapter, you'll learn how to build HTML forms to gather data from your visitors. Some forms are simple navigation aids, but others are much more sophisticated—and you'll learn how to use both.

SATURDAY MORNING

Designing
Web Forms

- ✿ All About Forms
- ✿ Designing Pages with Forms
- ✿ A Form Sampler

So far, you've learned how to design content that the user sees, but we haven't talked about how you can let the user talk back to you. The best web sites have at least one thing in common: they continually improve and change based on reader feedback.

In this session, you'll learn what forms are made of (just HTML; nothing to get worried about!), how they work, how to design them, and how to make your server accept form-based input. Let's get started by learning all about how forms work and how you define them in HTML.

All About Forms

Forms give you a way to get any kind of input you want from your users. With forms, you can provide a fast navigation tool, take orders, or ask for feedback—among many other uses. You can (and probably will!) use forms inside tables and frames.

How Forms Work

Every form is an HTML container. Inside the container, individual tags tell the browser to display pop-up menus, pushbuttons, radio buttons, text input fields, and checkboxes. (I'll call the form elements *widgets* from here on.) Displaying these widgets and taking care of user input is the browser's job; even though HTML is cross-platform, form elements retain the look, feel, and behavior of whatever platform the browser's running on. Figure 4.1 shows the same form on both a Mac and Windows NT machine; even though the content's the same, the presentation is different.

Your HTML defines how the form looks and what widgets it contains. In addition to whatever widgets you need to get data from the visitor, there will usually be two buttons at the bottom of the form: a Submit button, which sends the form's data back to the Web server, and a Reset button, which clears the form's widgets back to some default state. These buttons let visitors trigger the two basic form actions: sending the form's data to the server, and resetting the form back to its original state.

After the user has filled out the form, a click on the Submit button tells the browser to package up the form data and send it to the Web server. Part of the form definition is a URL, which tells the browser where to put the submitted data. This URL often points to a program on the server (usually called a *CGI script* or just *CGI,* after the Common Gateway Interface standard for moving form data from browser to server) that will

Figure 4.1

Forms take on the native look-and-feel of the browser, whether on a Mac or PC.

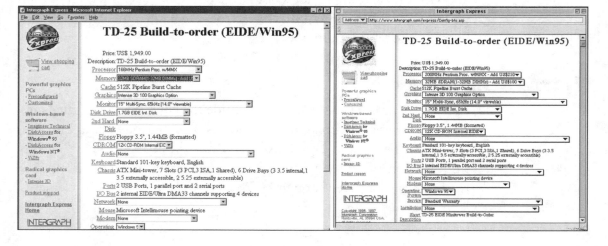

be run when the form data arrives. This CGI does whatever you want done with the received data; it can send e-mail, write to a file, look up things in a database, and so forth. Figure 4.2 shows some sample form data moving around from start to finish.

 NOTE   CGI programming may seem intimidating, but it's easier than you may think. Your *Internet service provider* (ISP) probably has a library of CGIs already installed that you can use for common tasks like sending e-mail; if not, you can often find a prewritten CGI that will do what you want with a little net searching.

Figure 4.2

Form data moves from the user to the server, with a stop at the browser

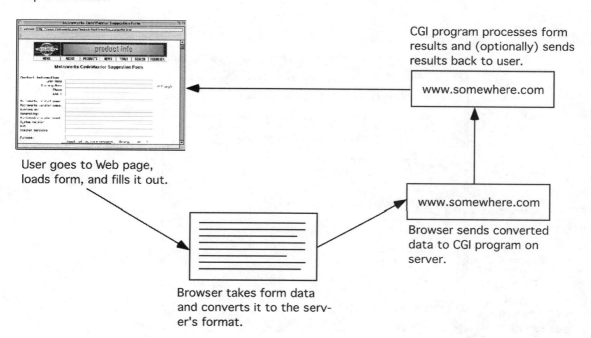

CGI program processes form results and (optionally) sends results back to user.

User goes to Web page, loads form, and fills it out.

Browser sends converted data to CGI program on server.

Browser takes form data and converts it to the server's format.

How Forms Are Defined

By now, you're used to the idea of HTML containers with many attributes; the `<FRAMESET>` container from Saturday morning's "Designing with Frames" session is only the most recent example. Forms are defined with the `<FORM>` container; that means that you can use other HTML tags inside a form. In addition to the form widget tags I'll discuss shortly, you can also use any other legal HTML tag inside a form container. In fact, you'll almost always *have* to so that your form widgets will be labeled so that the user can make sense of them.

Because all the parts of a form work together, I'll start by showing you what a simple form looks like on-screen and as HTML. Figure 4.3 shows a form that visitors can use to ask for help. In this case, they're asking for help with roses, but you can easily do something similar for your own pages. (In fact, your own forms will look better when you use the tricks you'll learn in the rest of this session!)

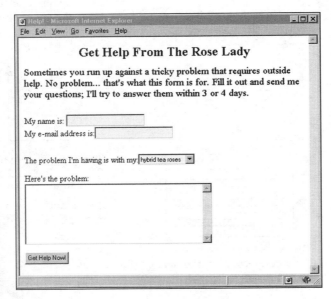

Figure 4.3

This form is surprisingly useful despite its simplicity.

The HTML that produces the form in Figure 4.3 is shown in Listing 4.1. The form itself has several parts:

- The form definition itself (<FORM ACTION . . . >) signals that this is a form and what the browser should do with it when it's submitted

- The form contents, starting with the caption ("Get Help From The Rose Lady") and including all the form widgets

- The Submit button (<INPUT TYPE="SUBMIT" . . . >), which you use to tell the browser when you're finished filling in the form

Listing 4.1 ROSELADYHELP.HTML

The form definition for the form shown in Figure 4.3.

```
<FORM ACTION="http://roses-online.com/cgi-bin/cgiemail/forms/
    ➥helpform.txt"
    METHOD="POST">
<H2 ALIGN="CENTER">Get Help From The Rose Lady</H2>


<P><FONT SIZE="4">Sometimes you run up against a tricky problem that
    ➥requires outside help. No problem... that's what this form is
    ➥for. Fill it out and send me your questions; I'll try to
    ➥answer them within 3 or 4 days.</FONT><BR>
<BR>
My name is: <INPUT TYPE="TEXT" NAME="Field" SIZE="25"><BR>
My e-mail address is:<INPUT TYPE="TEXT" NAME="Field7" SIZE="25"><BR>
<BR>
<BR>
The problem I'm having is with my:<SELECT NAME="Selection">
<OPTION SELECTED>hybrid tea roses</OPTION>
<OPTION>floribundas</OPTION>
<OPTION>mutt roses</OPTION>
```

```
</SELECT>
<BR>
<BR>
Here's the problem:<BR>
<TEXTAREA NAME="TextArea" ROWS="7" COLS="69"></TEXTAREA><BR>
<BR>
<INPUT TYPE="SUBMIT" NAME="Submit" VALUE="Get Help Now!"><BR>
<BR>
</form>
```

This listing may look a little intimidating at first, but don't let it worry you—it's much easier once you understand what each form part is for. The first part is ACTION, and its position at the beginning of the listing may seem backwards to you. However, as you probably can tell from its name, ACTION establishes where the data goes when the form is submitted.

Where Does the Data Go?

Part of the form container definition is an *action* that tells the browser what to do when the form is submitted. The key to understanding how forms work is knowing what this ACTION attribute does: it tells the browser where to send the form's data and how to encode it for the trip. You can specify any legal URL in the ACTION attribute; it needs to point to a CGI program on whatever server you're using. When the form is submitted, the visitor's browser will package up the form data according to the requested METHOD and then send it to the CGI. Two supported methods are GET and POST. They are quite similar; the big difference between them is exactly what format the browser uses when it packages the form data. Which one you use depends on what your CGI expects to see; you should consult the documentation, Web pages, or programmer for the CGIs you want to use to see what format they expect. There's no difference between the two methods for you, the Web page author.

TIP As an alternative, you can use a MAILTO URL to have the browser just mail you the form data. For example,

<form action="mailto:paulr@hiwaay.net" method="POST">

tells the browser to mail the form data to **paulr@hiwaay.net** instead of relying on a CGI program.

In our form, the definition looks like this:

```
<FORM ACTION="http://roses-online.com/cgi-bin/cgiemail/forms/
    ➥helpform.txt"
    METHOD="POST">
```

This tells the browser that we're defining a form whose data should be sent to the CGI at **http://roses-online.com/cgi-bin/cgiemail/forms/helpform.txt** according to the POST method. When the user clicks the Submit button, the browser will take care of the rest of the details. Speaking of the Submit button, let's move on to seeing how it works and what it does.

Submitting the Form's Data

The Submit button is special; when clicked, it instructs the browser to bundle up the form data and send it to the URL specified in the action attribute. Until the user clicks that button, the form will sit there like a lump, patiently waiting for that click. This is on purpose—that way, the user has time to fill out the form, check it for correctness, and so on, all at her leisure.

After the data is sent to the CGI, the browser will sit forever waiting for the CGI to send *something* back. If the CGI produces any HTML output, the browser will display it. Most CGI programs will at least produce a magic string that tells the browser not to keep waiting; Many will display a more elaborate page containing whatever results occurred when the

CGI was run. for example, a database search submitted through a form will probably display results, but a feedback form might not display anything other than a simple thank you message.

For our form, the Submit button is defined like this:

```
<INPUT TYPE="SUBMIT" NAME="Submit" VALUE="Get Help Now!"><BR>
```

The `INPUT TYPE="SUBMIT"` tells the browser that we're defining a Submit button; the `NAME` attribute can be whatever we want, and the `VALUE` attribute contains the label that the browser will display when it shows the button.

Using Form Widgets

Now that you know how the browser sends data to the form-processing CGI, you might be wondering how you build the form itself. I'm glad you asked! You build forms by putting form input widgets inside the form container; you may have noticed some of these widgets in Listing 4.1. The basic structure of form widgets is identical; the differences come in how they work when displayed.

◆◆

CAUTION If you put a widget outside the form container, that's illegal HTML. Some browsers may accept it; others may not. Be sure to keep your widgets inside the `<FORM>` . . . `</FORM>` area.

◆◆

Input widgets come in two basic flavors. Most widgets are defined with the `<INPUT>` tag; its `TYPE` parameter determines what the browser will display. Table 4.1 lists all these widgets. Other widgets, like pop-up menus, selection lists, and text areas, are defined as containers; this is necessary so that they can hold lists of values. The definitions for these widgets are shown in Table 4.2.

TABLE 4.1 FORM INPUT WIDGETS DEFINED BY THE <INPUT> TAG

What	How It's Defined	What It Does
Checkbox	`INPUT TYPE="CHECKBOX"`	Toggles on and off
Radio button	`INPUT TYPE="RADIO"`	Grouped items for making single selection from a group
Text field	`INPUT TYPE="TEXT"`	Allows input of one line of text
Submit pushbutton	`INPUT TYPE="SUBMIT"`	Sends the form's data to the server
Reset pushbutton	`INPUT TYPE="RESET"`	Resets the form fields to their defaults
Password field	`INPUT TYPE="PASSWORD"`	Like a text field, but displays "*" instead of text
Pushbutton	`INPUT TYPE="BUTTON"`	Sends value when clicked

TABLE 4.2 FORM INPUT WIDGETS DEFINED BY CONTAINERS

What	How It's Defined	What It Does
Pop-up menu	`<SELECT>...</SELECT>`	Presents several choices as a pop-up menu
Selection list	`<SELECT MULTIPLE>...</SELECT>`	Multiple-choice list box
Text area	`<TEXTAREA>...</TEXTAREA>`	Editable text field that can hold any amount of text

Each of these widgets requires a NAME attribute; that allows the receiving CGI to retrieve the value associated with it. If you assign the same name to more than one element, the CGI won't know which is which, and you'll get unpredictable results. In addition to NAME, there are several optional attributes—but which ones make sense vary depending on the widget! To clear up the confusion, let's look at each individual widget type.

NOTE You may have noticed that the ordinary pushbutton type is listed in Table 4.1 but isn't listed in its own section. Buttons are primarily useful with JavaScripts because you can run a JavaScript function when the button's clicked. That's too much to cover in a weekend, though.

Using Checkboxes

Checkboxes are so simple that we'll start with them. They're nothing more than the computer equivalent of a light switch: they provide an on-off toggle whose value you can use in your CGIs. Visitors can click checkboxes to toggle their state; each one changes its appearance when clicked to indicate whether it's set.

You build checkboxes with the <INPUT TYPE="CHECKBOX"> tag. As with every other type of widget, you should give each checkbox a unique name with the NAME attribute. You can also specify a value for the checkbox; the browser will return the value you specify if the checkbox is turned on. For example,

```
<INPUT TYPE="CHECKBOX" NAME="ShowAll" VALUE="yes" CHECKED>Show all
    available pictures
```

will return a value of "yes" for the object named ShowAll. You can also enable a checkbox by default by adding the CHECKED attribute, as I did in this example.

NOTE

Note to budding CGI programmers: a checkbox's value will only have something in it if the checkbox is on. If the checkbox is off, the value will be blank instead. That means that a button named CallMe and defined like this:

```
<INPUT TYPE="CHECKBOX" NAME="CallMe" VALUE="Yes">Have a
    salesman call me
```

will return "Yes" as the value *only* if the checkbox is set. Make sure that your CGIs can handle empty values!

Using Radio Buttons

Checkboxes are easy to use, but sometimes a single choice isn't enough. Radio buttons are the best way to let users choose a single thing from a list of mutually exclusive choices. For example, when you go to dinner, you can go to an Italian restaurant, a Chinese restaurant, a steak house, or a fast-food joint—but only one (unless you're really hungry!).

Radio buttons are defined with the same <INPUT> tag as checkboxes and buttons, but with TYPE="RADIO" at the end. As with other kinds of buttons, the VALUE attribute should contain whatever value you want the CGI to get when that button's selected.

Radio buttons have one key difference: you must give each button in a group the same name. This flies in the face of the recommended practice for other widgets, which should have unique names. There's a good reason for sharing radio button names, though; only one radio button in a group should be selected at a time. The browser can only take care of tracking which buttons in a group are on if it knows which buttons are in the group. To group radio buttons together, just give them the same VALUE, as shown in Listing 4.2. The code in Listing 4.2 is an excerpt from the code that produced the page shown in Figure 4.4.

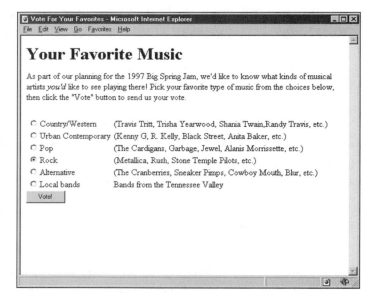

Figure 4.4

Radio buttons
make it easy to get
one, and only one,
choice from several
possibilities.

Listing 4.2 MUSICVOTE.HTML

The radio group's buttons all have the same VALUE attribute.

```
<INPUT TYPE="RADIO" VALUE="Country" NAME="MusicType">Country/
    Western: (Travis Tritt, Trisha Yearwood, Shania Twain,Randy
    Travis, etc.)

<INPUT TYPE="RADIO" VALUE="Urban" NAME="MusicType">Urban
    Contemporary (Kenny G, R. Kelly, Black Street, Anita Baker, etc)

<INPUT TYPE="RADIO" VALUE="Pop" NAME="MusicType">Pop (The
    Cardigans, Garbage, Jewel, Alanis Morrissette, etc.)

<INPUT TYPE="RADIO" VALUE="Rock" NAME="MusicType">Rock
    (Metallica, Rush, Stone Temple Pilots, etc.)

<INPUT TYPE="RADIO" VALUE="Alternative" NAME="MusicType">
    Alternative (The Cranberries, Sneaker Pimps, Cowboy Mouth, Blur,
    etc.)

<INPUT TYPE="RADIO" VALUE="Local" NAME="MusicType">Bands from
    the Tennessee Valley
```

Using Text Fields

Text fields provide a single-line input area for whatever the user wants to type in. They're perhaps the easiest type of form widget to use; all you have to do is give them a name, and the browser will take care of the rest. There aren't any length restrictions on the string, and the browser takes care of scrolling the field and handling Clipboard operations like cut, copy, and paste for you.

To define a text field, use the `<INPUT>` tag with a `TYPE="TEXT"` on the end. Two optional attributes might be useful to you. If you want, you can supply a width for the text field with the `SIZE` attribute, as shown in Figure 4.5. This width tells the browser how wide the field should be on-screen. The user can still type any length string into it; if the string's wider than the text field, the text will scroll to fit. The second attribute is `VALUE`; if you supply a value for the field, it'll be filled in by default.

If you don't want the text in the field to be readable, you can make it a *password* field instead. Password fields work just like text fields, and use the same `SIZE` and `VALUE` attributes. Instead of using `INPUT TYPE="TEXT"`, use `INPUT TYPE="PASSWORD"` to make a password field.

Figure 4.5

Text fields are simple but useful tools in your form arsenal.

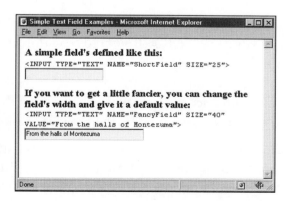

Using Pop-Up Menus

Pop-up menus are familiar to anyone who's used a Windows or MacOS computer—when you click on them, a menu springs into position and stays up until you either dismiss it or make a choice. You can easily use pop-up menus in your Web pages by taking advantage of the `<SELECT>` container.

Like the other form widgets you've seen in this session, `<SELECT>` widgets need to have a unique name. Like any HTML container, `<SELECT>` will also usually have items in it. Each item in the pop-up menu is defined by an `<OPTION>` element.

`<OPTION>` elements carry two key pieces of data: a value (which the browser sends on when the form is submitted) and some text (which is what the user actually sees). For example, a pop-up menu listing some of the things your local high school band's selling for a fund-raiser might be coded like this:

```
<SELECT NAME="BandFundraiser">
    <OPTION name="Oranges">Navel oranges</OPTION>
    <OPTION name="Tangerines">Tangerines</OPTION>
    <OPTION SELECTED name="Tangelos">Tangelos</OPTION>
    <OPTION name="Nuts">Shelled pecans</OPTION>
    <OPTION name="Chocolate">Bulk chocolate</OPTION>
</SELECT>
```

The `<SELECT>` container and each `<OPTION>` within it all have names; when the form is submitted, the selected option's name will be returned as the value of the `<SELECT>` container. The text inside the `<OPTION>` container is what the user actually sees when she browses the page and pops up the menu—that text isn't used by the browser or the form's CGI.

The only other interesting aspect of pop-up menus is that you can choose which element is used for the default selection with the `SELECTED` attribute. In the preceding example, the pop-up will always open with Tangelos selected, even though it's not the first item on the list.

Using Selection Boxes

Selection boxes are those list boxes that show several choices at the same time, like the one shown in the second row of Figure 4.6. The biggest difference between a selection box and a pop-up menu is obvious: you can see more than one item at a time in a selection box. The second-biggest difference is invisible at first—with a selection box, you can select more than one item, as shown in the figure.

Although their on-screen appearance is very different from pop-up menus, the HTML that defines selection boxes is practically identical to an equivalent pop-up menu definition. Browsers distinguish between them based on two attributes of the <SELECT> container:

○ If the MULTIPLE attribute appears as part of the <SELECT> definition, the browser makes a selection box because only they can allow multiple selections.

○ If there's a SIZE attribute, and its value is anything but 1, the browser makes a selection box.

Figure 4.6

Selection boxes can allow several simultaneous selections.

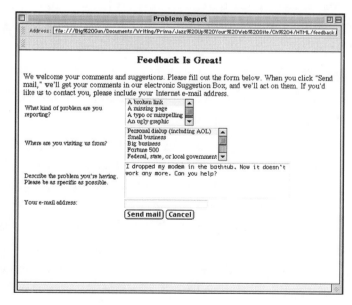

The browser will try to figure out a good width and height for the selection box; if you specify a SIZE value, it will be used to make the selection box the specified number of rows high.

Using Text Areas

Text fields are great when you want to get a single line of text, like an e-mail address. However, they don't work so well when you want to get two or more lines. But don't worry; there's a separate widget just for multiline text input: the <TEXTAREA> container.

<TEXTAREA> can handle any amount of text; the browser automatically handles scrolling, the system Clipboard, and so on. As with all the other form widgets, you have to give each text area a name with the NAME attribute. You can also specify an initial value for the container, but instead of using VALUE, you put the default text inside the container, like this:

```
<TEXTAREA NAME="Description">Describe the problem here.</TEXTAREA>
```

You can control how much space a text area takes up on-screen with the ROWS and COLS attribute. The text area uses a monospaced font, so the row and column settings really do match the amount of visible text. For example,

```
<TEXTAREA NAME="Feedback" ROWS="5" COLS="50"></TEXTAREA>
```

will build a 5-row by 50-column text area, though visitors can put more text than that if they want.

<TEXTAREA> also supports a unique attribute, WRAP, which tells the browser whether it should "wrap" the text area's text by adding end-of-line marks to it. This automatic wrapping can come in handy for you because it can eliminate the problem of strange line breaks in text sent to your CGI. There are three possible values for WRAP:

✿ WRAP="NONE" tells the browser not to do anything with the text. If the user pressed the Return key in the text, those line feeds will still be sent.

- ⚙ WRAP="VIRTUAL" tells the browser to break lines as the user types (like Microsoft Word or WordPerfect do). When the user types a word that would make the current line longer than the text area's width, the browser will break up that line and start a new one. However, when the text arrives at the CGI script, it's all one big line—the added line breaks only exist within the browser.

- ⚙ WRAP="PHYSICAL" breaks lines as the user types, but when the text goes to the CGI, the line breaks are kept as part of the form data.

◆◆◆

Don't use <TEXTAREA> to collect large text chunks. Many Web browsers and CGIs will fail if fed more than a few thousand characters. If you need to let people send you long text files, provide an e-mail address they can use instead.

◆◆◆

Using the Submit and Reset Buttons

Even though they look like ordinary buttons, the Submit and Reset buttons have special meaning to the browser. When a user clicks one of them, the browser treats it as a command and rushes to do the user's bidding.

You undoubtedly remember the Submit button—it tells the browser to pack up the form contents and send them along. The Reset button has the opposite function. It tells the browser to clear out all the form's widgets and reset them to their default values.

Both of these special buttons are handled entirely by the browser, so you don't have to do anything special in your forms to use them. The Submit button is required, because your users can't complete a form without it; the Reset button is optional, but it's a good idea to include it so that visitors have a quick way to clear out the form and start over.

Because these buttons are special, it makes sense that they're defined by special TYPE values: INPUT TYPE="SUBMIT" gets you a Submit button, whereas INPUT TYPE="RESET" makes a Reset button. Of course, you can name these buttons anything you want; whatever name you specify with the NAME attribute will be displayed as the button's label.

When Forms Are Appropriate

The flow of information in newspapers, television, and magazines is largely one-way. Sure, they may have a "letters to the editor" section, but the information flow is largely from them to you. Web pages offer a refreshing antidote—you can easily gather responses from your visitors by using forms, and you can design the forms to get whatever kind of information you want without overburdening the visitor.

In general, you can use forms any time you want to get information from someone who visits your site. This information might be complex (like a membership application or a family history form), or it might be simple (like an e-mail address or a URL). What you do with that information after the visitor submits it is up to you.

Unlike many of the other things you'll learn about in this book, there really aren't any places where forms *aren't* appropriate (although you'll learn some tricks a bit later to help keep your forms from being ugly).

What to Watch Out For

Because forms are complex, nested containers, you can make a number of easy mistakes. Fortunately, they're equally easy to avoid altogether. Here are the top five form mistakes and how to avoid (or fix!) them:

- *Forgetting the form action.* If you don't specify an action, the browser will either guess at an action or just sit there when the user clicks Submit. Make sure that your forms have actions defined, and that the actions point to valid, working CGIs on a server somewhere.

- *Forgetting the Submit button.* This is another easy-to-fix killer. If there's no Submit button, the user can't send in the form. Make sure that you have at least one INPUT TYPE="SUBMIT" button. (You can use more than one as long as you give them different values; this can be useful for complex forms backed up by smart CGIs.)

- *Mismatching the METHOD.* Your CGIs will expect to see form data sent with either the GET or POST methods. Make sure that your

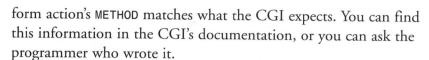

form action's METHOD matches what the CGI expects. You can find this information in the CGI's documentation, or you can ask the programmer who wrote it.

- *Missing or broken CGIs.* The form action has to specify a URL that points to your CGI; if the CGI's not at that exact location, the form submission will fail. In addition, CGIs are programs; sometimes they have bugs that make them fail. If your CGIs have these bugs, get someone to help you fix them.

- *Forgetting to close a container.* No, I'm not talking about leaving the top off the toothpaste. Instead, I'm talking about what happens when you open a text area, SELECT widget, or form and leave off the corresponding container end. You'll most often notice this problem when—all of a sudden—part of your form disappears.

Forms are best built with some kind of HTML editor; using an editor will help prevent these errors, and they'll make it easier to take advantage of the design tips you're about to learn. However, don't be afraid to look at your pages to see what HTML the editor's actually generating—it can be an enlightening experience!

Designing Pages with Forms

Now that you know what forms are made out of, it's time to learn how to use them on your pages, both alone and in combination with tables and graphics. The best way to make your forms look good is to play around with them: lay out a form with your editor; then load it into your browser and see how it looks.

Designing Forms

Designing paper forms is an art. A good designer can make even complex paper forms legible and clear, or even attractive—and it's the same for Web forms, except that you don't have to have already mastered typesetting or graphic design.

The first step on your form's journey is to list all the pieces of information you want to collect from the visitor. This list will help you organize related items into meaningful groups. Remember that visitors will have to enter every piece of data that's on your list and pare the list down to the minimum number of items you actually need.

After you've broken your list down into groups, put the groups into the order you want them to appear on the form. You can use paper forms to help you decide what sequence makes the most sense, or you can order them yourself. In general, most paper forms put information about the person who's filling out the form at the top, with the contents of the form in the middle. You can follow this model or not, but most visitors are used to seeing forms that follow this model, and it's always good to avoid confusing visitors.

Finally, lay out your forms using your HTML editor. Don't worry about formatting them; you'll do that once you have the basic layout arranged the way you want it.

Making Forms Pretty

Forms are a little harder to work with than many other HTML elements, in part because their exact appearance depends on the browser itself. There are three basic ways you can attack the problem of laying out and formatting your forms: ignore the problem, use preformatted text for alignment, or use tables. Let's look at how each approach works and when it's useful.

Taking the Raw Approach

The easiest way to build a form is just to slap some widgets together. The form shown in Figure 4.7 doesn't take advantage of any HTML formatting features. This approach sometimes makes sense; if you're building a simple form with only a few fields, you might be able to get away with it. More complicated forms usually look awful when built like this, though;

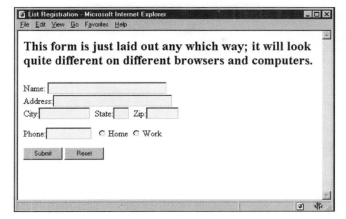

Figure 4.7

This form is
functional, but ugly.

the text labels don't align with each other, and the form widgets themselves have different sizes. The overall effect is a jumble.

Worse still, raw forms look very different on different browsers and computers—every version will be ugly in a slightly different way! Because you're reading this book, you probably want something better than "functional but ugly." The next step up the ladder is building forms using preformatted text.

Using Preformatted Text

Before the advent of computers, many forms and tables were typed with ordinary electric typewriters. To reduce the hassles of aligning items on the page, many typists would use a monospaced font—one where every letter is the same width. You've probably used Courier, the world's most popular monospaced font, in your own documents.

The <PRE> container is the HTML equivalent to the Courier font: it tells a browser to treat the container's contents as pure text, not HTML. In addition, browsers display the text exactly as it appears, with spaces, tabs, and line breaks intact. Before table support was added to Netscape, <PRE>

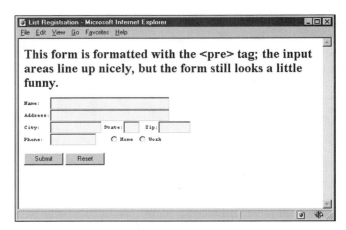

Figure 4.8

Preformatted text
makes it easier to
line things up, but
the form still has
that electric-
typewriter feel.

was often used as a substitute table maker; however, you can use preformatted text to align your forms, as shown in Figure 4.8.

Part of the code for this form is shown in Listing 4.3. Did you notice that the Name and Address labels are padded with spaces? These spaces are the key to making <PRE> work for you. You have to make sure that everything you want formatted is wrapped in <PRE> tags; then add or remove spaces and line breaks to get everything lined up properly.

Listing 4.3 REGISTER-PRE.HTML

Use the <PRE> tag to make monospaced form elements.

```
<PRE>
Name:    <INPUT TYPE="TEXT" NAME="Name" SIZE="40">
Address:<INPUT TYPE="TEXT" NAME="address" SIZE="40">
City:    <INPUT TYPE="TEXT" NAME="City" SIZE="15">State:<INPUT
    TYPE="TEXT" NAME="State" SIZE="2"> Zip:<INPUT TYPE="TEXT"
    NAME="Zip" SIZE="8">
...
</PRE>
```

This approach will work no matter what kind of computer or browser your visitor is using (though you can still make forms that are too big to fit on some screens). However, monospaced fonts look jarringly out of place on most Web pages—let's see if we can do better.

Putting Forms in Tables

In Saturday morning's first session, "Designing Pages with Tables," you learned how to use tables to give you more precise layout control. The good news is that you can use form elements in table cells, just like any other HTML contents. This is handy because it means that you can position forms where you want them on the page relative to everything else.

Look at the registration form shown in Figure 4.9. (The table borders are turned on for the picture, but normally they should be off.) It uses a four-column table to lay out the form's widgets; the two outermost columns are spacers, whereas the captions and widgets go in the two inside columns.

This form shows an example of how you can use tables to gain more control over the form's layout; of course, you can build more elaborate nested tables to control where on the page the form goes. (In a bit, you'll see how to wedge a navigational "jump menu" form into a page by using nested tables.)

It's worth remembering, though, that not all browsers can show tables. If you think visitors to your site might be using browsers other than Communicator and Internet Explorer, you can still get attractive forms with preformatted text.

Figure 4.9

Putting form elements in a table (like the four-column table shown here) gives you better control over the form's appearance.

```
                          List Registration
Address: file:///Big%20Gun/Documents/Writing/Prima/Jazz%20Up%20Your%20Web%20Site/Su

        This form's laid out in a borderless table; everything's nicely aligned,
                            and it still looks good.
        Name:     Paul Robichaux
        Address:  250 PowerPC Place, Suite G3
        City:     Austin          State: TX  Zip: 78759
        Phone:    n/a             ● Home  ○ Work
                  [ Submit ] [ Reset ]
```

Form Dos and Don'ts

I've often thought that new Web designers should have to sign a pledge that they'll only use their new superpowers for Good. In that spirit, let me present some things to do—and shy away from—when designing, building, and using forms on your pages. Like all the other "dos and don'ts" sections, these are suggestions. If you have a compelling reason to go against them, go ahead!

What to Do

Forms are already useful and effective tools, but they can be even more so if you follow three simple guidelines:

- *Group related things together.* Take a look at a paper form to see what I mean. For example, on a deposit slip from your bank, the amount and description lines are probably grouped together that so you can break down your deposit into cash and checks. You can put related elements into tables or separate them with horizontal rules to emphasize their relationships.

- *Use selections whenever possible.* Users can enter data into forms by clicking buttons, making selections from pop-up menus or list boxes, or by typing. Typing is the most labor-intensive of these, so don't make users type things into fields when a selection would work instead.

- *Clearly indicate which fields are required.* If you require that particular fields in a form be filled out, make it clear which fields are required. You can make their labels bold, put a small dingbat next to them, or do anything else that indicates that they're required. Don't forget to tell the user somewhere what your labeling means, perhaps by saying "Required fields are bold; if you submit the form without filling them all out, you'll have to come back and finish before the form will be accepted."

What to Avoid

There are only three "do" rules to remember; the good news is that there are only *two* things to remember not to do:

- *Don't overselect.* Remember the chunk theory from Friday evening's session? If you put more than seven or so items into a selection list, it's difficult for users to track which item they want. Instead, consider using a text input field (but remember the preceding suggestion about minimizing typing!). Sometimes it makes sense to put more than seven items in a list—the twelve months of the year are an excellent example.

- *Don't forget security.* Even a beginning discussion of Web security is a topic for an entire book, but I can boil it down to this: never ask for any information on a form that you wouldn't shout out in a crowded restaurant. Credit card numbers, social security numbers, medical data—any sensitive data can potentially be exposed, so don't ask for it unless you're sure you know what you're doing.

A Form Sampler

So far, you've learned what forms are made of, how to make them, and when and where to use them. Now let's take a look at some real-world forms being used to gather data from users in a variety of places and styles. The examples here represent only a smidgen of the different uses for forms; let them give you some starting ideas for your own pages!

Navigating: Apple Computer

Apple has taken the decisive step of using the Web as its main vehicle for communicating with Macintosh developers. This means that its developer info site (DevWorld, shown in Figure 4.10) has many pages covering every Apple product a developer might want to develop for or with: the Mac, Newton, digital cameras, OpenDoc, and so on.

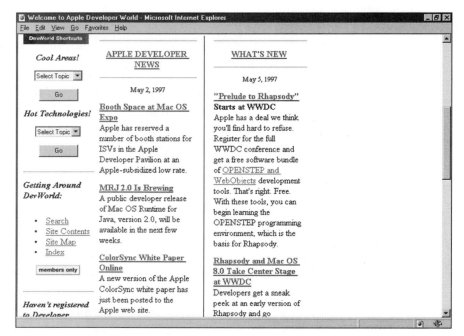

Figure 4.10

The two navigation areas combine a pop-up menu with a "Go" button to enable quick navigation.

The old-style solution to this problem would be to have a massive page with a big bulleted list of links. However, DevWorld is a news-oriented site too—it's how Apple gets news to developers, so space on its pages is at a premium. The jazzed-up solution is to use two jump menu forms, which appear on the left-hand side of the page. These menus—one for specific Apple technologies and one for Apple programs—give quick entry to specific areas of interest, without taking up much valuable screen real estate.

Jump menu forms are easy to build—you'll learn how to use them in your own pages in the section "Using a Jump Menu Form" later in the session.

Taking Orders: Intergraph

Computer manufacturers have discovered that ordering over the Web can be a gold mine. In early 1997, Dell Computer was processing more than $1 million of orders *per day* from its Web site. Intergraph (**http://www.intergraph.com/**), a long-time manufacturer of high-powered engineering workstations, turned to the Web to sell its Pentium and Pentium Pro personal computers.

Selling computers online can be a tricky business: if you offer a small number of fixed configurations, customers can't customize their machines. If you offer a customization capability, you must have a way to make sure that the configurations are valid. Intergraph solved this problem using a form-based interface, shown in Figure 4.11. The forms are

Figure 4.11

Intergraph's custom configuration forms let you specify exactly what equipment you want on your new computer.

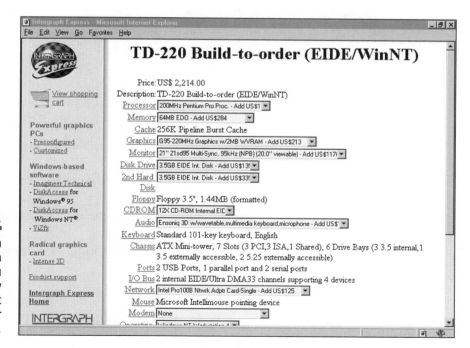

generated by scripts that run on the server; every time a visitor loads the page, the form and its widgets are customized to only show valid configuration choices.

The page is laid out with a two-column table; the right-hand column contains the configuration form, which changes depending on the type of system the visitor is interested in. Each configuration item is a separate table row, with a caption on the left side of the row and a pop-up menu that lists available options on the right. The HTML for a typical table row is shown in Listing 4.4.

Listing 4.4 HTTP://WWW.INTERGRAPH.COM/EXPRESS/

Each row in the "Configurator" table has its own pop-up menu.

```
<TR>
    <TD ALIGN=RIGHT VALIGN=TOP>
        <a href="/Express/Help/Helper.asp?TOPIC=GRAPHICS"
            target="help">Graphics</a>
    </TD>
    <TD VALIGN=TOP>
        <select name="GRAPHICS" size=1 >
            <option value="FOPT116">G76 Graphics Option 2MB DRAM
            <option value="FDSP971" selected>Intense 3D 100
                Graphics Option
            <option value="FOPT104">G95-220MHz Primary Screen
                Graphics
            <option value="FOPT104FMEM143">G95-220MHz Graphics
                w/2MB WVRAM
            <option value="FOPT104FMEM144">G95-220MHz Graphics
                w/6MB WVRAM
        </select>
    </TD>
</TR>
```

The caption is right-justified and aligned to the top of its table cell, whereas the pop-up menu is aligned to its cell's top—this makes the two line up properly. The VALUE for each option is the Intergraph part number; this makes it easy for the processing script to make out an internal order for the needed parts.

One other feature of note is the row of buttons at the bottom of the form (see the corresponding HTML in Listing 4.5). There's a Reset button, but the other three buttons are all Submit buttons! They each have different NAME attributes, so the CGI that processes the form can figure out what to do based on the value of the Submit button that it actually receives.

Listing 4.5 HTTP://WWW.INTERGRAPH.COM/EXPRESS/

Using more than one Submit button is easy—just make sure that your CGIs support it.

```
<TR>
    <TD align=left colspan=2><br><center>
        <input type="Submit" name="Calculate" value="Calculate
            Price">
        <input type="Reset">
        <input type="Submit" name="View" value="View Cart">
        <input type="Submit" name="ORDER" value="Add to Cart">
    </center></TD>
</TR>
```

Offering Help: Metrowerks Inc.

Metrowerks (**http://www.metrowerks.com>**) sells a line of programming tools called CodeWarrior. The tools run on the Mac, Windows 95, Windows NT, Unix, and the BeOS. Their customers are programmers from all over the world, which means that they're likely to want technical support in the middle of the night (programmers, like authors, keep odd hours!).

The solution to this problem is shown in Figure 4.12. Customers can fill out the form to specify exactly what's wrong; the form's contents are mailed to Metrowerks in a special format that allows them to quickly import problem results into their database. Everyone ends up happy: customers can submit their problems whenever they need to, and Metrowerks engineers can automate the process of accepting incoming questions and making sure that they get followed up.

A portion of the form's source is shown in Listing 4.6. First, the form action points to the cgiemail script. This script takes form input and mails it where you specify, with formatting you specify too. You'll learn more about it in the next section. The next important thing to notice are the two INPUT TYPE="HIDDEN" fields. cgiemail uses these to figure out what to display after the form's submitted; you can use hidden fields to pass data back and forth between browser and CGI when you start writing your own CGIs.

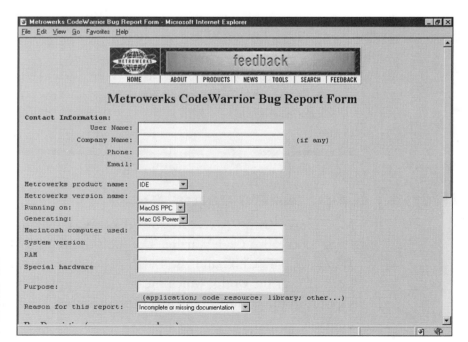

Figure 4.12

Metrowerks takes technical support questions via the Web.

Listing 4.6 HTTP://WWW.METROWERKS.COM/FEEDBACK/ CW_BUG.HTML

This feedback form is simple, straightforward, and effective.

```
<FORM ACTION="http://atlantis.metrowerks.com/cgi-bin/cgiemail/remote/
    mailforms/cw_bug.txt"
METHOD="POST">


<H2 ALIGN="CENTER">Metrowerks CodeWarrior Bug Report Form</H2>
<INPUT TYPE="HIDDEN" NAME="success" SIZE="-1" VALUE="http://atlantis.
    metrowerks.com/remote/mailforms/success.html">
<INPUT TYPE="HIDDEN" NAME="failure" SIZE="-1" VALUE="http://atlantis.
    metrowerks.com/remote/mailforms/failure.html"></P>
<PRE><B>Contact Information:</B>
                User Name: <INPUT TYPE="TEXT" NAME="required-name"
                    SIZE="50" MAXLENGTH="50">
                Company Name: <INPUT TYPE="TEXT" NAME="company"
                    SIZE="50" MAXLENGTH="50">   (if any)
                Phone: <INPUT TYPE="TEXT" NAME="phone" SIZE="50"
                    MAXLENGTH="50">
                Email: <INPUT TYPE="TEXT" NAME="required-email"
                    SIZE="50" MAXLENGTH="50">


...


<TEXTAREA NAME="required-desc" ROWS="15" COLS="70">Write a short
    description of your problem.
Include source code where possible.
If you can, reduce the problem to a snippet, and include the source
    and headers.
Please do not send more than 32K.


</TEXTAREA>
<CENTER>
<INPUT TYPE="SUBMIT" NAME="SUBMIT" VALUE="Send"></CENTER>
</FORM>
```

Some fields have names that start with `"required-"`. This convention tells `cgiemail` that those fields are required; it won't accept a form if any required fields are left blank.

The next interesting feature is the use of spaces to properly align fields in the "Contact Information" section. Although tables would have made the form look better, many Metrowerks customers are using browsers that can't handle tables. Because this report form is potentially important to every customer, tables got the heave-ho in favor of preformatting.

Finally, the text area includes a set of instructions as its default value; this guarantees that users will know what to do.

Tool Tips

Because forms depend on external programs to do something with the submitted data, this Tool Tips section is different from its relatives in other sessions. Instead of giving you tips on how to better use whatever tools you're using now, I'm going to teach you how to use two valuable CGI programs: `jump menu` for building jump menu forms and `cgiemail` for sending formatted form data through e-mail.

Using a Jump Menu Form

The pop-up navigation menus you saw in Figure 4.10 look like they would be hard to implement. The good news is that building these slick-looking widgets into your own pages is easier than you think.

As you'd expect, these menus are actually form widgets; the Go button is really a Submit button, disguised with a new label. Each entry in the jump menu is an `<OPTION>` container whose value holds a URL; when the visitor clicks Go, the URL gets sent to the CGI script, which sends the visitor to the appropriate place.

Using the CGI Script

The jump menu script is shown in Listing 4.7. Don't let it scare you! It's written in a language called Perl, which looks frightening but allows you to write powerful, compact programs for processing form output.

ON THE

CD

The script's also on the CD in the `IBM\Examples\SatMorn\Forms\JUMPMENU.cgi` folder.

Listing 4.7 JUMPMENU.CGI

This scary-looking Perl script handles the work behind the jump menu.

```perl
#!/usr/bin/perl
#
#
# Author: Brady P. Merkel     bpmerkel@ingr.com    01-JAN-1996
#

#replace $host with the path to your home directory, wherever it is
$host = "http://fly.hiwaay.net/~paulr";

&parseInput(*FORM);
foreach $link (split(/$;/, $FORM{goto}))
{
    if ($link ne "/")
    {
        printf "Location: %s$link\n\n", $link =~ /^http:/i ? "" :
            $host;
        exit;
    }
}
print "Location: $host/\n\n";

exit;
```

```perl
#
# Capture the CGI data into perl variables
#
sub parseInput
{
    local(*data) = @_;
    local($input, $pathinfo, $key);

    #
    # Capture the CGI input
    #
    $input = $ENV{QUERY_STRING};
        read(STDIN, $input, $ENV{CONTENT_LENGTH})
        if $ENV{REQUEST_METHOD} eq "POST";

    #
    # Append the path info to input string
    #
    if ($ENV{PATH_INFO})
    {
        $pathinfo = $ENV{PATH_INFO};
        $pathinfo =~ s/^\///;# remove leading slash
        $pathinfo =~ s/\//&/g;# replace others with "&"
        $input .= "&" if $input;
        $input .= $pathinfo;
    }

    #
    # Decipher the CGI input into an associative array
    #
    $input =~ s/\+/ /g;# + -> space
    foreach (split(/&/, $input))
    {
    $_ =~ s/%([\da-f]{1,2})/pack(C,hex($1))/eig;   # undo % escapes
```

```
        ($key, $_) = split(/=/, $_, 2);
            $data{$key} = $data{$key} ? "$data{$key}$;$_" : $_;
            }
    }
}
```

Exactly how you use the script will depend on how your Web server's set up. Your Internet service provider or local network administrator can help you put the CGI in the right place. Here are the general steps to follow:

1. Copy the script from the CD to your Web server.

2. Find out where CGI scripts need to live on your server; this will vary depending on how your server is set up and what operating system it's running, so you may need help.

3. Name the script (`jumpmenu.cgi` or `jumpmenu.pl` are good default choices) and put it wherever CGIs are supposed to go. Make sure that its permissions are set so that others can run it (if you need help, ask your server administrator).

4. Write down the path where you put the script. For example, on my server, the script's in `~paulr/jumpmenu.cgi`. You'll need this when building the jump form itself.

TIP

Ask your Internet service provider to put the jump menu script in a public directory on the server; that way, everyone on your server can use it!

If you're interested in learning how to write your own Perl programs, check out *Learning Perl* (O'Reilly & Associates; ISBN 1565920422).

That's it—after the CGI's installed, you can build any number of forms that use it.

Building the Form

My home page's jump menu form is shown in Listing 4.8. It's straightforward: the form only has a single <SELECT> container in it, plus a Submit button. The actual page is shown in Figure 4.13.

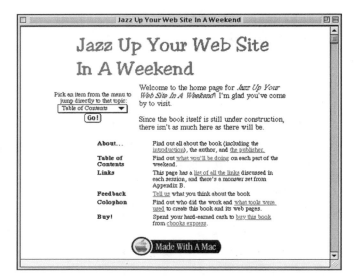

Figure 4.13

Putting form
elements in a table
(like the three-
column table
shown here) gives
you better control
over the form's
appearance.

Listing 4.8 PAUL-HOME.HTML

The jump menu form fits into a table cell.

```
<FORM ACTION="http://fly.hiwaay.net/~paulr/jumpmenu.cgi"
    METHOD="POST" ENCTYPE="application/x-www-form-urlencoded">
    <TD WIDTH="28%"><FONT SIZE="2">Select a topic, then click
        &quot;Go&quot; to jump there:</FONT></TD>
    <TD WIDTH="72%">
            <SELECT NAME="Selection">
        <OPTION value="http://fly.hiwaay.net/~paulr/books/11377
            /about.html">About...</OPTION>
        <OPTION value="http://fly.hiwaay.net/~paulr/books/11377
            /toc.html">Table of Contents</OPTION>
        <OPTION value="http://fly.hiwaay.net/~paulr/books/11377/
            biglinks.html">Links</OPTION>
        <OPTION value="http://fly.hiwaay.net/~paulr/books/11377
            /colophon.html">Colophon</OPTION>
        <OPTION value="http://www.cbooks.com/" SELECTED>Buy</
            OPTION>
```

```
            <OPTION value="http://www.apple.com/">Made With
                Macintosh</OPTION>
        </SELECT>
            <INPUT TYPE="SUBMIT" NAME="Go!" VALUE="Go!">
        </TD>
</form>
```

To build your own jump menu forms, you can use the script from Listing 4.7; install it according to the directions, and then build your forms. Here are four simple steps that will guarantee you perfect forms every time:

1. Step 4 of the script installation instructions told you to write down the path to the script. Add the path to your home page's base URL and use it as the form ACTION. For example, my home page is at **http://fly.hiwaay.net/~paulr/**, and my jump menu script is named `jumpmenu.cgi`. The combination gives me the action value for the form.

2. Build a single <SELECT> container named `goto`. You can change the name, but only if you change the corresponding line in the script. You can also use several of these forms on a single page, as long as each one is in its own form.

3. Inside the <SELECT> container, put one <OPTION> container for each item you want in the menu. The <OPTION>s can have any contents you want; the VALUE for each should be the URL you want to jump to when that option is selected. If the URL points to a directory (not an individual file), it must end with a "/" so that the script can figure out where to jump.

4. Add a Submit button, with whatever name and value you like. A click on this will trigger the script to work its magic.

If you want, you can have several jump menus on a single page, as Apple does on the page shown in Figure 4.10. You can reuse the same script for every jump menu on all your pages—install it once, and it's yours forever!

Using cgiemail

Sometimes all you want from a form is a mail message containing the form's data. By far, the easiest way to turn form data into nicely formatted mail messages is the `cgiemail` package from MIT. It's so popular that many Internet service providers have already installed it; if yours hasn't, you can send them to the main `cgiemail` home page at **http://web .mit.edu/wwwdev/cgiemail/**. (Don't worry; installing `cgiemail` takes about 10 minutes and is easy enough so that most system administrators won't mind doing it.)

NOTE `cgiemail` only runs on Unix Web servers. If you're using any other kind of server, you're out of luck.

`cgiemail` uses a *template file* that tells it how to format the form's data. Template files are just simple ASCII text files; you put in whatever text you want mailed to you, along with special tags that tell `cgiemail` where to insert data from the form.

Using the CGI Script

`cgiemail` is written with the C programming language. When your form specifies it as an action, `cgiemail` will pick apart the submitted form data and format it according to a template you specify. As part of this process, you can specify which fields are required, and `cgiemail` will present an error message to the visitor if she skipped any of the required forms.

If possible, get your system administrator or Internet service provider to install the program for you; if you can't resist doing it yourself, here are the basic steps:

1. Get the `cgiemail` source package from **http://web.mit.edu/wwwdev/cgiemail/cgiemail-1.2.tar.gz**.

2. Find out where CGI scripts need to live on your server; this will vary depending on how your server is set up and what operating system it's running, so you may need help.

3. Unpack the `cgiemail` archive with this scary-looking Unix command:

   ```
   gzip -dc cgiemail-1.2.tar.gz ¦ tar xvf -
   ```

   This will unpack all the parts of the archive into a directory named `cgiemail-1.2`.

4. Change to the `cgiemail` directory by typing **cd cgiemail-1.2**.

5. Run the automatic configuration finder by typing **./configure** (note the period before the slash).

6. Build the program by typing **make**.

7. Copy the `cgiemail` program file to wherever CGI scripts need to be on your server.

8. Test your installation by going to the URL for `cgiemail`. For example, if you put it in the `cgi-bin` directory on a machine named **www.hiwaay.net**, tell your browser to go to **http://www.hiwaay.net/cgi-bin/cgiemail**. If you get an error message, get your administrator to help; if you get a page titled "Using cgiemail," then your installation worked.

Building the Template

Building template files is easy. The key thing to remember is that `cgiemail` will use the template exactly as it is; all it will do is fill in values for any form tags you use in the template. Whenever you want a form value inserted, just put the widget's name in square brackets. Here's a simple example template, taken from the `cgiemail` user's guide:

```
To: strangeman@chasm.big
Subject: questions three

What is your name?            [yourname]
What is your quest?           [quest]
What is your favourite colour?    [colour]
```

When processed, this mail will have whatever values the visitor put into the widgets named `yourname`, `quest`, and `colour`.

The template starts by specifying where the mail will go; you may substitute any legal Internet mail address here. If you want to include the sender's e-mail address, you must add a line at the top of the template like this:

```
From:    [sender]
```
where *sender* is the name of the widget where the user puts her
    e-mail address.

You can freely use tabs, spaces, and blank lines with one exception: the header lines (at the start of the template) can't have any blank lines in them—the first blank line in the file must be the separator between the mail headers and the body of the template file.

If you want to make any field required, just put `required-` before the name. For example, I could build a template like this for handling reader questions submitted through a Web page:

```
To: paulr@hiwaay.net
CC: [required-email]
Subject: [JAZZ] question from    [required-visitor]
```

```
Visitor's name                          [required-visitor]
Visitor's e-mail                        [required-email]
Question:                               [required-question]
```

This template will bounce any form where the `required-visitor`, `required-email`, or `required-question` fields are left blank.

After you're finished with your template file, save it somewhere in your Web pages' folder structure; `cgiemail` will need to be told where it is in the next step.

Building Your Form

Building `cgiemail` forms is mostly the same as building any other kind of form. The hardest part is making sure that you get the form's ACTION right. The `cgiemail` user's guide suggests doing the following:

1. Start with the URL that points to your template file (for example, **http://fly.hiwaay.net/~paulr/forms/jazz.txt**).

2. Split the URL in two: the first half is the name of your server (**http://fly.hiwaay.net/** in this example), and the second is the path to your template (**~paulr/forms/jazz.txt**).

3. Add the path to the `cgiemail` program between the two halves. In this case, the program is in `/cgi-bin/cgiemail`. That makes the final URL **http://fly.hiwaay.net/cgi-bin/c giemail/~paulr/forms/jazz.txt**.

4. Specify the path from step 3 as the ACTION for your form.

After you have the form action set up right, double-check to make sure that the widget names in your template match the actual names in your form. That's it!

Wrap It Up!

It's been a long Saturday morning so far—congratulations on sticking with it! You've learned how to design effective, attractive, attention-getting pages using the Big Three elements: tables, frames, and forms. When properly combined, they'll make your pages look like they were designed by a mega-expensive pro instead of a weekend Web warrior.

In the next session, you'll learn how to design and select great graphics for your pages—images, backgrounds, textures, accents, and photographs can really jazz up your pages with relatively little effort.

Adding Graphics, Backgrounds, and Accents

- ✪ Adding Effective Web Graphics
- ✪ Adding Effective Backgrounds
- ✪ Accenting Your Pages

In the preceding three sessions, you learned how to design and create attractive pages by using tables, frames, and forms. In this session, you'll learn how to design, create, and use graphics to improve the appearance and appeal of your pages.

Adding Effective Web Graphics

Back in "the old days," most Web pages were text only. This was partly because early Web authors didn't have as much incentive to make pages with many graphics, and partly because their tools and browsers were less capable. Today, no page is complete without graphics. However, like condiments on a hot dog, too many can spoil the taste. The trick is knowing how many to use, along with where to put them and how to design them. The first step is knowing the difference between the basic graphic file formats used for Web images; then you can move on to building images and using them well on your pages.

Understanding Graphic Formats

The Web has one major format for content: HTML. As you saw in Friday evening's session, that format is splintered by browser-specific extensions and a variety of competing standards efforts. Graphics on the Web use several formats, each with its own strengths and weaknesses.

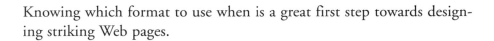

Knowing which format to use when is a great first step towards designing striking Web pages.

GIF

The *Graphic Interchange Format* (GIF) was originally developed by CompuServe for use in its online service. It caught on as the preferred format for use in exchanging images across the Internet, and GIF images are still the most common type used on Web pages.

Image contents are compressed using a scheme that takes advantage of patterns in images. Each recognizable pattern is assigned a unique code; when the pattern reappears, the code is used rather than the pattern itself.

GIF compression is *lossless*: the compressed image contains just as much information as the uncompressed image. Most Web graphics have enough regular patterns to get good compression from GIF, but GIF images are limited to using no more than 256 colors. This limited color palette poses a problem for some images, like photographs.

GIF supports *transparency*, so that one color in every image can be made "invisible" and won't appear in the image. Figure 5.1 shows two images; the first is opaque, so it looks funny because its background color doesn't match the page's color. The second image has a transparent background, so it appears to "float" above the background.

In addition, GIF images can be *interlaced* so that they can be displayed while being downloaded. Interlaced GIFs are slightly larger than their non-interlaced counterparts because they store image data differently— instead of storing each line of the image in sequence, the lines alternate. Browsers that can understand interlaced images display each chunk of image data as it arrives, copying it onto adjacent lines whose data hasn't arrived yet. A typical interlaced GIF will display every fourth line first and then the remaining three. The resulting images are blocky, but they can often be recognized well before they're completely downloaded.

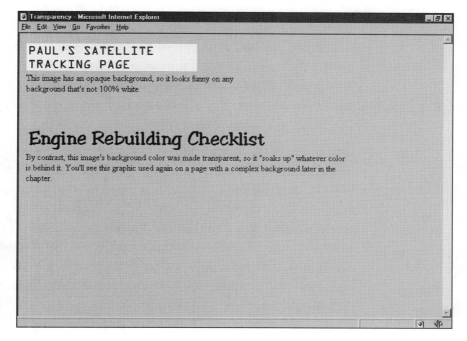

Figure 5.1

The image on the top isn't transparent, but the image on the bottom is.

There's one final feature of GIF files that's worth discussing: they can be animated. Animated GIFs contain a sequence of ordinary GIFs, plus some timing information that tells the browser how long to flash each successive image on the screen. I'll talk more about animated GIFs in Saturday evening's session.

Most Web images have many regular patterns: squares, circles, text, and so forth. GIF gives good compression for these images, and almost every graphic tool (except for the ones that come standard with Windows 95 and the Macintosh) can save images in GIF format.

TIP

■ ■

Use GIF images for banners, backgrounds, bullets, toolbars, and other non-photographic images.

■ ■

JPEG

GIF isn't ideal for every use. In particular, it doesn't work very well for photographs. The Joint Photographic Experts Group gave its name, *JPEG*, to a compression method designed from the outset to give good results for photographs. JPEG also includes a number of other features that make it a useful Web format.

First of all, JPEG images can use up to 24 bits of color compression. This means that JPEG files can display up to 16.7 million colors, as opposed to GIF's 256. More significantly, JPEG uses *lossy* compression. If you take a photograph, compress it with JPEG, and uncompress it again, the newly uncompressed version of the image will have subtle differences from the original. Although this might seem like a terrible problem, in reality it doesn't perceptibly affect most images. The JPEG compression code has been carefully tuned to compress data according to how human eyes actually see images, so it won't throw away critical details of an image. Of course, if you're digitizing something where detail is critical— an ultrasound of your unborn baby, or an aerial photograph—you'll want to avoid using any lossy compression format, including JPEG.

JPEG also supports a "quality" parameter, which can range from 0 to 100. This setting, often called "Q" for short, governs how much leeway JPEG has to compress the image. High Q values produce good-looking, but large, images; smaller values achieve better compression at the cost of some image quality. You can adjust an image's final appearance by saving it with different Q settings and eyeballing the results; for most purposes, a Q of 60-75 is adequate. For example, Figure 5.2 shows two versions of the same JPEG image. The left image was saved with a Q of 100, where-as the right image was saved with a Q of 40. The difference is evident, but the Q=40 picture still looks acceptable.

TIP Use JPEG for photographs. Experiment with the Q value for each image—strive to get the smallest possible file that still looks good on-screen.

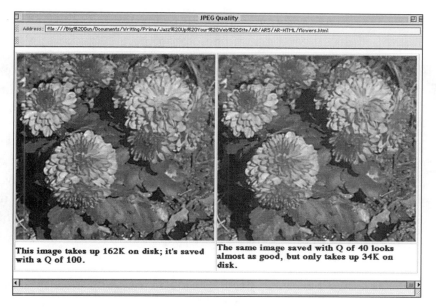

This image takes up 162K on disk; it's saved with a Q of 100.

The same image saved with Q of 40 looks almost as good, but only takes up 34K on disk.

Figure 5.2

The image on the left has a Q setting of 100; the one on the right has a Q of 40. See the difference?

JPEG images can also be interlaced; these *progressive JPEG* images bring the speed benefits of interlaced display at a slight cost in file size and decompression time. Most tools that can create JPEG files can also make them progressive.

PNG

The fundamental part of GIF compression is a formula patented by Unisys in 1977. For many years, Unisys didn't require GIF-using tools to license its patent, but that changed in 1994 when it became obvious that the Internet was here to stay. The licensing terms were simple: paraphrased, they were "license our patent if your program creates or uses GIF images, or we'll sic our lawyers on you."

This heavy-handed approach didn't sit well with many netizens, including a group led by Thomas Boutell. Boutell's group defined a new graphics standard, called the *Portable Next Generation* or PNG format (just say "ping!" and you've got it). PNG was designed to eventually replace GIF

as the preferred non-photo compression method of the Internet, and it does a good job on photos, too.

FIND IT ON ▶
THE WEB
The complete PNG specification is part of Thomas Boutell's home page; if you're interested in the advanced technical features of PNG, drop by **http://www.boutell .com/png/png.html**.

PNG supports up to 48 bits of color information and 256 transparent colors in each image. Its compression is as good as, or better than, GIF for graphic images. It supports interlacing for progressive display of large images, and it can be extended to use new algorithms in the future, meaning that it should never become obsolete. Perhaps best of all, PNG compression isn't encumbered by patents, so it can be freely implemented in commercial, freeware, and shareware tools.

With all these advantages to its credit, you might wonder why PNG hasn't already taken over the Web. The answer is simple: right now, you can only display it with a plug-in. Several freely available PNG plug-ins are available on the Internet, but PNG isn't yet a part of Navigator or Internet Explorer. Although it's a great format, with a lot of future potential, it's not widely used yet. Until this changes, you should probably only use PNG when you're sure that visitors will either have or be willing to get the plug-in.

Vector Formats

All the formats discussed so far are *raster* formats: their images are made up of individual pixels. If you build an image of a circle, it's stored as a collection of pixels arranged in a circle. As the circle gets bigger, so does your image file.

Vector graphics take a different approach that brings some unique benefits—our imaginary circle would be stored as a center point, a radius, a line width, and perhaps a fill pattern. The vector data file doesn't change size as the circle does. Vector graphics are intelligent, meaning that they can be rescaled, resized, colored, shaded, or filled in with patterns (as in an architectural or engineering drawing) without changing the file size.

Take a look at the circuit displayed in Figure 5.3. The GIF version on the top takes up 2,784 bytes, but the Computer Graphic Metafile, or CGM version, on the bottom is only 1,252 bytes! (CGM is a popular vector format that many graphics packages can handle as-is.)

Many competing vector formats are on the Web, but they all have a few things in common:

- They all require the use of plug-ins to display their content. Most viewer plug-ins are free, but some users won't bother to install them.

- Most of the vector formats are incompatible, so each format must be created with a separate tool and viewed with a separate plug-in.

- Some vector formats (like Macromedia's Flash) support animation and sound, whereas others (like Intergraph's ActiveCGM) support hyperlinks and scaling. The feature set for each format tends to be slightly different.

Figure 5.3

The two versions of the circuit look identical on-screen, but the CGM file at bottom is 54% smaller than the GIF version.

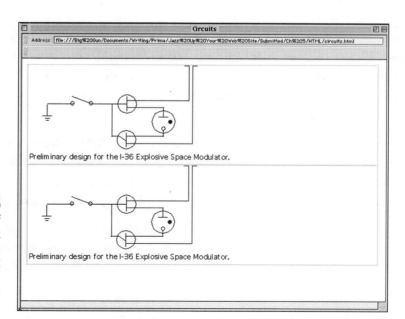

PLUG IN, TURN ON, WATCH OUT

When Netscape designed Navigator 2.0, they had the foresight to include a way for third parties to write small programs, called *plug-ins*, that could handle non-HTML data in a browser window. Plug-ins can display data in the browser, or they can do something else, like play music or audio data or recognize spoken commands.

FIND IT ON ▶
THE WEB   The BrowserWatch site has a directory of plug-ins, indexed both by name and platform. Check out http://browserwatch.iworld.com/plug-in.html.

Sounds great, doesn't it? You can use any kind of data you want on your Web pages, and as long as there's a plug-in for it, everyone will be able to see it.

Here's how plug-ins work: when the browser recognizes that some data on a page is meant for a plug-in, it will load the plug-in if it's installed and give it the data. If the needed plug-in isn't installed, both Internet Explorer and Navigator will tell the user, "Hey, you don't have the right plug-in for this format." Users must then go get the plug-in, install it, and return to your page.

In practice, though, there are a few rough edges to the plug-in concept. The biggest problem is that neither major browser ships with a rich set of plug-ins. This means that if you use embedded data on your pages, visitors will have to go somewhere else to get a plug-in. Some will, but some won't bother; of those who do go get the plug-ins, not all will come back to your page when the plug-in is installed.

To make things worse, not all plug-ins are available for all platforms. Many plug-ins only run on the Mac or Windows 95; some of the ones that run on both don't run under Windows 3.1; and almost no plug-in writers port their product to Unix. This fragmentation means that members of your target audience may not be able to get your plug-in even if they want to.

In general, the rule I recommend is this: use plug-in data to enrich your pages with video, sound, speech, and whatever else you want, but make sure that your pages still make sense when viewed without the proper plug-ins.

Even with these limitations, vector images are very useful for displaying data already in a vector format. House plans, design or drafting documents, maps and other non-photographic images can often be built as very small vector files rather than multi-megabyte scanned images.

Animation Formats

Besides GIF animations, you can build animated content for your pages using any of a large number of animation formats. Almost all use vector representations of your images, meaning that individual frames are very small. You can create striking animations with formats like Object Dancer, Apple Internet Graphics, or Macromedia Flash.

Each format has its own tool for creating animations in that format; Which one you use largely depends on whose tools you like and how much you're willing to pay. Of course, all these animation formats require plug-ins, so their availability may influence your choice.

FIND IT ON ▶
THE WEB   For a good sample of what you can do with GIF animations, check out **http://www.ani-zone.com/**.

Shockwave and Flash

Two animation formats are used widely enough that they merit special mention: Macromedia's Shockwave and Flash. Shockwave combines animation and interactivity into a single file format; it's possible to build games, product catalogs, or other interactive content without using Java or ActiveX. In fact, Shockwave is probably more common than either of these precisely because non-programmers can create useful, entertaining material without outside help.

Flash is like a lightweight Shockwave: it uses small, vector-based animations to produce cool interactive content. It can't do everything Shockwave can do, but the Flash creation tools are easier to use, the resulting files are smaller, and the required plug-in is smaller and takes up less RAM.

At present, you can only create Shockwave and Flash animations with tools from Macromedia, and your visitors must have the appropriate Macromedia plug-in for their browsers. Even with these requirements, "shocked" or "flashed" pages can offer content that's not easily duplicated with other tools.

Building Good Graphics

The first step to having good graphics on your pages is building them. Of course, if you're using photographs or images supplied by someone else, you may not be able to control everything about them, but you can still have a surprising amount of influence.

The two key steps to making your graphics stand out are to build good images in the first place and to put them into an appropriate format. (The real fun begins when you start putting images on your pages; I'll talk about that in the next section.)

Building Good Images

Graphic artists and other design professionals are used to thinking about color, size, and balance when they draw or design. For the rest of us, these are often afterthoughts that enter our drawings when most of the work is done. I can't teach you how to draw attractive pictures (mostly because I don't know how either!), but I can teach you how to get the best quality for whatever you *do* draw.

One key factor that affects image quality is how big your images are—that is, how many horizontal and vertical pixels they have. The size of your images affects not only how much space the image takes but also how the image looks when used on your page.

Large images tend to dominate the surrounding area, whereas small images get along better with their neighbors. When creating images, don't forget to size them according to how much real estate you want them to use.

Remember, too, that the viewer's browser has to have enough RAM to hold all the *uncompressed* images on your page. A 20K compressed GIF can expand to 200K or even more when it's uncompressed, and if you use many images, you can quickly suck up all the free memory in the visitor's computer. Be mindful of the total uncompressed size of all the images on any particular page.

The number of colors used in your images also influences both how images appear and how much space they take. If your image editor supports minimizing the number of colors in an image, taking advantage of this feature can shrink your images quite a bit.

Finally, bear in mind that your audience may have different viewing capabilities than you do. A richly detailed 640×480 image that looks great on your monitor might not look so good on a different computer or monitor.

Building Good Photographs

Many Web page authors use photographs on their pages; there's often no substitute for a photograph of whatever it is you're talking about in your pages. I can't help you find or take pictures; however, after you take the picture, you still need to get it into a size, color range, and format that will fit onto your page.

Before you start snapping pictures, decide how you're going to get your pictures into the computer. If you have existing prints, slides, or negatives, you can scan them with an optical scanner. These scanners "look" at the picture and convert it to a sequence of pixels. The more resolution and color depth your scanner has, the better; it's better to take a high-resolution image and *downsample* it to reduce its size than to start with a low-resolution version. You may also be able to find a film processor that can convert your existing images to PhotoCD format. PhotoCD images come in several resolutions, so you can pick the most appropriate one for your images and copy it right off the CD.

If you don't want to bother with a scanner, there's an alternative: you can send your film to a firm like Seattle FilmWorks (**http://www.film-works.com**), and they'll process your film, make prints, *and* scan your images. You can choose to get your pictures as old-fashioned prints, via e-mail or the Web, or any combination. It's inexpensive, too, especially when compared with the cost of a scanner.

If you're taking new pictures, you can go the conventional film-to-scanner-to-computer route, or you can consider using a digital camera. Digital cameras are getting cheaper, and better, every day. Even an inexpensive camera, like those from Kodak, Agfa, and Canon, takes pictures that are perfectly adequate for Web pages; these cameras have helped many amateurs get great pictures for their Web pages without a lot of hassle.

No matter how you capture the original image, the next consideration is which image format you'll use on your pages. Which formats you have available will depend on the scanner or camera you're using; all the major scanner packages can capture GIF, JPEG, BMP, and other formats. By contrast, most consumer cameras store pictures in one of three ways: the standard JPEG format, GIF format, or a proprietary format like Kodak's KDC. No matter where your images come from, the best format for general purpose Web use right now is JPEG because it's designed for compressing still photographs. PNG offers excellent compression, but still requires a plug-in, making it a poor choice for some uses.

The sharper and clearer your original image is, the better the JPEG version will look, even with low Q values. JPEG compression works by reducing the amount of color data in an image, so a good-looking image will still look better after compression than a fuzzy one.

After you have the image in JPEG format, you can experiment to minimize the color palette. You should also save the final with different Q settings until you find a setting just low enough to make the image look good while still keeping its size as small as possible.

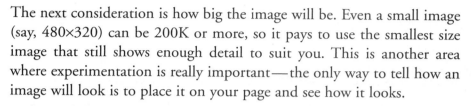

The next consideration is how big the image will be. Even a small image (say, 480×320) can be 200K or more, so it pays to use the smallest size image that still shows enough detail to suit you. This is another area where experimentation is really important—the only way to tell how an image will look is to place it on your page and see how it looks.

To apply the finishing touches to your images, you can use the image editor of your choice to resize, crop, retouch, or otherwise fiddle with the picture until you're happy with it.

ON THE

CD

The CD includes WebImage, an easy-to-use image editing tool for Windows (it's in IBM\multimed\webimage). With WebImage, you can crop, retouch, rotate, and adjust pictures until you're satisfied with their appearance.

Choosing the Right Format

With so many graphic formats to choose from, it's understandable if you're puzzled by the variety. Don't worry; finding the right format for your images is much easier than you think. You can make this complex decision simple by answering just a few questions:

- ☼ *What are my images?* If they're not photographs and they have fewer than 256 colors or many fine details, use GIF. if they have more than 256 colors, use JPEG. If they're photographs, use JPEG.

- ☼ *Are my images static?* If they are, any format will work fine. If you need animation, animated GIFs may work, or you may need a more complex format. See Saturday evening's session for more in-depth coverage of animation.

- ☼ *Is it safe to use exotic plug-ins?* If your target audience won't mind plug-ins, you can freely use PNG, Shockwave, or other formats. if not, stick with GIF or JPEG.

Beyond these questions, your skills and tools will determine what formats you use. If you find that a particular tool is easy for you to use, then use it and encourage visitors to get the appropriate plug-in or browser software they need to view your creations.

Putting Graphics on Your Pages

ON THE

CD

The HTML and graphic files used to generate many of the examples in this section are on the CD in the IBM\examples\satmorn directory. Mac users, you can read the files, too.

Now that you know how to size, capture, and color your images for the best look and smallest size, it's time to put them on your pages. As with the earlier sessions on tables, frames, and forms, I'll focus on what the HTML tags can do instead of the process of knowing which button to push. By the time you make it here, you'll already have some images; let's dive in and get them in front of your visitors.

Sizing Graphics

Every raster image has a finite size because the image is made out of pixels. You can display the image larger or smaller than its true size, but that true size stays the same.

To display an HTML page properly, a Web browser must know how big each element on the page is. When loading an image, the browser can do one of two things: It can uncompress the image and see how big it is, or it can rely on hints that tell it how much screen space the image needs. The first approach means that the browser must either wait to draw the page until all images have been loaded, or it must redraw the page every time an image download finishes. First-generation browsers like the original Mosaic took these approaches, and it was annoying.

A better solution is to give the browser hints telling it how big the image is. You do this with the WIDTH and HEIGHT attributes; they attach to the <IMG> tag like this:

```
<img src="/images/flowerpot.gif" width="80" height="40">
```

When the browser reads this tag, it knows to block out an 80-by-40 area on the page for that image. This knowledge makes it possible to quickly lay out the page text while the browser is still fetching images.

Any competent HTML editor will automatically insert these attributes for you when you place an image on the page. However, you can adjust the values yourself to get some interesting effects. For example, you can use the single-pixel image trick you learned in Saturday morning's tables session to space page elements as much as you want. You can also make quick bar graphs by adjusting the image's WIDTH attribute, as shown in Figure 5.4.

Preloading and Caching Graphics

Another trick you can perform with the WIDTH and HEIGHT attributes can make your Web pages seem to be super-fast. Normally, Web browsers will keep local copies of images and HTML pages you've already seen. When you go back to a page, the browser can use its local copy instead

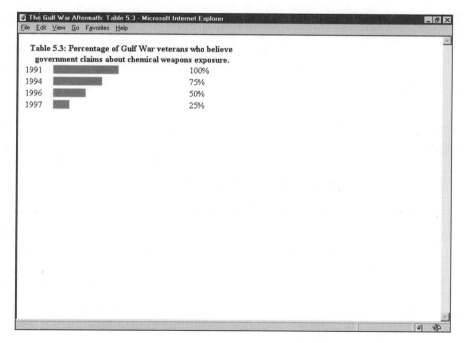

Figure 5.4

The top bar is shown at 100% of its size; the other bars are scaled using WIDTH to make a bar chart.

of making another potentially slow visit to the server. You can make this behavior, known as *caching*, work to your advantage in your pages by hiding tiny versions of your images on one of the first pages a visitor sees. When the visitor goes to the page that actually *uses* the images, they'll already be in her cache! Here's how to use this trick on your pages:

1. Figure out which images you want to preload. The best candidates are images frequently reused on your site, like navigation bars or category icons. Don't use large images—because they'll be pre-loaded while the visitor is reading something else, if she clicks on a link before the image is preloaded it'll have to be fetched again.

2. Decide which page will hold the images to be cached. Your home page may be a good choice, but another page may be better—it depends on what images you're caching and where they're used. If the images will be buried several links away from your home page, don't weight down the home page with images that few visitors will ever see.

3. Open the page, either with a text editor like Notepad or Alpha or with your HTML editor.

4. At the end of the page (but within the <BODY> container), add the following HTML for each image you want to preload:

```
<img src="whatever" width="1" height="1" alt="[preload]">
```

Of course, you'll need to replace "whatever" with the image you want preloaded.

Aligning Graphics

With the tricks you learned in Saturday morning's session on tables, you know how to put images where you want them on the page—but you can also get fairly precise control over how images line up with their neighboring text. The original HTML specification didn't give page authors much leeway in image placement; the current version is much better, thanks to prodding from Web page authors and browser vendors.

By default, images are aligned to the left margin of the page or table where they appear, as shown in Figure 5.5. If your image is very wide, this can look all right. In the figure, though, you can see a lot of unsightly white space between the picture and the right margin.

You can force images to the center or right margins in a number of ways. The easiest is to precede the image with a `<P>` tag and an alignment attribute; `<P ALIGN="center">` will center the image, whereas `<P ALIGN="right">` will force it to the right margin. Figure 5.6 shows a right-aligned version of the satellite tracking page from Figure 5.5.

A slightly more advanced method is to use *divisions*. HTML 3.2 supports the concept of divisions in a document; like sections in a Word document, divisions let you change style settings for one part of a page. The page shown in Figure 5.7 uses the `<DIV>` tag to align the image *and* page caption; the source to do this is shown in Listing 5.1.

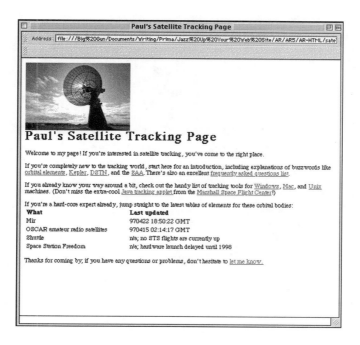

Figure 5.5

Images are left-aligned by default.

Figure 5.6

This image is right-aligned with the <P ALIGN= "right"> tag.

Figure 5.7

Centering the image helps to make the page more balanced.

TIP

■ ■

The biggest difference between the `<DIV>` and `<P ALIGN>` approaches is that the `<DIV>` tag is a container, so its alignment applies to everything in the container. Use `<DIV>` to align more than one item, as in the figure; use `<P ALIGN>` for individual items.

■ ■

Listing 5.1 SATELLITE-CENTER.HTML

The `<DIV>` tag lets you specify alignment for multiple items.

```
<div align="center">
<IMG SRC="../Artwork/Satellite.JPG" WIDTH="192" HEIGHT="128"
    ALIGN="BOTTOM" BORDER="0"><BR>
<H1>Paul's Satellite Tracking Page</H1>
<P>Welcome to my page! If you're interested in satellite tracking,
    you've come to the right place.
</div>
```

Of course, images have two dimensions, so it's natural that you should be able to align them in both dimensions. The `align="center"`, `align="right"`, and `align="left"` attributes control horizontal alignment. There's also a second set of attributes for controlling vertical alignment:

✪ `ALIGN="TOP"` tells the browser to align the top of the image with the top of whatever text is next to it, as shown in the top portion of Figure 5.8.

✪ `ALIGN="MIDDLE"` (which many editors and browsers use by default) aligns the image center with the text centerline; the middle part of Figure 5.8 shows an example.

✪ `ALIGN="BOTTOM"` aligns the bottom of the image with the baseline of the text, as shown at the bottom of Figure 5.8

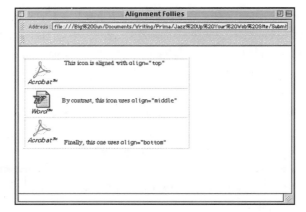

Figure 5.8

You can control the vertical relationship between text and images.

However, when you use the vertical alignment attributes, you'll quickly notice the problem shown in Figure 5.9. Notice that the caption text is neatly aligned next to the image—until the text is wrapped to the next line! The best way to solve this problem is to use a two-column table to hold the image and text together, as shown in Figure 5.10.

Figure 5.9

The vertical alignment tags only work until the end of the current line.

Figure 5.10

Using a two-column table fixes the alignment problem.

Using LOWSRC Images

Web pages that use many images can be frustrating to visitors who are using modems or other relatively slow links to the net. Without waiting for an image to be downloaded and decompressed, you often can't tell whether it's *worth* waiting for. Decompressing images can be a slow process; in addition, it can't take place until after the image has been completely downloaded.

Netscape thoughtfully added a way to work around these annoyances: let page authors specify a small, fast-loading version of their big, ornate graphics. Their idea was such a good one that it made it into the HTML standard. This bit of magic is the LOWSRC tag.

When used as part of an <IMG> tag, LOWSRC tells the browser that an alternate, low-resolution form of the image is available. The browser can fetch the low-res version and display it immediately, while it downloads the high-resolution one. You use it like this:

```
<img src="http://www.ljl.com/images/armadillo.gif"
        lowsrc="http://www.ljl.com/images/lowdillo.gif">
```

A browser that reads this HTML will immediately load and display lowdillo.gif while simultaneously downloading the larger armadillo.gif. When the big image is completely loaded and decompressed, the browser will display it in the same space. You can use LOWSRC with any image you can put into an <IMG> tag; it's not limited to use with GIF images as shown here. Figure 5.11 shows an example of the same image in high- and low-resolution forms.

Many graphics editors can automatically create a graphic suitable for LOWSRC. If yours can't, you can fake it by blowing up your original image to 400% of its normal size, then forcing it back to the original size, and saving it separately.

Figure 5.11

The same image can be shown in high- and low-resolution forms.

TIP

You can also cheat on creating LOWSRC graphics by using the WIDTH and HEIGHT attributes. Just take your big image and scale it down to 25% or so of its original size; then use it in a LOWSRC tag. For example, if your big image is 320×240, create a small version that's only 80×60; then use it like this:

```
<img src="http://yoursite.com/images/big.gif" lowsrc="http://your-
    site.com/images/small.gif" width=320 height=240>
```

The browser will helpfully scale the 80x60 image up to the full size; it'll be chunky, but it will load fast, and it'll disappear when the full-size image is loaded.

Using Client-Side Imagemaps

You can make any image a link by enclosing its <IMG> tag inside of an <A HREF> container. However, this approach limits you to using squares or rectangles for your links—you can't attach multiple links to different parts of a single image.

Figure 5.12 shows a simple navigation tool. If the table were a single image (as opposed to a table with four images), there would be no way to have each quadrant link to its own page.

Imagemaps provide you an escape from this restriction by letting you map arbitrary parts of an image to any links you choose. You can use imagemaps for almost any image, because you can use circles, rectangles, or oddly shaped polygons to establish the link. To apply an imagemap to

Figure 5.12

This navigational block is really an imagemap.

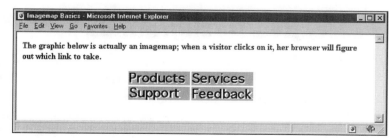

the navigational block in Figure 5.12, you use the HTML shown in Listing 5.2. The image has two new attributes: ISMAP tells the browser that this image has a map, and USEMAP tells it which map to use when someone clicks this particular image.

Listing 5.2 IMAGEMAP1.HTML

The imagemap code ties regions of the image to HTML links.

```
<P ALIGN="CENTER"><IMG SRC="../Artwork/navblock.gif" WIDTH="258"
    HEIGHT="63" ALIGN="BOTTOM" BORDER="0" USEMAP="#navblock" ISMAP>

<MAP Name="navblock">
    <AREA Shape="Rect" coords = "117,29,232,58" HREF="feedback.html">
    <AREA Shape="Rect" coords = "4,28,118,58"  HREF="support.html">
    <AREA Shape="Rect" coords = "118,3,232,29" HREF="services.html">
    <AREA Shape="Rect" coords = "4,3,118,29"   HREF="products.html">
</MAP>
```

The map itself is just a list of areas. Areas can be rectangles, circles, or polygons with any number of sides. Each area has a COORDS attribute, which defines its clickable area, and an HREF attribute that specifies which link to take when the area's clicked.

ON THE CD

The CD includes two excellent Windows imagemap editors: Thomas Boutell's Mapedit (IBM\webtools\mapedit) and MapThis! (IBM\webtools\mapthis). In addition, many HTML editors include imagemap editing functions.

Adding Effective Backgrounds

Background images are supposed to be just that—in the background, where they're barely noticed. The background of a page can make or wreck its visual appeal. A good background will emphasize and reinforce the colors and designs of the page "above" it, whereas a poorly chosen one will make the page difficult, or even impossible, to read.

Background images can be any size. If the image is smaller than the browser window, the browser will tile it to fit. Tiling is both horizontal and vertical; the joining of adjacent tiles can result in some interesting effects, as shown in Figure 5.13. If the image is larger than the browser, the excess part isn't displayed.

Background images can be GIF files, although you can't use an animated GIF as a background. You may also use JPEG files for your background, although the extra time needed to decompress them argues against using them. Although it's possible, you should avoid using interlaced or progressive images for backgrounds because the background image will usually be loaded first.

Background Dos and Don'ts

Nature has all sorts of interesting textures: wood grain, grass, silk, ocean foam, and orange peel are just a few examples. However decorative, many

Figure 5.13

The background image on the left is small, so it's tiled; the one on the right is a hefty 1600 pixels wide, so it doesn't tile.

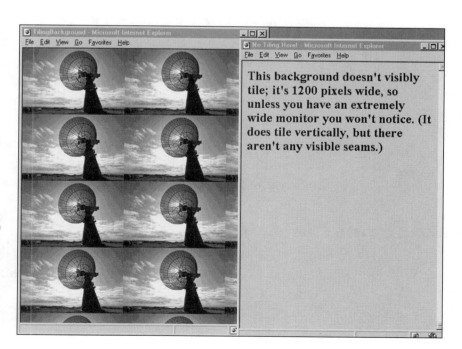

of these textures would be worthless for use as backdrops—imagine trying to read a newspaper printed on elephant skin or pine bark! In real life, most backgrounds are carefully chosen so that they don't detract from whatever's in the foreground.

Many of these physical textures have been made into backgrounds that you can use in Web pages or images. However, just because you *can* use pineapple skin for a background doesn't mean you *should*. Here are a few simple rules to follow when choosing backgrounds:

- *Pick good colors.* Just like with background colors, you have to make sure that people will still be able to read your text over whatever background you pick. If you're using light text, pick a darker background, and vice versa—people's eyes depend on contrast to distinguish letter shapes.

- *If you're using patterns, pick a good pattern size.* A finely detailed pattern may look pleasingly intricate, but if you overlay it with small text, it may be hard for people to read. In addition, remember that some visitors will be using relatively low-resolution screens—don't get carried away.

- *Pick a good tile size.* Browsers will take your background pattern and *tile* it to cover the entire screen. The bigger your pattern image, the fewer copies the browser will need for tiling, but the longer it takes to download.

- *Don't get too busy.* If your pattern has too many details or colors, it'll be difficult for people to pick out the text; most surfers will quickly give up on pages that make their heads hurt.

Backgrounds in Action

Although most pages still use solid color backgrounds, the idea of subtly enhancing pages with well-chosen backgrounds is catching on. Let's look at a few real-world examples.

Using Natural Textures

Nothing feels quite like a piece of expensive paper; a heavy bond with high fiber content has a substantial, expensive feel to it. Maybe that's why high-cotton bond is used for U.S. currency! If your Web page is something (like a resume or CV) that you'd normally print on expensive paper, why not use a paperlike background like the one shown in Figure 5.14? It won't help if the visitor prints your pages, but it adds a nice touch anyway.

ON THE

CD

For a great starting set of textures, check out AusComp's 101 Backgrounds, on the CD in the `IBM\multimed\Auscomp` folder. Mac users, you can use these too.

Of course, you can always use backgrounds that mimic the look of other paper types, too; see Figure 5.15 for a good example. You could instead use graph paper, a shopping list, or any other kind of paper for a similar effect.

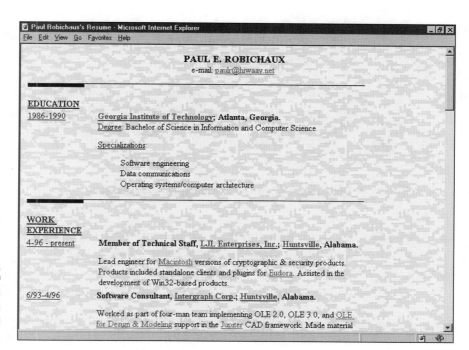

Figure 5.14

The paperlike background gives this resume a little extra boost.

Figure 5.15

Nothing says "checklist" quite like a yellow legal pad.

You can also use backgrounds like stone, rock, or fabric; these can lend your pages a bit of flair with little effort. (Remember the preceding rules, though, or people might miss your content while staring at your backgrounds!)

Using Stripe Backgrounds

In Saturday morning's frames session, you learned how to use multicolumn tables to give your pages margins and borders. You can combine tables with striped backgrounds to make the Web page equivalent of a casserole—it's easy to whip up, looks good, and will please your guests. Check out Figure 5.16 for an example.

Stripe backgrounds work best when you keep them to two or three colors. To avoid unsightly tiling for users with big screens, I always make my stripes at least 1200 pixels wide; a 1200×10 stripe is only around 9-10K.

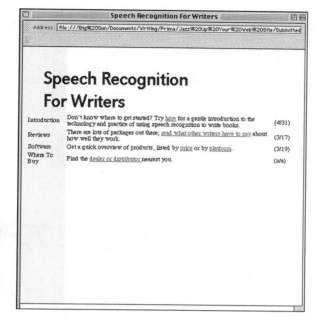

Figure 5.16

Combine stripe
backgrounds with
multicolumn tables
to add interest to
your pages.

Using Accent Stripes

An alternative to the solid-color stripes from the preceding section are accent stripe backgrounds. You can create these the same way as ordinary stripe backgrounds; the only two differences are that you'll usually have a single striped area, and that the stripe will be narrower than ordinary stripe backgrounds. Figure 5.17 shows a sample; you can use any repeating pattern, or even a solid color.

Where to Find Cool Backgrounds

Now that I've whetted your appetite, you're probably wondering where you can get backgrounds for your pages. The good news is that you can get great backgrounds in a number of ways, and you can build a good collection without spending a lot of money. Here are four suggestions to help you get started:

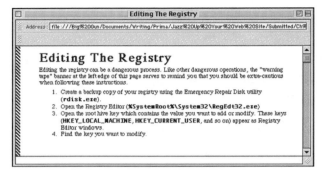

Figure 5.17

The "construction" stripe warns readers that they're about to do something particularly dangerous.

○ *Draw them yourself.* Especially for stripe backgrounds, drawing your own backgrounds can be an easy way to get even more pride of ownership in your pages.

○ *Scan or photograph them.* If you have a particular texture you want to capture, why not take a picture and get it scanned? If you have access to a scanner, this can be an excellent way to capture textures for use in backgrounds.

○ *Get them from the Web.* Zillions of textures are available on the Web; a quick InfoSeek or AltaVista search for "texture background" will turn up several dozen worthwhile sites. In particular, check out Kaleidoscope (**http://www.steveconley.com/kaleid.htm**) for a great list of links to other texture sites.

○ *Get them on CD.* Many companies sell texture libraries on CD; these range in price from $49 to several hundred dollars, depending on the number and quality of textures you get. Although this is the most expensive route, you can get great textures that might be impossible for you to reproduce yourself.

Accenting Your Pages

Now that you've filled your pages with graphics, you'll be pleased to know that you can add even more flair to your pages with a few simple changes.

After your pages are designed and written the way you want them, these tweaks can make them look even better.

Unload Your Bullets

One of the first changes I always recommend is to get rid of bullets. Why? Because all they do is break up the visual flow of a list. If you've been keeping your lists to no more than seven items, you don't need the extra markings. In particular, don't replace the standard browser bullets by using your own GIF images as bullets; this makes the standard clutter of a bulleted list even worse.

If you feel like your lists absolutely require some kind of visual markings, I recommend using indentation. You can use HTML "dictionary lists," or you can put each list item in its own table cell as described in Saturday morning's session on tables.

However, even die-hard bullet haters have to admit that there are times when bullets are useful—for example, when giving lots of dry technical information like engine specifications or baseball statistics. Use your own sense of what looks good and what doesn't to guide you.

Rule Out Horizontal Rules

Take a look at almost any print publication. You won't see horizontal rules used to separate adjacent pieces of text. Of course, paper designers still have a few tricks up their sleeve that Web page designers can't use yet, but that's no excuse.

Instead of using horizontal rules, you can separate text by using table borders. Better still, use tables and spacers to put white space where you want it, and let the white space separate your text instead.

If you just want to set off a block of text like a signature or a company address, consider using a *dingbat*. Dingbats are those funny little characters you've probably seen in the Zapf Dingbats font; they were originally

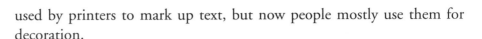

used by printers to mark up text, but now people mostly use them for decoration.

The dingbat shown in Figure 5.18 is simple: a plain blue square that I drew in about 45 seconds. It's small, but it adds a dash of color and interest to an otherwise ordinary page.

Separate Text Runs

Speaking of white space, you probably haven't noticed it, but most books use indentation to separate paragraphs instead of using blank spaces between paragraphs. There's a good reason for this: indentation is the best way to signal the reader's eye that something new is starting. You can indent paragraphs yourself by using a single-pixel transparent GIF as a spacer, or by using the <spacer> tag discussed in Saturday morning's tables session.

Figure 5.18

The square blue dingbat marks off the text from the fancy signature.

Tool Tips

Although you can create Web pages without any sophisticated tools, not many people can create graphics files without some sort of image editor. Here are some suggestions and tips for getting the most from whatever image editor you're using.

Minimize, Minimize, Minimize

The fewer colors and patterns your images use, the smaller their files will be. Several excellent books on Web graphics can give you the excruciating technical details on shrinking your files to the smallest possible size; you don't have to go to complete extremes, but it's worth learning whether your image editor can automatically reduce the color palette for an image. If it has that feature, use it—your visitors will thank you for it.

Use Superpalettes if You Can

Normally, every image on your pages will have its own color palette. This is fine if all your images use similar colors. However, because Netscape can only display 216 colors at a time, if you have two images that together use more than 216 colors, one or both will be dithered, and it'll end up ugly.

BoxTop's PhotoGIF and GIFmation (for Macintosh; in the `Macintosh\webtools` directory) can automatically create superpalettes for images, as can many Windows image editors.

Your image editor may be able to create a *superpalette* for all images on a page or site. A superpalette is just a common palette that all images share; using one helps to ensure that your images have consistent colors and look good when displayed.

Get a Map Editor

Imagemaps are really cool, but editing them by hand is a time-consuming, error-prone, laborious process. Rather than spending your time counting pixels, I recommend that you get a good map editor and use it for your imagemaps. (The CD includes MapEdit and MapThis for Windows.) You'll be glad you did!

Wrap It Up!

Earlier, you learned how to design pages. Now you've learned how to fill them with graphics. When you're comfortable building graphics for your pages, you'll find that there's literally nothing you can't do! Your design skills will continue to improve as you practice.

Think of this session as getting ready for a night on the town: now that you're all scrubbed clean and dressed up, it's time to paint the town red by adding animation, sound, and video to your pages. You'll do all that, and more, in the next session.

Adding Animation, Sound, and Video

- ✿ Spicing Up Your Pages with Animated GIFs
- ✿ QuickTime — A One-Man Band
- ✿ Adding Sound and Music to Your Pages
- ✿ Adding Video to Your Pages

Now it's Saturday evening—jazz clubs all over the world are packed with eager listeners who've come to soak up hot jazz. Meanwhile, you're about to learn how to add hot Web multimedia—animation, sound, and video—to your Web pages. Soon you'll be able to rival your local jazz club for audience appeal!

In the preceding sessions, you learned how to use tables, frames, and forms to structure the information on your pages. These elements give you a great way to present static text or graphic information, but you can't use them alone to enliven your pages with movement or sound—that's what this session is all about.

You'll learn the basics behind the graphic, sound, and video formats that make the Web come alive—and how to use them! You'll start by building animated GIF images and then move on to capturing sound and video and using them on your pages. Grab your director's megaphone and let's get started!

Spicing Up Your Pages with Animated GIFs

The original GIF format specified how to make static, two-dimensional images, and for a long while that was fine. In 1988 or so, CompuServe (originator of the GIF format) wanted to create moving images, like animated weather maps, for use on its online service. Because CompuServe was already planning on revising the GIF format to include transparency and interlacing, some bright soul came up with the idea of extending the GIF format to support animations—and the animated GIF was born!

What's an Animated GIF?

Basically, an animated GIF is a sequence of individual images—but you probably guessed that! In all seriousness, the biggest difference between an animated GIF and its static counterparts is that the animated GIF file contains more than one image. The images follow one another like box-cars in a train. Rather than a locomotive, however, a chunk of data specifies how many images are in the sequence, how long to pause between successive images, and so on.

When a browser (or other program) loads an animated GIF, it decodes the instructions that tell it how many frames there are and how long to pause between frames. It then uncompresses all the frames and starts displaying them in sequence. Browsers that don't understand the animation instructions treat the animated GIF like an ordinary GIF and just display the first image.

You can use an animated GIF anywhere you would use a static GIF—in a table cell, as a header or footer, or wherever else you want. First, though, you'll have to build them.

 NOTE Don't confuse animated GIFs with other Web animation formats like Macromedia Flash, Apple Internet Graphics, or TotallyHip Sizzler. These formats require plug-ins, but most browsers can display animated GIFs without additional software.

Building Animated GIFs

So, how do you build animated GIFs? One frame at a time! Just like Chuck Jones (creator of Wile E. Coyote and the Road Runner), you'll have to start by building each frame of your animation as a separate image. The easiest way to do this is to make a *storyboard* of your animation idea; the storyboard can be a list, set of drawings, or whatever else helps you organize your thoughts about what will go in the sequence. After you have your ideas in order, it's time to build the individual images.

There are three simple rules to follow when building your images:

- ✿ *All your images should be the same size.* Animated GIFs don't provide for having frames of different size, so every image in the animation sequence needs to have the same width and height.

- ✿ *All your images should use a similar palette.* The final animated GIF can use a maximum of 256 colors *total,* so if you have three images and each uses a unique set of 128 different colors, you're in trouble! Many tools (like BoxTop's GIFmation) can automatically adjust the animation's palette to include all the needed colors.

- ✿ *All your images should have the same transparent color, if any.* If you're using transparency effects in your animation, all frames should use the same color as the transparent color.

The easiest way to meet all three of these requirements is to start off by creating the first frame of your animation sequence; then copying it and editing the copies to make subsequent frames. This ensures that your images all match, and it's easy to do besides.

Building Animated GIFs with AniMagic

In writing this book, I've tried to avoid endorsing or giving instructions for particular tools—focusing instead on providing useful advice that would help you no matter what tool you were using. I'm going to break that rule to talk about AniMagic, a Windows 95 program for building animated GIFs. Although most of you will already have settled on an image editor and an HTML editor that you prefer, not many people have chosen an animated GIF editor yet, and this one is easy to use, so I'll cover it briefly.

ON THE

CD

A 30-day trial version of AniMagic is on the CD (it's in `IBM\Webtools\AniMagic`). Mac users, don't feel left out: BoxTop Software's GIFMation is on there too in `Macintosh\Webtools\GIFMation`.

The first step, as discussed earlier, is to build the individual frames you're going to use in your animation. AniMagic can use GIF, Windows bitmap (`BMP`), and PCX files; it can also import text files and draw them as animation frames. The frames I'll use in this example are shown in Figure 6.1.

After you've installed AniMagic on your computer, you'll see its main window, as shown in Figure 6.2. Within the AniMagic window, you'll see two floating palettes. The Frame List window shows all frames in the current animation; you can move between them by using the arrow keys or clicking a frame with the mouse. After you click a frame in the Frame List, it's displayed in the main window area. The Palette window shows the color palette necessary to display the entire animated GIF. AniMagic automatically minimizes the palette by removing redundant entries as you add new frames.

Figure 6.1

The sample animation has six different frames.

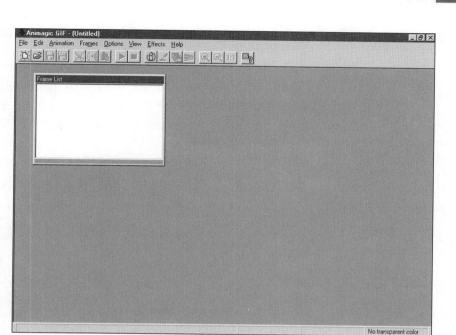

Figure 6.2

AniMagic lists available frames in the Frame List window and draws the selected frame in the background.

The two commands you'll need to use to put frames into your animation are both in the File menu: File, Insert Frame and File, Append Frames. When you insert a frame, it's added *before* the selected frame in the Frame List. When you append a frame, it's added to the *end* of the Frame List.

Here's how to build an animation with the sample frames included on the CD.

1. Open AniMagic and use the File, Insert Frame command to insert the file 1.gif from the CD. You'll see a window like the one shown in Figure 6.3; the Frame List will include the frame you've just inserted.

2. Use the File, Append Frames command to add the remaining six frames, 2.gif through 7.gif. As you add each frame, notice how the Palette window changes to include new colors added with each subsequent frame. When you've added all seven frames, your animation will look like the picture in Figure 6.4.

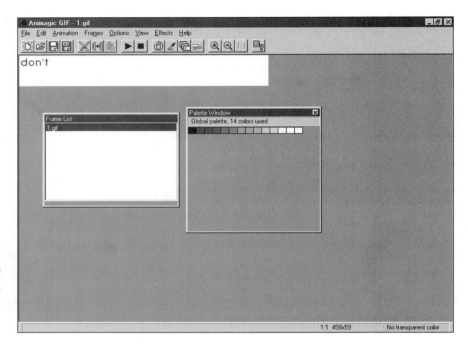

Figure 6.3

The AniMagic
window with a
single animation
frame.

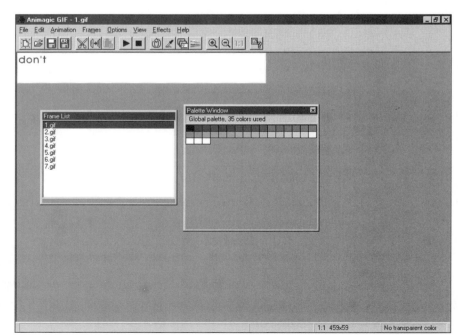

Figure 6.4

The complete
animation has a
bigger palette than
the initial frame.

3. Use the <u>F</u>ile, <u>S</u>ave Anim command to save your animation; then use the <u>A</u>nimation, <u>P</u>lay command to see it in motion.

Now that you've built an animation, there are still a few things you should do to it before putting it on your Web pages. Before you unleash your new creation on the net, you need to make a few small adjustments to control its behavior and appearance.

Preparing Your Animation for the Web

The first step in getting your animation ready for the Web is to control its playback speed, or *frame rate*. The frame rate governs how fast the animation plays, thus how long it takes to display from beginning to end. AniMagic has a flexible set of frame rate controls, which you get to with the <u>A</u>nimation, <u>F</u>rame Rate command.

The Frame Rate dialog box is shown in Figure 6.5. Here's what the controls do; by using them, you can affect the overall speed of your animation, and you can also make any single frame linger longer, or disappear faster, than its brethren.

- ✿ The list on the right-hand side of the dialog box shows all frames in the animation.

- ✿ The All Frames group controls the playback speed for the entire animation. Use the Milliseconds per frame control to adjust how long you want each frame to stay on-screen; the Frames per second counter will adjust to show you how many frames per second your setting will yield.

- ✿ The Selected Frame controls how long the selected frame in the right-hand list will stay on-screen. The Repeat control lets you specify how many times you want the frame to repeat; the number of repetition times the Milliseconds per frame value from the All Frames group gives the total on-screen time for the selected frame, as shown in the Milliseconds this frame field.

By default, AniMagic assumes that you want your animation to *loop* forever. It will play endlessly until the visitor moves to another page. This

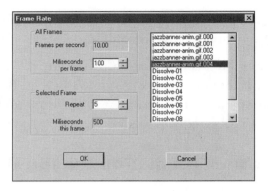

Figure 6.5

The Frame Rate
dialog box lets
you specify how
long each frame of
the animation will
stay on-screen.

endless looping tends to annoy visitors, and it can distract their attention from the rest of your page's content. To turn off looping altogether, you can click the loop icon in the toolbar (it's the green circular arrow next to the "stop playing" icon.) If you want to allow a small number of loops, you can instead use the Animation, Loop Count command to set the number of repetitions you want to allow.

After you've adjusted the loop count appropriately, it's time to consider the size of your animation. Your animation will be as big as the sum of its individual frames, but you can save a little space by optimizing the animation's palette to remove unneeded colors. To do this, use AniMagic's Options, Global Palettes menu to turn on automatic optimization; AniMagic will take care of shrinking your palette for you.

If your image has more than 32 colors, consider using the Animation, Reduce Color Depth command to shrink the palette further. This will have some effect on image quality, but the size savings will make it worthwhile.

Adding Special Effects

One of the coolest things about AniMagic is its built-in special effects. The Effects menu lets you build in several types of visual effects, including fades in and out, dissolves, and side-to-side wipes. When you choose any of the effects, you'll get a dialog box like the one shown in Figure 6.6, which is for the wipe effect. Each effect has its own unique settings, but they all do

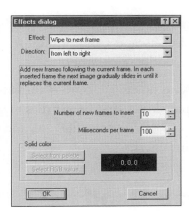

Figure 6.6

The Effects dialog box lets you insert effects into your animation sequences.

the same thing: they insert a sequence of frames into your animation to implement the effect. You control how many frames should be used for the effect and how long each frame should linger. By experimenting with these settings, you can get just the visual effect you're looking for.

Putting Animated GIFs on Your Pages

After you've built your animated GIFs using AniMagic, GIFMation, or whatever other tool you're using, you're ready to include it in your pages. As you learned in the previous session, you'll use the <IMG> tag to tell the browser what image to display.

For animated GIFs, it's especially important to use the WIDTH and HEIGHT parameters to tell the browser how much space to reserve for the animation. Placement is important too because your image is animated. Visitors' eyes will be drawn to the motion, so you can put your animated image in a spot on your page where the attention it attracts will go to good use.

Now would be a good time for me to remind you of one of the key things I hope you learned from Friday evening's session: don't overdo it. This is especially important for two reasons. First, having several animated GIFs moving around at once is distracting to your visitors. In fact, enough people have expressed annoyance with overuse of animated GIFs that Internet Explorer 4.0 and Netscape Communicator 4.0 both include options to turn off GIF animation altogether.

The other reason, of course, is download time—animated GIF files tend to be bigger than not-animated files, and bigger files means more waiting for your visitors. Be aware of how big your files are, and your visitors will thank you for your thoughtfulness.

QuickTime—A One-Man Band

Before I go any further, it's time for a brief digression to talk about how visitors will view the fancy sound, music, and video you're about to learn how to put on your pages. In addition, you'll probably need some software to create (or edit) that content yourself. QuickTime provides both capabilities, and it runs on the Mac and Windows both.

FIND IT ON ▶
THE WEB If you don't already have QuickTime on your computer, you can get it from **http://www.quicktime.apple.com**.

What Is QuickTime?

Many types of computer data have their own structure. Databases, word processing files, spreadsheets, and so on each have a format that defines the file's content. Some types of data are dependent on the passage of time. For example, video and sound clips must play at a certain rate to be intelligible—too fast and you can't understand them, too slow and they don't make sense.

QuickTime was Apple's answer to the problem of how to accurately capture, time, store, and play back this time-based data. It's not just a piece of software; instead, it's a framework for capturing, editing, and viewing this data.

The QuickTime standard quickly caught on in the market and is now the backbone for products ranging from high-end video editing systems for professionals to CD-ROM based games, Web pages, and even TV commercials.

Although the preceding may sound like an Apple commercial, Quick-Time really *is* the fundamental base for time-based media on the Web. Netscape includes a QuickTime plug-in for its browser as a standard part of the navigator and Communicator installations, and many Internet Explorer users have it as well.

As of this writing, QuickTime supports several data types of interest to Web page authors. In addition to compressed video and sound, QuickTime can play back MIDI and digitized sound files, MPEG movies, AVI movies, and QuickTime VR panorama files. (Don't worry if you don't recognize all these formats; they'll be described in more detail later in this session.)

NOTE As of this writing, QuickTime 2.5 is the current version for Macs, and QuickTime 2.12 is the current Windows version. Apple has promised to release QuickTime 3.0 during summer 1997 for both Mac and Windows, so check its site often.

QuickTime *isn't* an editing tool in and of itself—if you want to create your own sound or video clips, you'll need appropriate hardware and tools. Appendix C discusses some popular editing and capture software and hardware and tells you how to choose the right setup for you.

Getting and Installing QuickTime

You'll need the QuickTime software yourself if you want to test and view the sound and videos you're going to add to your pages. Fortunately, it's simple to install and use, and it's free! The exact procedure differs depending on whether you have a Mac or a Windows box.

For a Macintosh

Because QuickTime is an Apple product, it's been bundled on the MacOS system software CD for a few years now. If you have a MacOS 7.5, 7.5.5,

7.6, or 8.0 CD, it will have a QuickTime installer on it, with instructions. QuickTime uses the standard MacOS installer, so you already know how to use it—run the installer, click Easy Install, and go get a cold drink while the installer does all the dirty work. (If you don't have a CD, you can get the software from **http://www.quicktime.apple.com**.)

The MacOS QuickTime runs on any 68020, 68030, 68040, or Power-PC Macintosh, and the installer will automatically load the right components for the type of machine you have.

For a Windows Machine

If you want to install QuickTime for Win95 or Windows NT, your first step is to visit the QuickTime Download Page at **http://www.quick-time.apple.com/sw/qtwin32.html**; it's shown in Figure 6.7. You'll be able to choose between an "Easy Install" download that includes the QuickTime software core, the QuickTime plug-in for Internet Explorer

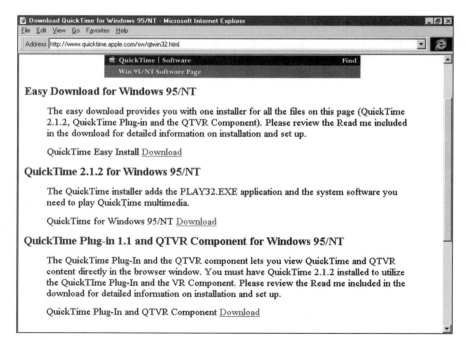

Figure 6.7

The QuickTime Download Page is where you get started with QuickTime by downloading the installer.

and Netscape, and the QuickTime VR component for using QuickTime VR 3D movies.

After you've downloaded the installer, uncompress it (using PKZip, WinZip, or your favorite file utility) and run the setup program, QTEASY32.EXE. You'll be asked to confirm that you really want to install the software. When you say yes, the InstallShield-based installer will start doing its work. You'll be asked to confirm various file checks and installation options; then the installation will load QuickTime onto your computer.

After it's finished, you'll have to wait while the installer loads the Quick-Time plug-in for you; the installer will ask whether you want to install the plug-in for Netscape or Internet Explorer if you have both on your computer—otherwise, it's smart enough to figure out which one to install. After the plug-in install finishes, that's it!

Part of the QuickTime for Windows installation is a control panel, shown in Figure 6.8, that you can use to see exactly what drivers and components QuickTime is using. QuickTime is careful to pay attention to your hardware setup, so you probably won't ever have to change these settings—it's still nice to know they're there!

Figure 6.8

The QuickTime control panel doesn't yet know the difference between Win95 and Windows NT 4.0.

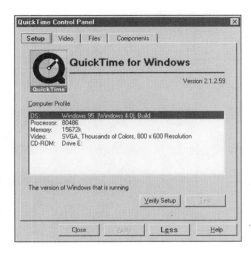

Checking Out QuickTime

After you've installed QuickTime, test it to make sure that it works on your Mac or Windows machine. Fire up your browser and visit **http://www.quicktime.apple.com/sam/** for a great gallery of sample movies and sound files.

For an added treat, drive over to **http://www.rearden.com/webcam.html** — the guys at Rearden Technology have a live Web camera overlooking San Francisco Bay. Great scenery!

Pointing Your Visitors to QuickTime

Even though Netscape includes the QuickTime plug-in as part of the standard Communicator and Navigator installations, not every visitor to your site will have it. Of those who do, not all will already have the QuickTime software. You've probably seen the "Netscape Now!" and "Download Internet Explorer" logos that Netscape and Microsoft encourage page authors to use—Apple has one too, as shown in Figure 6.9. To signal your visitors that they'll be seeing QuickTime-based content, just paste this HTML into your pages:

```
<A HREF="http://www.quicktime.apple.com"><IMG
    SRC="http://www.quicktime.apple.com/graphics/downQT.gif"
    WIDTH="77" HEIGHT="37" ALIGN="BOTTOM" BORDER="0"
    ALT="Get QuickTime Now!">
```

Of course, you can't install it *for* your visitors, but the process is pretty simple, so you shouldn't encounter any problems.

Figure 6.9

Apple's "Download QuickTime Now" logo is free for your use.

Adding Sound and Music to Your Pages

Web pages were once totally silent. Some pages would include sounds in Sun's audio format, but the technical capacity to deliver live audio or music didn't exist, and most people didn't have hardware that could capture sounds.

Of course, that has changed. Macs and PCs routinely now include sound-capture and playback hardware, and software manufacturers have produced tools for capturing, editing, and delivering sounds from computer to human with a minimum of technical tomfoolery.

Understanding Sound and Music Formats

It seems like everything on the Internet comes in several formats: even plain old HTML has Netscape and Microsoft versions. Sound and music are no exception; there are several different formats for capturing sounds on a computer for later playback, and sometimes it seems like no two of them can be interchanged. Most sounds come in one of five flavors, though—MIDI, WAV, .AU, .SND, and AIFF. Let's see how each works.

MIDI

MIDI stands for *Musical Instrument Digital Interface*; it was originally designed as a standard way for musical instruments to talk amongst themselves, as well as to enable them to exchange musical data with computers. The MIDI format is like sheet music: it's a list of musical notes, along with timing information and codes that tell sound software or hardware which instruments to use when playing each note.

You usually create MIDI files by using a music composition program or an external musical keyboard. You play music on the keyboard, and the software turns your playing into a stream of MIDI instructions. Of course, you can switch between several instruments to get that well-rounded sound. After you've created a MIDI file, anyone with a MIDI-capable computer or sound card can play it back; Windows and QuickTime both include MIDI drivers that interpret the notes, make appropriate noises, and send them to the sound hardware for playback.

MIDI files are usually used as background music or sound effects on a Web page. They offer a compact representation of music—the visitor's computer has to do all the hard work of decoding the notation and turning it into sounds. As a bonus, they're easy to create: just plug a musical keyboard (available for under $100; see Appendix C) into your computer and start jamming!

.WAV, .AU, .SND, and AIFF Files

If MIDI files are sheet music, these other formats are like tape recordings. Instead of recording the notes and instruments to be used when playing back the sound or music, these formats actually capture the sounds, convert them to digital patterns, and turn them back into audible information when they're played back.

WAV files, identified by their .WAV extension, are the native Windows sound format. The Windows 95 and Windows NT sound recorders, as well as the multimedia recorders provided with many popular sound cards, record sounds in this format.

The .AU file format was pioneered by Sun Microsystems; it is similar to, but incompatible with, the wave format. Most programs that can capture sounds from an external microphone or other source can save in this format. Likewise, the .SND format is the native Macintosh format, recorded by the Mac's onboard sound recording circuitry; unlike Sun's format, the Mac format is understood by many non-Mac applications.

The *Audio Interchange File Format* (AIFF) was developed to provide a standard way for computers to share sounds, but it never became as popular as wave or .SND files, though you'll sometimes see these files out on the Web.

Streaming Audio

All the formats just described share one common characteristic: they're recorded and stored for later playback, so they don't work well for live broadcasts. The cure for this problem was the invention of new audio formats that send sound data out in little squirts. RealAudio (from Progressive Networks; **http://www.real.com**) was the first streaming audio format, and it remains the most popular. Streaming audio is commonly used for live broadcasts of news events, concerts, sporting events, and computer-industry trade shows. After you've built an audio stream, you can store it and serve it to visitors, who can jump to any point in the stream— great for skipping the boring parts of sporting events or speeches!

As the name implies, a *stream* is a continually flowing sequence of data. The faster your Internet connection is, the "deeper" a stream you can receive and play back—with more bandwidth, you can dip into the stream and grab a picture or sound bite for display more often. Unlike the audio schemes outlined previously, streaming audio formats are designed to cope with low-bandwidth links by dropping sounds and adjusting their compression to compensate for the narrow channel.

The biggest drawback to streaming audio is that all the available streaming formats require special software to take digitized sound and turn it into a stream. This software is fairly expensive, and using it is outside the scope of this book. At least for the near future, you probably won't have any streaming audio on your site.

Getting Sound and Music into Your Computer

Before you can start serving sounds to your visitors, you have to get it into your computer. The exact process by which you do this depends on whether you're using Windows or a Mac, and what, if any, extra software you're using; for that reason, I won't talk about it here (if you need more details, see Appendix C). Instead, I want to examine the basic process behind capturing sounds and making MIDI music.

Making Music with MIDI

MIDI was originally designed for musicians who wanted to control a bunch of synthesizers and drum machines with one set of instructions. For example, you can connect a keyboard and drum machine together and control the drum beats by playing notes on the keyboard. It didn't take long for musicians to realize the value of using computers with their instruments, too, and that's how most MIDI gear is used now.

MIDI files are sequences of notes; the notes carry timing and instrument information, so that one note might say "play C-sharp with a steel drum for 1/4 second" and another might say "play D-flat two octaves up, with a pipe organ, for 2 seconds." These notes are all relative to a *time base* that lets all the different synthesizers synchronize.

You create MIDI files with a piece of software called a *sequencer*, the sequencer gets its name because you can blend many instruments together by assembling one instrument at a time. The sequencer takes care of correcting the time base and issuing the right "play a note" commands at precisely the right time.

How does the sequencer get the notes in the first place? Easy—you put them there, either by using a musical keyboard to play them or by using a music composition program (sort of like a word processor for sheet music). Not everyone has enough musical ability to create new music from scratch, but a number of Web sites and companies offer every conceivable type of music in MIDI form.

TIP   There aren't many books on MIDI; the best one I've found is Rich Grace's *The Sound and Music Workshop* (1996, Sybex; ISBN 0782118011).

After you've put a single instrumental track into the sequencer, you can add additional tracks. For example, you could lay down a drum track first and then add a trumpet, piano, and saxophone in their own tracks. After all the instruments are recorded, you can use the sequencer to rearrange the music, change its tempo or pitch, or do practically anything else you want to it. When you're finally finished, the result is a MIDI file that you can embed into your Web pages or use as a soundtrack in a QuickTime or MPEG movie.

Recording Sounds

When you record sounds, you're converting the sound source into a digital representation. To do this, you'll use a sound card (or Mac sound hardware) that takes care of converting the voltage changes produced by the microphone (or tape recorder, or whatever else you're using as a sound source) into a stream of bits. However, there are some things you need to know about before you jump into recording.

Recorded sound files are made up of a sequence of *samples*. Each sample represents a small time interval when the audio hardware takes a snatch of sound from the sound source and digitizes it. The *sampling rate* for sound is a measure of how often the computer grabs samples from the sound source. The higher the rate, the better the sound quality—but the bigger the files! The two most common rates are 44.1KHz (the same sampling rate used for audio CDs) and 22.5KHz, although other, lower, rates are sometimes used for telephone-quality audio.

The size of each sample also influences the sound quality. Almost all sound hardware can record 8-bit samples; many newer sound cards can record 16-bit samples. The larger sample size gives better audio quality at the cost of larger files. As a final complication, you can record in either mono or stereo; a stereo file will be bigger because it has to accommodate an extra sound channel.

The combination of these two factors gives a spectrum of quality versus size: at the high end, 44.1KHz 16-bit stereo audio can be every bit as good as what you get from a music CD, but the files are quite large. At the low end, 8KHz 8-bit mono audio is the same sampling arrangement used when you use your telephone; it doesn't sound as good as the CD-quality files, but it's much smaller.

ON THE

CD

If you look on the CD in IBM\multimed\goldwave, you'll find GoldWave32, a full-featured and easy to use sound editor.

For Web use, I usually recommend 11KHz 8-bit mono recording for speech clips. This level is good enough for most uses, but for music I recommend trying several different sampling rates until you find the optimum balance between size and quality. It doesn't do any good to capture 16-bit 44.1KHz audio from a scratchy LP or a tape recording of an AM radio broadcast, so you can often use lower sampling rates without any perceptible decrease in quality.

Putting Sound and Music on Your Pages

Sound can be a powerful way to add interest to your pages. When properly used, it provides a counterpoint to the images and text on your pages, and with careful planning you can provide punchy sounds without making your visitors wait forever. There are three basic ways that you can get sound onto your pages; let's begin with the simplest.

CAUTION

◆◆

There are many music and sound files on the Web. Many of them are copyrighted. Be careful not to use someone else's work without permission—not only is it impolite, it can get expensive if record company or film studio lawyers start calling you!

◆◆

Using Downloadable Sounds

The easiest way to add sounds to your pages is as downloadable files. To do this, all you need to do is put the files on your Web server and create links to them, like this:

```
<A HREF="/sounds/welcome.wav">Welcome message</A>
```

This is a fast way to get some sounds on your pages, and it has the advantage of not requiring your visitors to have any particular plug-in. However, when you make the visitor break away from whatever she's looking at to jump somewhere else and download a sound, you break her train of thought—so use downloaded sounds as a temporary measure until you're comfortable with embedded sounds.

ON THE

CD

There are a bunch of cool sounds you can use on your pages on the CD in the back of the book look in the `IBM\multimed` and `Macintosh\multimedia` directories, put the files on your server, and link away.

Making Background Music with Microsoft's Extensions

Microsoft has its own proprietary HTML tag for background sound and music: `<BGSOUND>`. As with most of Microsoft's HTML extensions, other browsers will ignore it when it appears, so it's fairly safe to use if you don't mind the fact that only visitors with Internet Explorer will hear your sounds.

`<BGSOUND>` takes two parameters. The first, `SRC`, specifies the URL of the sound you want to play. The sound can be a `.WAV` file or a MIDI file; the browser will play either type when it finds one. The second parameter, `LOOP`, is an optional setting that tells the browser how many times to replay the sound. If you leave it off, the sound will be played once. If you specify a number, the sound will be played that many times. If you specify `LOOP="INFINITE"`, your visitors will hear the same sound over and over until they leave your page.

Here's a simple example of `<BGSOUND>` in action:

```
<bgsound src="midi/amadeus1.mid" loop="infinite">
```

In this case, it's okay to use `LOOP="INFINITE"` because the MIDI file is fairly long; in general, though, it's best not to make your background sounds loop because there's no way for the visitor to turn them off.

FIND IT ON ▶
THE WEB

There are many cool MIDI files on the Web; for starters, try the MIDI Farm at **http://www.midifarm.com**. In addition, Electronic Music magazine maintains a great site at **http://www.electronicmusic.com**.

Embedding Sounds

There's an alternative way to put background music or sounds onto your pages, one that works with any browser provided that it has the proper plug-in. This approach embeds the sound (or video, but more about that later) as part of your page. When the browser reads through the page contents, it sees the <EMBED> tag and asks the server to start delivering the embedded data. When the data arrives, it's sent to the plug-in that handles that embedded type. If that plug-in isn't on the visitor's computer, he'll either see a funny icon in place of the embedded content or nothing at all; both Internet Explorer and Navigator will offer to take him to a page listing plug-ins available for download. Of course, if you stick to QuickTime, the odds are very good that the visitor will already have it.

ON THE

CD

LiveUpdate's Crescendo plug-in plays MIDI files quite well, and it's included on the CD. (Mac and PC versions; look in `IBM\Multimed\crescen` or `Macintosh\multime-dia\crescendo`.) LiveUpdate also has an excellent embedding tutorial at **http://www.liveupdate.com/embed.html**.

The first step in embedding sounds or music into your pages is to get the sound files onto your Web server. They can be in the same directory as your Web pages, or in a different directory, as long as the Web server has access to files in that directory. After the files are there, you're ready to start embedding.

NOTE You'll notice me using the word "movie" to refer to QuickTime sounds and movies—that's because to QuickTime, *everything's* a movie, regardless of whether it actually has any visual data.

The <EMBED> tag only has a few required parameters, but there are many optional ones—and which optional ones you can use depends on the plug-in! Let's start with the required parameters first:

```
<EMBED SRC="worm.mov" WIDTH="256" HEIGHT="256">
```

The <EMBED> tag itself only needs these three parameters to function. The first required parameter is the SRC attribute, which tells the browser where to find the embedded content. This can be a full URL or a file name alone. If the browser can't retrieve the specified file, it will display an icon to indicate that something's missing from the page.

As with images, Java applets, and several other HTML tags, the WIDTH and HEIGHT attributes tell the browser how much space to reserve for the embedded item. For an embedded sound, it's safe to make these values very small.

QuickTime supports four extra attributes that are useful with embedded sounds. These attributes apply to all movie types, so you can also use them with any other kind of QuickTime movie:

- The HIDDEN attribute tells QuickTime to keep the embedded item hidden. Although this makes no sense for movies, it's useful for sounds because it keeps the plug-in from displaying anything. By default, the embedded data will be visible unless you specify otherwise.

- CONTROLLER controls whether QuickTime displays its controller next to the plug-in frame (the controller is that sliding bar with the play, pause, and stop buttons). By default, the controller will be visible—to turn it off, use CONTROLLER="FALSE".

- Like its counterpart in the <BGSOUND> tag, LOOP controls how many times the sound clip will play. The default value is LOOP="FALSE"; you can also specify LOOP="TRUE" (which has the same effect as LOOP=INFINITE for BGSOUND) or LOOP="PALINDROME", which makes the sound play alternately forwards and backwards.

- AUTOPLAY tells the browser to start playing the sound or music clip as soon as possible. The default is AUTOPLAY=FALSE. Beware—if you hide the movie or the controller, and AUTOPLAY is off, the user won't be able to play your movie!

There are some other useful, but optional, attributes for the <EMBED> tag, but they're primarily useful with video, so I'll save them for later.

Adding Video to Your Pages

Not so long ago, video playback on computers was a distant possibility, somewhere out on the horizon. Now almost all new computers being sold today can play back full-motion, full-screen video from disk or CD, and the emerging DVD format promises to make desktop video even more common in the future.

Video on the Internet has been slow in coming for several reasons. First, video takes up lots of space, meaning that not many people have had adequate bandwidth to download it. Of course, there hasn't been much video to download, because video capture hardware and software has been expensive and difficult to configure and use. Finally, Internet software hasn't been up to the task of displaying and using video well.

All these factors are changing. More and more people are buying fast connections, and video compression software has improved to the point where you can deliver watchable video over a 56K modem. Apple has been building video capture hardware into most new Macintoshes, as have a few PC vendors. For those who don't have built-in video, manufacturers like Avid and miro are delivering inexpensive add-on boards that do a very good job of capturing and compressing video at low cost. Finally, software vendors—not just Netscape and Microsoft, but smaller vendors with specialty products—have done a great job of making Internet products video-ready.

There are several formats for video on the Web, so we'll start there and then move on to the details of how you put video into your pages.

Understanding Video Formats

There are a number of ways to store and compress video images for playback on the Web, and you're likely to encounter all of them as you surf. When the time comes for you to build your own video clips, a knowledge of the formats can help you decide on the best scheme for your needs.

QuickTime

Earlier on, I called QuickTime a framework, and you can see that clearly when you examine how it handles compressed video. Anyone can write a video compression/decompression component (called a *codec*) and plug it into QuickTime—and many vendors have done just that. The broad array of available audio, video, and still-image codecs makes QuickTime extremely flexible—in fact, it handles the MIDI, WAV, AU, and Macintosh sounds, and the MPEG and AVI video formats I'm about to discuss.

Most desktop-based video production systems still run on the Mac with QuickTime, so much of the professionally produced video on the Web is in QuickTime format. In addition, Macs have had built-in video capture equipment for a few years now, and many Web authors have put it to use for producing their own Web-based video content.

MPEG

In the previous session, you learned about the JPEG compression scheme for still images. There's a similar compression scheme for moving images, designed by the Motion Picture Experts Group (hence its name). MPEG actually refers to a family of standards that handle everything from CD-quality Digital audio to the digital satellite systems sold to millions of consumers throughout North America.

A complete technical description of MPEG is a book in itself (and a dull one at that!). In brief, MPEG takes a snapshot of the video stream every so often; then stores each succeeding frame by figuring out what changed since the previous frame. Making MPEG movies used to require special-purpose hardware, and for heavy-duty applications like satellite TV, it still does. For the most part, MPEG isn't less common on the Web than AVI and QuickTime, but it's still a contender.

AVI

AVI was originally designed by Microsoft and Intel as a compact format for compressing video. Like many other Microsoft innovations, it became widely used because it's widely available. The standard Windows multi-media tools can work with AVI files, and almost all video capture and editing software can generate AVI files as well.

A great deal of Web and Internet video content is in AVI format, but QuickTime is rapidly gaining on it. Microsoft also has a video format called Active Movie, but it is almost completely unused on the Web at present, and there's no way to tell whether it will ever catch on.

Streaming Formats

All the formats described previously compress video, but most were designed for efficient playback of video stored on CD-ROM or disk. Even a slow CD-ROM can deliver 150KB/second of bandwidth—considerably more than most Internet users have available. Several enterprising software companies saw a market opportunity for video compression that would work at relatively low bandwidth and rushed off to start developing compression schemes that would allow video delivery over standard modem lines.

The key difference between these new formats and the others described in this section is that the new formats use streams of video, like the streaming audio formats described earlier. QuickTime, AVI, and MPEG all work by taking a video sequence and compressing it. The compressed version is what visitors download and play back. Streaming formats compress the video only when the visitor requests a playback; this allows the video server to tune its compression to the amount of available bandwidth.

The rush to get usable video out of a 28.8Kbps modem channel has delivered several incompatible formats from various vendors. The RealVideo format from Progressive Networks and the VDOlive format from VDO are the most prevalent right now, but there are a host of others. Further confusing things, Apple added streaming support to QuickTime, so it now supports streaming and non-streaming video.

Like audio streams, video streams require special (and expensive) software to produce, so you're not likely to use them on your own site, but it's useful to know what they are.

Getting Video into Your Computer

Like marriage, video capture is not something entered into lightly, but it can be rewarding and great fun besides.

Turning a videotape or video camera image into a playable movie is a fairly simple process, but the specifics of how you do it vary depending on your hardware and software setup. The basic process is the same, however, no matter what kind of computer or video capture equipment you're using.

First, you must have a way to get video into your computer. These *digitizers* or *sequence grabbers* can capture full-motion video; there are also *frame* grabbers that capture individual frames as snapshot still images. Whatever you call them, these devices do the same thing: they decode the video signal from its source; turn it into a block of bytes containing color, brightness, and image data; and feed it to the computer as a single frame.

The number of frames a device can capture in one second is its *frame rate*. Each frame has a fixed size; for example, you might capture a video clip at 15 frames per second (fps), where each frame is 320×240 pixels. The final movie size increases as you capture more frames per second or capture bigger frames; naturally, bigger movies can take longer to play back, and they surely take longer to download.

A number of companies make inexpensive PCI cards that you can drop into your Mac or PC to capture video. Most of these cards can capture at least 320x240 at 15fps. Compression is relatively slow, and usually can't be done in real time. That means that you have to capture all the video you want to use and *then* compress it—so the amount of video you can capture at once is usually limited by the amount of space you have in your computer. Most capture software can capture to RAM (fast but there's not much of it) or to disk (there's more space, but pausing to write to disk means that you may miss some frames). Appendix C has more details on choosing the right video capture hardware for your needs and budget.

After the video actually has been captured, you can edit it with a program like Speed Razor, Avid Cinema, or VideoShop. These editors let you insert special visual effects like dissolves and fades, add or remove sound and music tracks, overlay captions, and do all the other fancy things you think of when you hear "digital video." You can cut and paste video just like text, so it's easy to edit out parts that you don't want and rearrange sequences of video into whatever order you want.

Finally, when you're finished editing, you'll compress the video for delivery. Which compression method, or codec, you use will depend on what you're doing. Different codecs work better on different video; for example, one codec is optimized for compressing animation, and others are designed to work best when compressing video enough to be played back from a double-speed CD-ROM.

NOTE If all this seems rather vague, it's only because the specific steps for capturing and editing video depend on the hardware and software you choose. Appendix C goes into the details of capturing video, including detailed instructions for using the USRobotics Bigpicture and Avid Cinema systems, so you can get a feel for the process with one particular hardware-software package.

Putting Video on Your Pages

Assuming that you have some video to put on your pages, the actual process is fairly easy. No matter how you plan to deliver video to your visitors, the first step after completing your video masterpiece is to put it onto your Web server, in whatever directory is convenient. If you're creating video on a Mac, make sure that you select the Playable on non-Apple computers and Make movie self-contained settings in your video editor's save dialog box, as shown in Figure 6.10.

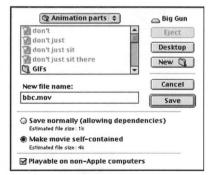

Figure 6.10

Make sure to set these checkboxes when saving video for the Web on a Mac; if you don't, Windows and Unix users won't be able to read your files.

After the videos are safely on your Web server, it's time to deliver them to your visitors.

Putting Downloadable Videos on Your Pages

Earlier in this session, you learned how to put links to sounds on your pages so that visitors could download them and listen at their convenience. This approach works even better for movies because movies tend to be large, and visitors often prefer to download them in the background and play them when they're not on-line.

You add links to movies the same way you add any other kind of link: with the <HREF> tag. However, it's a good idea to grab a single frame of your movie from your editing tool and then use it as part of the link so that visitors will have some idea what the movie's going to look like. For example, CNN does this with its Video Vault pages (shown in Figure 6.11). It's also good Web etiquette to show the file size of your movies next to the links, so that visitors will know what size download they're getting into *before* they click the link.

One more suggestion: you can mix the best of embedded and downloadable movies by putting a two- or three-second long "preview" version of your movie on your page and making it link to the full-length version. That gives your visitors a free sample of the long version without making them suffer through a long wait.

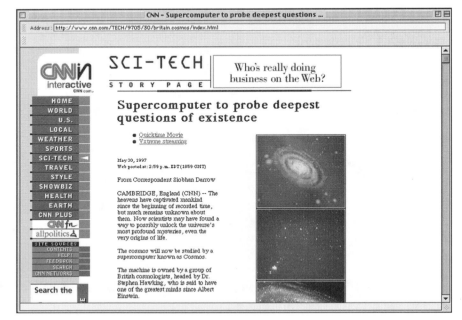

Figure 6.11

CNN uses single
frames to give
visitors an idea
what a video looks
like and contains
before they
download it.

Embedding Movies

Embedding video works in much the same way as embedding sounds. This isn't surprising because, as far as QuickTime is concerned, sounds are just a movie with no video content. In addition to the embedding parameters listed earlier in the section on embedding sounds, there are some additional parameters that you can use with embedded video.

First, a quick review: you always need the SRC, WIDTH, and HEIGHT attributes along with the <EMBED> tag itself. You can use the HIDDEN attribute, but doing so doesn't make much sense for a video you mean visitors to see. You can show the movie's controller or not; if you do show it, you need to add 24 to the video's height to allow for the extra space taken up by the controller.

As with music and sound files, you can use the AUTOPLAY parameter to tell the browser to start playing the movie as soon as possible. If your movie was saved with the proper options (the two I mentioned earlier), the browser can download the first few bits of the movie and start playing them while it downloads the rest. You can also use the LOOP parameter, and using LOOP="PALINDROME" is especially cool because it will play movies forwards and then backwards!

There are several other useful optional parameters that you can use to control embedded movies. Let's see what they do:

- The VOLUME parameter tells QuickTime how loud to play sounds in the movie. This doesn't have anything to do with the system volume on your computer—if you set the QuickTime volume to 128 (half its maximum), it will play half as loud as a normal sound at the volume you have set. You can specify volumes from 0-256; 256 is the default.

- CACHE tells the browser to put the movie in its cache so that it won't have to be downloaded again when the visitor reloads the page. By default, this parameter is always on, and you should leave it on (even though only Netscape supports it at present). If for some reason you don't want visitors to cache your movies, use CACHE=FALSE to turn it off.

- When visitors don't have a plug-in needed for displaying data, the browser doesn't know where to find it, so visitors usually get an unhelpful dialog box telling them only that something is missing. The PLUGINSPAGE parameter lets you specify a URL where the visitor can go to get the plug-in if she doesn't have it. For QuickTime movies, you should use PLUGINSPAGE="http://quicktime .apple.com", but other plug-ins can use other pages, and if you have a page listing all the plug-ins used on your site you can use it instead.

- You can resize a movie with the SCALE parameter, which scales the movie to fit. Using TOFIT forces the movie to fit in the space you define, no matter how big or small it is. Using ASPECT scales the movie but maintains its width-to-height ratio. Using a number scales the movie by that number; for example, SCALE=2 displays the movie at twice its normal size. Scaling takes time, and it can make your movie play back slowly, so avoid it unless you need it.

✪ Normally, QuickTime will play as many frames as possible. On slow machines, it will skip frames when it needs to so that it can keep up. Some frames, called *key frames*, are guaranteed to always be played. PLAYEVERYFRAME="TRUE" (the default is FALSE) lets you tell QuickTime not to skip any frames, and to slow down the movie as much as necessary. This is useful when your movie is a sequence of stills or an animation where skipping frames would meet the movie look funny. However, when you use PLAY-EVERYFRAME="TRUE" QuickTime will turn off any audio tracks in the movie to avoid making *them* sound funny.

✪ You can make a movie into a link with the HREF parameter. Just like its HTML counterpart, specifying a URL with this parameter will take the visitor to that URL when she clicks on the movie.

✪ TARGET works hand-in-hand with HREF; you use it to specify where the link given in an HREF parameter will be displayed. You can specify a frame name or one of the special frame targets you learned this morning: _top, _self, and so on.

FIND IT ON ▶ Apple maintains a helpful page for people who want to use QuickTime on their Web
THE WEB pages at **http://quicktime.apple.com/dev/devweb.html**. It's a good place to learn about the more advanced parameters that the QuickTime plug-in understands.

Tool Tips

There's no denying how cool a well-designed multimedia site can be—the combination of sound, video, and text is more powerful than any one of them alone. To help you maximize your multimedia, here are some suggestions and hints.

Clean Up Your Act

QuickTime, AVI, and MPEG all compress video "as best they can"; they don't have any special knowledge about how the video will be delivered. They *do*, however, have many adjustable settings that you can change—but how do you know which ones to change and what to change them to?

Apple and I both recommend two excellent tools from Terran Interactive (**http://www.terran-int.com/**): Media Cleaner Pro and the WebMotion plug-in for Movie Cleaner. Media Cleaner uses wizards to interview you about your movies, their intended audience, and how they'll be delivered; it then determines the best compression settings and compresses the movie. In addition, it has pre-processing features that work before compression (such as adaptive noise reduction); these features make highly compressed movies look better when played back.

The add-on WebMotion product has built-in settings for compressing movies for transmitting over the Internet. It uses a wizard that shows you several different versions of *your movie* and asks which one looks the best to you—a nice change from the conventional process of "compress, view, shake head in dismay, repeat" that most video editors make you go through.

Good Things Come in Small Packages

You can get a lot of effect from a relatively small number of bits if you choose them wisely. Animated GIFs are very bandwidth-efficient, as are MIDI files, and they're both easy to create. Moving a notch up the size ladder, you can make great animations by taking a sequence of still images and turning them into a QuickTime movie. Experiment to find motion and sound effects that highlight your pages while minimizing the amount of bandwidth used—it's a challenge, but a rewarding one!

Wrap It Up!

In earlier sessions, you learned how to make good-looking static pages. Now you know how to blast those pages into orbit with animation, sound, and video. Although too much of a good thing is, well, *too much*, the right amount of multimedia can make a killer first impression on new visitors and keep your site fresh and interesting for repeat visitors.

You may need to take a nap before the next session—you're going to activate your Web pages with Java and ActiveX, a combination guaranteed to energize you *and* your audience!

Adding Java and ActiveX to Your Pages

- ✪ Understanding Embedded Program Content
- ✪ Java and ActiveX Basics
- ✪ Adding Java to Your Web Pages
- ✪ Adding ActiveX to Your Web Pages

It's almost impossible to read about the Internet and not encounter some mention of either Java or ActiveX. Both technologies allow designers (that's you!) to attach programs to Web pages. When a visitor downloads the page, the program comes along with it, and it can do almost anything—from displaying graphics to searching the Internet for requested information.

Many books give the details of writing these attached programs, so I won't go into the details here. Instead, in this session, you'll learn how to use other people's Java applets and ActiveX controls on your own pages. Although this may not sound like much fun, there are lots of cool Java and ActiveX goodies that you can put in your pages, and you'll learn where to go to find them and what to do with them when you're finished.

First, though, it's worth starting with an overview of how embedded programs work. Next, you'll learn about the similarities, and differences, between ActiveX and Java; then we'll plunge into putting each type of program into your own pages.

Understanding Embedded Program Content

In the beginning, Web pages could contain only HTML and GIF images. This was enough for many applications, but it didn't equal what a good designer could do with a page layout program like PageMaker. As time passed, the HTML standard gained new features that added tools for better control over fonts, color, images, and layout. Although these changes were welcome improvements, they still didn't add one key feature—there wasn't any way to make pages change after they had been loaded.

Many designers wanted to build pages whose colors, images, or content would change in response to user typing or mouse actions. A few revolutionaries even wanted to be able to run programs that would interact with the user on her own machine, but this would require a portable language that would run on many different types of computers.

The idea underlying both Java and ActiveX is that someone (an individual programmer, a large company, or whoever) can write a program and put it on his Web server. Instead of running on the Web server like a CGI program, though, the program would be downloaded to the visitor's Web browser and would run on the visitor's computer. The result? You can embed programs in your pages to let visitors play games (as shown in Figure 7.1), display data, or do practically anything else you want.

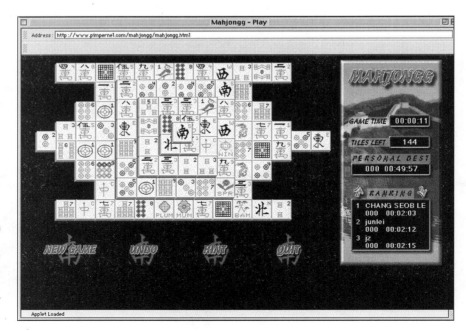

Figure 7.1

Games are fun, and it's easy to add them to your pages with embedded Java or ActiveX code.

They are called *embedded programs* because you embed a reference to them in your page. When a compatible browser downloads the page, it also downloads the embedded program and runs it. What that program does when run is up to the developer. (Although both ActiveX and Java impose security restrictions; more about that later.)

Java and ActiveX Basics

Java and ActiveX actually have more in common than you'd think from reading about them. This is mostly due to the intense rivalry between Sun Microsystems, creator of Java, and Microsoft, which advocates ActiveX. Understanding their likenesses is important for understanding where it makes sense to use each technology and what they can do.

Isn't Java an Island?

Java began life as a language called Solid Oak. It was originally designed as a way to write programs for those cable TV boxes that sit atop your TV. Sun figured that there would be a market for tools that would ease the process of writing fancy, cable-based interactive TV applications.

One of the key design concepts behind Solid Oak was that programs would live on a central computer that would send them out to the set-top boxes on demand. Because of this, Solid Oak included a rich set of networking capabilities that were easy to use. Because there are several manufacturers of set-top boxes, another important design goal was to come up with a way to write a program only once and have it run on different manufacturers' boxes without any changes.

Sun designed what's called a *virtual machine*, or VM, for Solid Oak. The VM is nothing more than a computer simulator. It simulates a particular computer's design and programming language. By using a VM, Sun could write one VM for each type of cable box and then have its programs run on the VM.

When you download a new applet, it's in the form of code that the Java VM can run. Because the VM has to translate this *byte code* into the *native code* your computer's CPU normally uses, Java code runs slower than native code. To fix this, most VM vendors have developed *just-in-time compilers*, which translate the entire applet into native code and store the result. This translates into vastly better performance at the cost of a slight increase in load time.

Unfortunately, there wasn't much demand for cable-box programming languages—but some smart marketing people at Sun recognized that Solid Oak would make a great language for writing dynamic programs that could run across the Internet. The name was changed to Java, Sun inked a deal with Netscape to get Java support into Navigator 2.0, and the rest is history!

Java has four key features:

- *Platform independence.* Java programs run on the Java VM, so as long as there's a VM, any Java program can run. Of course, there are VMs for the Mac, Windows, and Unix, but there are also VMs for handheld computers like the Newton, and at least one manufacturer of cellular phones is working on a Java-capable phone!

- *Built-in Internet capabilities.* The Java language specification includes a healthy set of network capabilities, including HTTP and FTP. There are also classes for working with GIF and JPEG images, picking apart form data, and a number of other common tasks.

- *"Sandbox" security.* Sun realized that no one would want to download programs from the Internet unless their computers could be protected. The answer to this was to keep Java programs in their own "sandbox." When an application is in the sandbox, it can't access files on the local computer, and its network communication capabilities are limited. The Java VM includes a number of features that check the programs it runs for bad behavior.

- *Elegant design.* Engineers and programmers like clean, functional designs, and Java's an excellent example of how a small team can produce a beautifully engineered product. This elegance has helped spur many programmers' enthusiastic acceptance of Java technology.

ActiveX: OLE By Any Other Name . . .

Object Linking and Embedding (OLE) is a cool feature of Windows that lets you put documents created by one program into documents belonging to another. For example, you can put an Excel chart in the middle of a Word document and then put the Word document—still with its embedded Excel object—into an Imagineer Technical blueprint.

When Microsoft saw how enthusiastically the rest of the software world was embracing Java, it was forced to decide between boarding the Java bandwagon or striking out on its own path. Characteristically, they chose both routes: Microsoft developed its own Java VM for Windows, but it also announced the ActiveX technology to directly compete against Java.

The premise behind ActiveX is similar to that of Java: write small programs that are downloaded to the visitor's computer and do whatever they're supposed to. Instead of using a VM like Java, Microsoft adopted the existing OLE embedding model for ActiveX. This allows ActiveX controls to be embedded into almost any OLE application, not just Web browsers, and it freed developers from having to deal with several potentially different VMs on any one computer.

Initial acceptance of ActiveX was slow, because it's harder to write ActiveX controls than Java programs, and they only run on computers running Windows. Microsoft turned its considerable marketing muscle behind ActiveX, though, and it's starting to become more popular as time passes. Internet Explorer 4.0 relies heavily on ActiveX controls to integrate the Web with the Windows desktop.

Despite having an intent similar to Java's, the list of ActiveX's key features is quite a bit different from the Java list. First of all, ActiveX controls are all native code; there's no byte code and no VM. This gives ActiveX a potential performance advantage at the cost of portability. There are some other key differences, too:

- *Full access to Windows.* ActiveX controls can do anything a Windows program can do, so they can take full advantage of the Windows user interface and whatever other ActiveX-capable software the user has on his computer. However, controls that use these capabilities aren't very portable and can't easily be made to run under the ActiveX for Macintosh service that Microsoft now delivers.

- *OLE technology.* OLE applications let you build a single document that contains pieces from other application documents, and ActiveX controls build on that capability to let you put them anywhere you could put part of a Word document. This greatly extends their flexibility.

- *Consistency.* The downside to Java's portability is that differences between VMs mean that some programs run fine in one Web browser and don't work at all on another. Although ActiveX doesn't make any promises to run anywhere, it does run the same way on the platforms that support it.

- *It's Microsoft's.* Whether you admire or loathe them, Microsoft is still a formidable presence in the software market. Many page designers and programmers are using ActiveX because it's Microsoft's, and they expect it to be successful on that basis alone.

Adding Java to Your Web Pages

Adding Java programs (or *applets*) to your pages is surprisingly easy. There are only four steps to the whole process:

1. Find an applet you like well enough to put on your pages.
2. Move the applet files to your Web server.
3. Use the <APPLET> tag to actually link each applet to the pages where you want it to appear.

4. If you want to, and if the applet supports it, customize the applet's settings, or *parameters*, to make it do exactly what you want.

Before You Begin

You might think that, of all places on the net, JavaSoft's (the division of Sun in charge of Java) pages would be filled with flashy Java applets—after all, they invented Java! If you go there, though, there aren't many animated billboards and the like. Why not?

The answer should be familiar by now: time. Java applets take time to download, just like any other Web content. On top of the download time, your visitors will have to wait while their Java VMs run the applets they just downloaded. Sometimes users are willing to wait, and sometimes they're not. For example, NASA's Marshall Space Flight Center has a nifty Java application called J-Track at **http://liftoff.msfc.nasa.gov/ JTrack/welcome.html**. It's shown in Figure 7.2. On a 28.8Kbps modem,

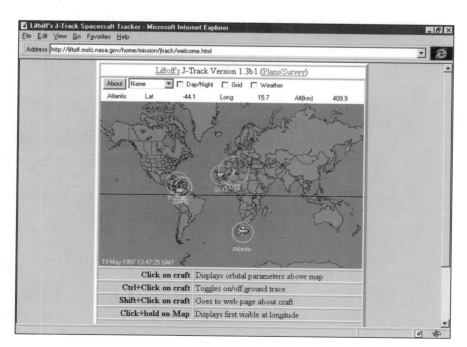

Figure 7.2

J-Track tracks the space shuttle, the Russian space station, and several other interesting satellites.

it takes a minute or so to load, and most users who are interested in tracking satellites are willing to wait. The same users probably wouldn't want to wait a minute just to see a flashing ad banner or a scrolling text marquee.

Another thing to consider is how well your applets behave on different VMs. The theory behind Java is that one applet can run equally well on any VM. However, the reality is that all VMs have bugs in them—but different VMs have *different* bugs! The only way to make sure that all visitors will be able to see your applets as you intend is to test them on several browsers. At minimum, you should check them with Netscape navigator and Microsoft Internet Explorer on both the Mac and a Windows machine. (Of course, because you'll probably be using someone else's applets, they may have already done so.)

Finding Cool Applets

Now that you know how to put applets on your pages, you're probably wondering where you can go to find cool applets. The enormous popularity of Java has led to the development of many Java-oriented sites. Many of them have libraries full of applets that you can download and use; like with most other Internet-related tools, some are free, some are trial versions of commercial tools, and some are shareware.

Gamelan

Gamelan is literally "a Javanese orchestra"; the term originally referred to Indonesian music and orchestra, played with iron, bronze, wood, and wind instruments. Like almost every other word having any relationship to Java, the original meaning of Gamelan has been co-opted—it also is the name of a large database of Java applets, samples, and resources. It's kept at **http://www.gamelan.com**; see Figure 7.3 for its home page.

JARS

The Java Applet Review Service, or JARS, lives at **http://www.jars.com**. JARS is basically a large database of reviews of Java applets, along with the

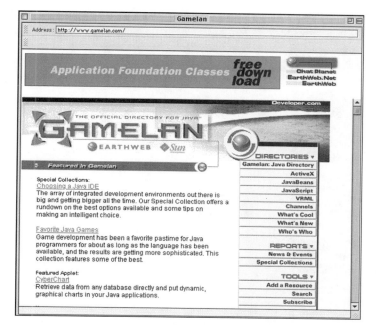

Figure 7.3

Gamelan has it all: sample applets, documentation, even ActiveX controls.

applets themselves. Applets are grouped together based on how JARS thinks they stack up against their peers. For example, the page shown in Figure 7.4 shows JARS's pick for the best 5% of all applets on the Web— and that's a good place to start!

Everywhere Else

Most programmers who have written general-purpose applets are likely to submit them either to Gamelan or JARS. However, during your travels on the Web, you're likely to see other cool applets and think "Hey, that would really look nice on my page!"

Many sites will have custom-made Java applets that do specific things, like the satellite-tracking application from NASA. Just because these applets only do one thing doesn't mean they're not interesting; it only means that they may not be as widely distributed as applets that everyone can use.

Figure 7.4

The top 5% category at JARS represents their picks for the best applets on the Web.

When you see an applet that you think would be useful to you, send some e-mail to the author or webmaster of the page where you found it and ask whether you may use it. You'll be surprised by how often the answer is "yes," and you'll quickly build up a nice arsenal of applets that make sense for your site.

On the CD

The CD bound to the back of this book also includes some applets that you can use on your pages; here's a partial list:

- ○ KzmAdvertise, discussed in more detail in the later section "Adding Dynamic Banners with KzmAdvertise," provides animated advertising banners.

- ○ RiadaCartel is a tool for making "marching LED" signs like you've seen at sports stadiums and other public places.

⚙ The Coffee Cup HTML editor includes "Built-In Java," a feature that lets you use Coffee Cup's Java applets on your own pages.

Putting Your Applets on the Server

Applets fall between CGI programs and ordinary Web pages. Like CGI scripts, they are really executables. Unlike CGIs, and like Web pages, the server doesn't run them; it just delivers them to the browser for it to interpret. This means that you have to put your applets somewhere that the browser can reach them.

Java applets often reference other applets. For example, the KzmAdvertise animated banner applet you're about to use is actually made up of three separate files. You'll embed one of these files in your page, and the browser will load it. During that loading process, the browser will notice that the file it loaded needs the other two files to run, so it will fetch them too.

In general, you should keep all the Java applets on your site in a single directory. I suggest creating a directory named applets or something similar and using it as the applets' holding tank. However (as you'll see in the next section), there's a way to give the browser the exact URL of your Java applets so that it can find them no matter where they are.

Some applets are packaged in *archives*, which have the familiar .zip extension. Java archives can contain one or more applet files, GIF or JPEG images, or anything else the applet needs to run. If the applets you're using aren't packaged as archives, make sure not to leave out any required files when you put the applets on your server.

Finally, don't forget that Java applets are executable files! When you put them on your server, you have to treat them like other binary files; make sure to use the "binary" option if you transfer the files with FTP.

Using the <APPLET> Tag

Now that you've found some applets that you want to use and put them on your server, it's time to embed them into your pages. You do this with the <APPLET> tag, which started life as a Netscape extension but has been incorporated into the HTML 3.2 standard and is supported by browsers from Sun, Netscape, Microsoft, and others.

Dissecting the J-Track Example

Let's start off with an example, taken from the J-Track page shown earlier in Figure 7.2; this HTML tells the browser to load and display the J-Track satellite tracker:

```
<APPLET CODE="GroundTrack" WIDTH="484" HEIGHT="360" ALIGN="BOTTOM"
    align="baseline" archive="GroundTrack.zip">
    <PARAM NAME="cabbase" VALUE="GroundTrack.cab">
    <PARAM NAME="bggif" VALUE="noweathert.gif">
    <PARAM NAME="miniMode" VALUE="false">
</APPLET>
```

Each of the <APPLET> tag parameters has a special meaning to the browser. CODE, WIDTH, and HEIGHT are required, but all the other attributes are optional. Here's a dissection of the J-Track applet tags:

✿ CODE tells the browser the name of the applet it's supposed to load. Unless you specify otherwise, the applet named in CODE must be in the same directory as the HTML file that contains the <APPLET> tag. CODE is just the name, not the URL, of the applet.

✿ WIDTH and HEIGHT work the same way as they do for images: they tell the browser how much space to reserve for the applet's drawing area.

✿ ARCHIVE tells the browser that the applet and its supporting files all live in a single archive with the given name.

✿ ALIGN also works like it does in the <IMG> tag. You can align the applet's contents along the left, right, top, middle, or bottom of the drawing area. You can also combine any ALIGN attribute with the ALIGN="baseline" attribute; when you do, the browser will align the applet relative to the text baseline instead of the drawing area.

✿ The PARAM attributes let you communicate with the applet, which can retrieve the value of any <PARAM> whose name it knows. In this example, there are three PARAM attributes, each of which tells the applet something it needs to know. Some applets will have more, some less—the number of <PARAM> tags and their contents depends on the applet.

Helping the Browser Find Applets

When a browser downloads a Web page, it will also try to get any applets embedded in the page so that it can run them. By default, browsers assume that applets live in the same directory as the page that references them. For example, if a page at **http://www.bellsouth.net/~garden/roses.html** pointed to an applet named FlowerPlanner, the browser would try to load **http://www.bellsouth.net/~garden/FlowerPlanner**. If the applet's not there, the browser can't load it; instead, it will display an error.

You can override this behavior with the <APPLET> tag's CODEBASE parameter, which specifies the URL where the browser should expect to find your applets. If you put all your applets, archives, and supporting files into one directory, you can use the same CODEBASE everywhere. This will ease your ongoing maintenance burden because you'll always know right where your applets are stored, and your pages will continue to point to the right place even when you move pages around on your server.

Supporting Non-Java Visitors

Throughout the book so far, I've emphasized that it's important to include alternate content for visitors whose browsers might not be able to display your main content. For images, you use the <ALT> tag; for frames, you use the <NOFRAMES> container, and for sound and video you use downloadable and streaming versions. Guess what? You should do the same for your Java applets.

First of all, you should display a meaningful message to visitors whose browsers don't handle Java. You do this by putting HTML in the <APPLET> tag itself, like this:

```
<APPLET CODE="Mahjongg.class" WIDTH=750 HEIGHT=380>
    <H2>If you are reading this, your browser doesn't support
        ➥Java-applets.</H2>
    <H3>Please use a Java-compatible Browser,<BR>
    like Netscape Navigator 2.x/3.x or Microsoft Internet
        ➥Explorer 3.x</H3>
    <TABLE><TR>
    <TD><A HREF="http://home.netscape.com/comprod/mirror/index.html">
        <IMG SRC="http://www.pimpernel.com/images/now20_button.gif"
        ➥BORDER=0
        ALT="Goto Netscape"></A></TD>
    <TD><A HREF="http://www.microsoft.com/ie/ie.htm">
        <IMG SRC="http://www.pimpernel.com/images/ie_animated.gif"
        ➥BORDER=0
        ALT="Goto Microsoft"></A></TD>
    </TR></TABLE>
</APPLET>
```

You can see the results of this HTML in Figure 7.5; the lower window has the Java applet, and the upper window shows what non-Java visitors will see.

There's another case to consider, though: what if your visitor's browser *can* do Java but she has Java loading turned off? The Java designers thought of this problem already and provided a solution: the <ALT> tag can be used with an applet just as it can with an image. Make sure to put <ALT> tags on your applets!

Now that you've seen how to find applets and put them in your pages, it's time to apply your newfound skills! This section will lead you through the process of adding applets to your pages: one applet will get you cool animated banners, whereas the other will let you host discussion groups without a dedicated server.

You may have already decided what pages you want to put applets on. If you haven't, there's no need to postpone reading this section—after

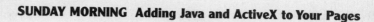

Figure 7.5

The same page viewed in two browsers: one with Java, and one without.

you've built the proper applet tags, you can use them anywhere, so don't be afraid of plunging ahead.

Adding Dynamic Banners with KzmAdvertise

In Saturday evening's session, you learned how to use animated GIF images on your pages. These GIF files consist of a series of GIF images that the browser plays back in sequence. If you want special effects like fades, dissolves, or fancy scrolling, you have to add them yourself with Photoshop or another image editor.

Luckily, there's an alternative: you can use a Java applet to sequence a series of images for you, including transition effects. I've chosen Alex Garbagnati's KzmAdvertise applet for use as an example. KzmAdvertise has more than 20 transition effects, and it's easy to integrate with your pages. Here's what's in the package:

KzmAdvertise is on the CD in the `SundayMorning\Applets` folder. It's also on the Web at **http://www.kazuma.net/**.

- ✿ The three mysterious files whose names end with `.class` (`KzmEffects.class`, `FileVector.class`, and `KzmAdvertise.class`) are the actual Java files that make up the applet. The `.class` extension identifies these files as Java applet pieces; you need all three of them for the applet to work properly.

- ✿ The `banners` folder holds the GIF or JPEG images you want to use as banner material.

- ✿ The `advertise.txt` file holds a list that tells the applet which banners to show, what order to show them in, and where to link each banner image to.

- ✿ `effects.html` explains what each of the visual effects do, and `index.html` is a sample page showing `KzmAdvertise` in action.

Getting to the Applet

Before you'll be able to use any Java applet, you have to know where it is. You can use some Java applets without copying them to your local server—just set the `CODEBASE` attribute of the `<APPLET>` tag to point to the URL where the applet lives. For example, to use the `KzmDClock` digital clock, build an `<APPLET>` tag like this:

```
<APPLET CODEBASE="http://www.kazuma.net" CODE="KzmDClock" WIDTH="80"
    HEIGHT="24"
    ALIGN="BOTTOM" align="baseline">
    <PARAM NAME="backcolor" VALUE="0 0 100">
    <PARAM NAME="copyright" VALUE="Alex 'Kazuma' Garbagnati, kazu-
    ma@energy.it">
    <PARAM NAME="size" VALUE="small">
</APPLET>
```

You can always put applets on your own server; in fact, you'll have to if the applet requires local configuration files, because Java's security model

doesn't let the applet read or write files from anywhere except the server that provided the applet in the first place.

To use KzmAdvertise, you'll have to copy it from the CD or its home Web site onto your server. Remember where you put it; you'll need that location when you build the <APPLET> tag a little later in this session.

Building Banners

The next step in bannerizing your pages is to get your banners together. Images can be in GIF or JPEG format, and you may freely mix the two types. You can use any size image you want, but they should all be the same size. KzmAdvertise won't scale images up or down, but will instead use the drawing area you give it in its <APPLET> tag. In addition, you should keep the images to a reasonable size because your visitors will have to wait for *all* of them to load before the animations start.

NOTE Because KzmAdvertise is an applet, it can be run on any kind of Web server—Windows, MacOS, Unix, or anything else, unlike some CGI-based banner tools.

You can use any number of images in a banner list. After you have assembled all the banners you want to use, put them in a directory on your server. You can either use the same directory you use for other graphics, or you can create a new directory just for the banner images—whichever suits you.

Building a Banner List

After your banners are assembled, it's time to build a banner list. This is nothing more than a text file that lists each banner image and tells the applet what to do with it. The banner list that comes with the applet looks like this:

```
b_cattivi.jpg,H_HORCLOSE,5,http://www.cattivipensieri.it/,_self
b_jis.jpg,H_VERCLOSE,4,http://jis.rmnet.it/,_self
```

```
b_bowling.jpg,T_BOTTOPBOT,4,http://www.bowling.it/,_self
b_simurg.jpg,Q_DIAGONAL,5,http://www.simurg.it/,_self
b_pharos.jpg,Q_TOPRIGBOTLEF,4,http://www.pharos.it/,_self
b_energy.jpg,D_BOTTOMLEFT,4,http://www.energy.it/,_self
```

As you can see, each line in the list has five pieces of information in it:

- The banner name specifies the name of the graphic file to use, without folder or directory names.

- The transition effect tells the applet how to draw the banner when it's time to show it. See Table 7.1 for a complete list of transitions. If you misspell or make up a transition name, KzmAdvertise will just ignore it.

- The number of seconds to leave the image in place before moving on to the next one.

- The target URL to jump to when the visitor clicks the banner image.

TABLE 7.1 TRANSITION EFFECTS FOR KzmADVERTISE

Transition	What the Banner Does	Abbreviation
None	Nothing at all	NONE
Drop from top	Comes down like a curtain	TOP
Rise from bottom	Rises from the bottom	BOTTOM
Move from left	Slides from left to right	LEFT
Move from right	Slides from right to left	RIGHT
Diagonal top-left	Slides down from top-left corner to middle	D_TOPLEFT
Diagonal top-right	Slides down from top-right corner to middle	D_TOPRIGHT

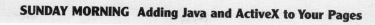

Transition	What the Banner Does	Abbreviation
TABLE 7.1 TRANSITION EFFECTS FOR KZMADVERTISE (continued)		
Diagonal bottom-left	Slides up from bottom-left corner to middle	D_BOTLEFT
Diagonal bottom-right	Slides up from bottom-right corner to middle	D_BOTRIGHT
Half top & bottom	Left half of image descends, right half rises	H_TOPBOTTOM
	Left half of image rises, left half descends	H_BOTTOMTOP
Half left & right	Top half of image slides in from left; bottom half from right	H_LEFTRIGHT
	Top half of image slides in from right; bottom half from left	H_RIGHTLEFT
Horizontal close	Two halves slide in and meet in middle	H_HORCLOSE
Vertical close	Two halves slide up and down to meet in middle	H_VERCLOSE
Quadrants	One quarter of image arrives from each corner	Q_DIAGONAL
	Quarters of the image arrive from top, right, right, bottom and left	Q_TOPRIGBOTLEF
	Quarters of the image arrive from left, top, right, bottom	Q_LEFTOPRIGBOT
Thirds top & bottom	Left and right thirds come down; middle third rises	T_TOPBOTTOP
	Left and right thirds come up; middle third descends	T_BOTTOPBOT
Thirds left & right	Top and bottom thirds move in from left; middle third in from right	T_LEFRIGLEF
	Top and bottom thirds move in from right; middle third in from left	T_RIGLEFRIG

⚙ The target frame to put the target URL into. `self` tells the applet to display the new URL in the main browser window, but you can use any of the other legal targets. (See Saturday morning's "Designing Pages with Frames" session for a refresher on frame targets if you need it.)

To create the list, use a text editor like Notepad, SimpleText, or your HTML editor. For each banner, put a line in the file that contains the five pieces of information presented in the list preceding Table 7.1. When you're finished, save the file and put it on your Web server; it needs to go in the same directory as the `KzmAdvertise` applet and its other support files.

Embedding the Applet in Your Page

The last thing you actually have to do is add an `<APPLET>` tag for `KzmAdvertise` to your page. Here's how to do it (the bold lines in each step represent the new HTML you add in that step):

1. Create a new `<APPLET>` tag, like this:

   ```
   <APPLET>
   </APPLET>
   ```

2. Add the name of the applet you're using and tell the browser where to find it:

   ```
   <APPLET CODE="KzmAdvertise.class" CODEBASE="http://fly.hiwaay.net/~paulr/books/11377" ">
   </APPLET>
   ```

3. Assign a width and height for the banner area; this should match the size of your banner images. You can also add an alignment attribute if you need one:

   ```
   <APPLET CODE="KzmAdvertise.class" CODEBASE="http://
   fly.hiwaay.net/~paulr/books/11377"
       WIDTH="360" HEIGHT="40" ALIGN="bottom" ALIGN="base
       line">
   </APPLET>
   ```

4. Add the copyright parameter:

```
<APPLET CODE="KzmAdvertise.class" CODEBASE="http://
fly.hiwaay.net/~paulr/books/11377"
     WIDTH="360" HEIGHT="40" ALIGN="bottom" ALIGN="base
     line">
<PARAM NAME="copyright" VALUE="Alex 'Kazuma' Garbagnati,
     kazuma@energy.it">
</APPLET>
```

5. Tell the applet where to find your banner list, and the banners it contains, by adding the SCRIPTFILE and IMAGESDIR parameters. Remember that the applet expects to see both of these files in the same directory where it is:

```
<APPLET CODE="KzmAdvertise.class" CODEBASE="http://
fly.hiwaay.net/~paulr/books/11377"
     WIDTH="360" HEIGHT="40" ALIGN="bottom" ALIGN="base
     line">
     <PARAM NAME="copyright" VALUE="Alex 'Kazuma'
          Garbagnati, kazuma@energy.it">
     <PARAM NAME="scriptfile" VALUE="banners.txt">
     <PARAM NAME="imagesdir" VALUE="banners ">
</APPLET>
```

6. Add alternate text so that your visitors who aren't using Java will know what they're missing:

```
<APPLET CODE="KzmAdvertise.class" CODEBASE="http://
     fly.hiwaay.net/~paulr/books/11377"
          WIDTH="360" HEIGHT="40" ALIGN="bottom"
          ALIGN="baseline"
          ALT="LadyWorks advertising banner">
     <PARAM NAME="copyright" VALUE="Alex 'Kazuma' Garbag
          nati, kazuma@energy.it">
     <PARAM NAME="scriptfile" VALUE=" banners.txt">
     <PARAM NAME="imagesdir" VALUE="banners ">

     This Java applet displays an animated sequence of
     banners to try to entice you to buy one of my books.
</APPLET>
```

7. (Optional) `KzmAdvertise` can display a message to tell visitors what it's doing while it loads images; you control the message with the `welcome` parameter:

```
<APPLET CODE="KzmAdvertise.class" CODEBASE="http://
    fly.hiwaay.net/~paulr/books/11377"
        WIDTH="360" HEIGHT="40" ALIGN="bottom"
        ALIGN="baseline"
        ALT="LadyWorks advertising banner">
<PARAM NAME="copyright" VALUE="Alex 'Kazuma'
    Garbagnati, kazuma@energy.it">
<PARAM NAME="scriptfile" VALUE="banners.txt">
<PARAM NAME="imagesdir" VALUE="banners ">
<PARAM NAME="welcome" VALUE="Please wait— I'm loading
    some images.">
This Java applet displays an animated sequence of banners
to try to entice you to buy one of my books.
</APPLET>
```

The finished banner, and the page that hosts it, is shown in Figure 7.6.

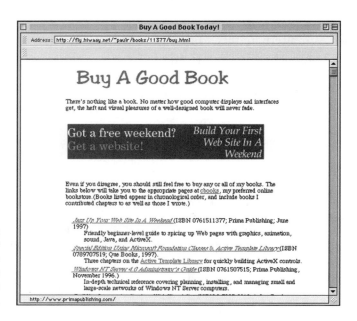

Figure 7.6

KzmAdvertise in action on the "please buy my book" page.

Troubleshooting Java Applets

The first few times you build applets into your pages, it's easy to make mistakes that keep things from working. Here are the most common problems you're likely to run into with KzmAdvertise, or any other applet for that matter.

- ✿ *I just see an empty square where the applet should be.* This is probably because your browser can't find the applet—it knows how big the drawing area should be, but with no applet it can't draw anything! Check the applet's name in the CODE parameter and make sure that the CODEBASE parameter points to where the applet is actually stored on the server.

- ✿ *I see the welcome message, but the banners never appear.* This means that KzmAdvertise can't find either your script file or the banners it references. Make sure that they're in the same directory as the applet and that the SCRIPTFILE and IMAGESDIR parameters are correct.

- ✿ *The applet window says "problems in reading script file. . . . "* KzmAdvertise displays this message when it can't find the script file. Double-check the SCRIPTFILE parameter.

- ✿ *Some of my banners show up, but some don't.* The applet will skip any banners it can't find. Make sure that your banner list has the correct names for all banners you want displayed.

ON THE

CD

As an alternative to KzmAdvertise, the CD includes Banner*Show/32, a Windows program for creating JavaScript-based banners in your pages.

Adding ActiveX to Your Web Pages

ActiveX controls are easy to add to your Web pages. When you find a control you like, you have only three steps to complete:

1. Put the control's files on your Web server.
2. Add an <OBJECT> tag to your page to make the control display.
3. Customize the control by adding JScript, VBScript, or PARAM attributes.

Before You Begin

You must carefully consider a number of things before putting ActiveX controls on your site. Because your main goal is to build a site for your visitors, it pays to think through adding ActiveX to make sure that it makes sense for your site.

The biggest stumbling block you're likely to face is that only one browser supports ActiveX: Microsoft's Internet Explorer for Windows 95 and Windows NT. (The Mac version supports it too, but almost no one is making ActiveX controls that can run on the Mac.) Unlike Java applets, ActiveX controls aren't portable, so only visitors who use Microsoft's browser can see them. If you don't mind limiting your site (or parts of its content) to a potentially smaller audience, then you can use ActiveX without reservations.

NOTE nCompass (**http://www.ncompass.com**) has written a plug-in for Windows versions of Netscape Navigator that lets ActiveX controls run in Navigator; but it costs money, so it's not widely deployed.

Another possible bugaboo is download time. Depending on how they're written, individual ActiveX controls can be as big as a megabyte or even more—for one control! Unlike Java, though, after the control is installed, it doesn't have to be downloaded again the next time the visitor accesses the page.

You must balance these obstacles against the fact that you can do things with ActiveX controls that just aren't possible with Java right now. For example, ActiveX controls can take advantage of other ActiveX controls on a visitor's machine to view and edit Windows documents, including those produced by Microsoft Office. Dozens of ActiveX controls are available for playing surround video, QuickTime videos, sound files, and other multimedia types that usually require plug-ins.

Finding Cool Controls

The hardest part about using ActiveX controls is likely to be deciding which ones to use! Hundreds of controls are available as I write this, with dozens more coming every day. Microsoft is doing everything it can to encourage (and in some cases subsidize) ActiveX control development, and the demand from users and webmasters is speeding the development of ActiveX library sites like the ones in this section.

Gamelan

Even though they're still primarily a Java resource, Gamelan has recognized the groundswell of interest in ActiveX and added an ActiveX control resource directory at **http://activex.developer.com/pages/Gamelan .related.activex.tools.general.html** (see Figure 7.7).

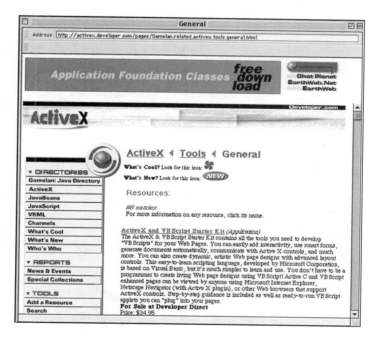

Figure 7.7

Gamelan's ActiveX directory includes a description and link for every listed control.

As with Gamelan's Java site, some controls here are free, others are shareware, and still others are demo versions of commercial products. Each control is linked to a page that describes it, so you can browse before you download.

BrowserWatch

When Dave Garaffa started BrowserWatch, he wanted it to keep track of the fast-changing state of the Browser Wars. Since Mecklermedia began paying for the site, it has really blossomed. It now features a comprehensive list of ActiveX controls at **http://browserwatch.iworld.com/ activex.html**, as shown in Figure 7.8.

ActiveX.com

The same folks who brought us the clNet television program and the **news.com** Web site have struck again with **http://www.activex.com**,

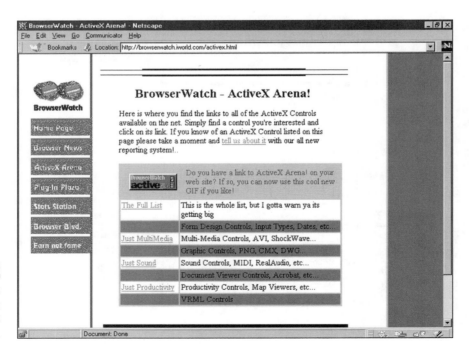

Figure 7.8

BrowserWatch's ActiveX Arena includes comments on each control.

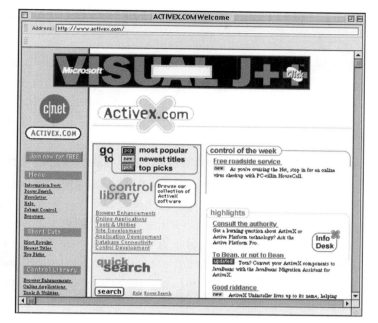

Figure 7.9

ActiveX.com has a ton of useful resources.

shown in Figure 7.9. In addition to dozens of controls, a number of good tutorials and learning resources are available, so you can even learn to write your own ActiveX controls! Many examples of how to use ActiveX on your own Web pages are given, so you can explore the nuances after you've mastered the basics.

On the CD

The CD bound to the back of this book includes a batch of the best ActiveX controls on the net. You can use them to enrich your pages with cool features like an automatic tip of the day or an automatic stock ticker.

Everywhere Else

You might find some other ActiveX resource sites useful, even though they don't focus on making controls available. For example, Ziff-Davis maintains the ActiveX Files at **http://www.zdnet.com/activexfiles/**.

Among other things, it contains a large number of ActiveX-related magazine articles from ZD Press.

In addition, many ActiveX controls are written by individuals or small companies, and there aren't as many ActiveX collections as there are for Java applets. This means that hundreds of controls are floating around on the net that aren't listed in catalogs or sites like Gamelan's.

Putting Your Controls on the Server

ActiveX files are usually packaged in `.cab` files. *Cabinets* (as Microsoft calls them) are similar to Java archive files; they can contain any number of ActiveX controls or supporting files. In addition, `.cab` files can point to other cabinets. This makes it possible for the visitor to automatically get, and install, all the pieces needed for a control. If you've ever waited to download a program and then had to go get a library or DLL that it needed, you'll understand why this is a benefit.

`.cab` files are just ordinary binary files, so you can transfer them to your server with the FTP tool of your choice. Once there, where you put them is up to you. Like Java applets, some ActiveX controls require access to other files on the server, and they'll usually need to be in the same directory as the needed files. Other controls, like the Tip of the Day control you'll be seeing shortly, can go anywhere on the server.

As with Java applets, I recommend keeping all your ActiveX controls in a single directory if possible; having them all in one place makes it much easier for you to keep track of, and maintain, these files when needed.

Using the <OBJECT> Tag

When you want to put an ActiveX control in your pages, you use the <OBJECT> tag. It's not yet officially part of the HTML standard, but it's being considered for inclusion in the next version of the standard. Because <OBJECT> supports many other things besides ActiveX, it's pretty much a shoo-in for inclusion.

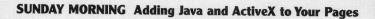
`<OBJECT>` is just like most other HTML tags; you can put ActiveX controls in table cells, frames, or anywhere else, as long as you leave enough space for the control to draw itself.

Dissecting the Tip of the Day Example

The Tip of the Day ActiveX control lets you put a rotating Windows 95-like "tip of the day" on your Web site. You can supply the tip text and images, and the control takes care of drawing and animating them for you. The page shown in Figure 7.10 uses this control to give an up-to-date pointer to interesting books about Web design and the Internet.

Here's what the actual `<OBJECT>` tag looks like. You'll notice the similarities to the `<APPLET>` tag; future versions of the HTML standard may combine the two because Java and ActiveX are two sides of the same

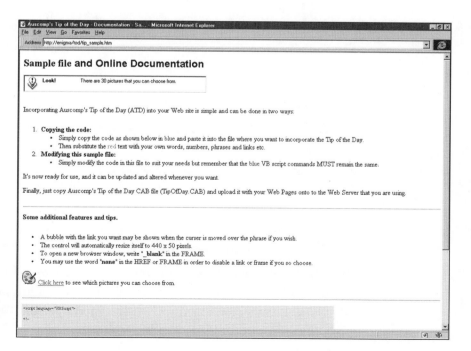

Figure 7.10

The Tip of the Day adorns this page.

thing. The CLASSID attribute is required, and all the others are optional.
Here's the HTML that produced the page shown in Figure 7.10:

```
<OBJECT ID="TipOfDay" WIDTH="439" HEIGHT="60"
    ALIGN="top" border=0 hspace=8 vspace=0
    ALT="Tip Of The Day"
    CLASSID="CLSID:FCA59C8F-7D8E-11D0-8713-0080AD11822F"
    codebase="http://fly.hiwaay.net/~paulr/applets/TipOfDay.CAB">
If your browser can't show ActiveX, you're missing the Tip of
    the Day.
</OBJECT>
```

- ☼ ID provides a "short name" for the control. The browser will identi-fy the control by its CLASSID, but that's unwieldy for humans. You can use the ID attribute in a VBScript or JScript script to send commands to, or get data from, the control.

- ☼ WIDTH and HEIGHT work the same way as they do for applets: they tell the browser how much space to reserve for the control's draw-ing area. Controls can have a default size that they'll use when you don't specify a size, but not all controls do.

- ☼ HSPACE, VSPACE, and BORDER work just as they do for images and Java applets: they tell the browser how to draw the control in its bounding rectangle.

- ☼ ALIGN works just like it does in other HTML tags. You can align the control to the left, right, top, middle, or bottom of its drawing area.

- ☼ CLASSID provides the unique ID for this control. Every control (or any other kind of OLE or ActiveX object) has its own CLASSID, and no two are the same. You'll have to know the correct value for a control when you add it to your pages, or the browser might load the wrong control, or none at all.

- ☼ The CODEBASE attribute tells the browser where to look for the con-trol's files. If the browser doesn't already have a local copy of the control, it will look at the URL specified by CODEBASE.

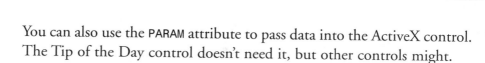
You can also use the PARAM attribute to pass data into the ActiveX control. The Tip of the Day control doesn't need it, but other controls might.

Supporting Browsers That Can't Use ActiveX

Because only Microsoft Internet Explorer supports ActiveX, you need to add some type of content to your controls so that visitors who aren't using MSIE will be able to know why they don't see anything. You do this by putting HTML within the <OBJECT> container; whatever you put there will be displayed by browsers that can't handle ActiveX.

You should also use the ALT attribute of the <OBJECT> tag to cover visitors who have ActiveX-capable browsers but who have turned off ActiveX controls. In general, you should use ALT on all HTML tags that support it, and this is no exception.

Adding a Tip of the Day

Tips are usually short, helpful messages that point out a feature or time-saving trick of software (or books!). One of the most welcome features of Windows 95 was the "tip of the day" window that appears at startup; it dispenses a tip every time you start Windows 95. Microsoft adopted this feature for Office 95, and it stayed around in Office 97, Windows NT 4, and many non-Microsoft products. Thanks to AUSCOMP's Tip of the Day control, you can add this feature to your own Web pages.

ON THE

CD

The Tip of the Day ActiveX control is on the CD in the IBM\webtools\JavaApps folder, or on the net at **http://www.auscomp.com**.

Here's what comes in the distribution package:

🌣 The actual control is in the TipOfDay.cab file. The .cab also contains a few extra images for use as tip icons (most of the icons are already part of Windows). This file will have to go on the server.

🌣 The start.htm file shows an example of the tip mechanism; it also links to the AUSCOMP Web pages.

- Several other .htm files make up the rest of the online documentation for the control.

- Each icon has its own GIF file, so that you can see what they look like. You don't need to put these on the server.

Getting to the Control

The .cab mechanism makes installing this control easy: just move the single TipOfDay.cab to the appropriate place on your server. (But remember its location; you'll need it to when you build the <OBJECT> tag.)

Building the <Object> Tag

The <OBJECT> tag for this control is fairly simple because there aren't any parameters. The only tricky part is getting the CLASSID right. Apart from that, it's almost exactly the same as building an <APPLET> tag: you specify a width and height, an alignment if you want one, and alternate text for visitors who don't use ActiveX.

You also need to give the <OBJECT> an ID parameter so that you can refer to it from the accompanying VBScript. Finally, you must specify the CLASSID (in this case, it's CLSID:FCA59C8F-7D8E-11D0-8713-0080AD11822F). Here's a simple example version that you can use to get started:

```
<OBJECT ID="TipOfDay"
    ALT="Tip Of The Day"
    CLASSID="CLSID:FCA59C8F-7D8E-11D0-8713-0080AD11822F">
    No ActiveX, no Tip of the Day.
</OBJECT>
```

Putting the VBScript on Your Page

Some ActiveX controls require you to embed VBScript or JScript scripts in your pages. These scripts let the control get notification when the browser does something. Writing your own scripts isn't difficult, but it's too much to cover here. However, you can easily paste the necessary scripts into your pages when they come with the control, as they do here.

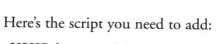

Here's the script you need to add:

```
<SCRIPT language="VBScript">
<!—
    Sub Window_onLoad()
        TipOfDay.Additem "INTERVAL:5"
    end sub
    —>
</SCRIPT>
```

As you can see, the actual script is enclosed in a <SCRIPT> container. The comment marks (the <!— . . . —>) mark the script as a comment for browsers that don't understand VBScript. The rest of the script is code that gets called when the browser first loads the page (hence the onLoad name).

To use the script, you have to paste it into your HTML editor as HTML. If you use the normal editing mode of Netscape Composer, FrontPage 97, or another editor, it will think the script is text that you want to display. You can open your pages with Notepad, or use an editor that supports showing you the actual HTML for a page.

Writing Your Tips

Now that you've added the VBScript to your page, you can add the actual tips you want the control to display. Each tip has five pieces of information: the picture and title to display when showing the tip, the text of the tip itself, a URL to load when the user clicks the tip, and the target frame for the URL. The latter two are optional.

You assemble a tip from several parts. The first part combines the ID of the <OBJECT> tag you built earlier with the control's AddItem command. The combination is actually an instruction to the control to add whatever item you specify to its internal list of tips.

The next part is the tip itself. You can specify the four pieces of tip information in any order, and you separate them with the # character.

- **PIC**: tells the control which picture to use. `PIC:Tip` tells it to use the standard Windows "tip" icon, for example. You have to use the same capitalization as the names in the sample icon list, or the control won't draw anything.

- **TITLE**: contains the title text you want shown next to the tip icon. You can leave it blank, but if you do the visitor might not understand what the tip's for.

- **TEXT**: contains the actual text of the tip. You can safely fit three or four lines of this in the tip window, but no more.

- **HREF**: tells the control where to jump when the visitor clicks on the tip window. You can leave this off or use `HREF:none` if you don't want to link the tip to a page.

- **FRAME**: specifies where the URL specified by the `HREF` tag should be displayed. `FRAME:none` means to use the parent window; you can also use `FRAME:_self`, `FRAME:_top`, or any of the other frame target tags.

Here are two examples of how all the pieces go together:

```
TipOfDay.Additem "PIC:Tip#TITLE:Did you know?#TEXT:It's amazing-
ly
    simple to use ActiveX controls on your
pages?#HREF:none#FRAME:none"
TipOfDay.Additem "PIC:About#TITLE:Get the scoop!#TEXT: For the
latest on the
    computer book industry, come check us
out!#HREF:http://www.studiob.com
    #FRAME:none"
```

ON THE

CD

The tip icons you can use are shown in the `tip_picture.htm` file in the `Sunday-Morning\Applets` directory of the CD.

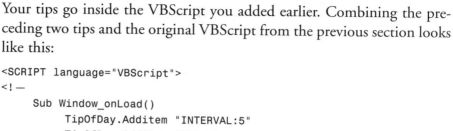

Your tips go inside the VBScript you added earlier. Combining the preceding two tips and the original VBScript from the previous section looks like this:

```
<SCRIPT language="VBScript">
<!—
    Sub Window_onLoad()
        TipOfDay.Additem "INTERVAL:5"
        TipOfDay.Additem "PIC:Tip#TITLE:Did you know?#TEXT:It's
    amazingly
            simple to use ActiveX controls on your
    pages?#HREF:none#FRAME:none"
        TipOfDay.Additem "PIC:About#TITLE:Get the scoop!#TEXT: For
    the latest on the
            computer book industry, come check us
    out!#HREF:http://www.studiob.com
        #FRAME:none"
    end sub
    —>
</SCRIPT>
```

Add your tips to your page; then save it, and you're done!

Troubleshooting ActiveX Controls

ActiveX controls are pretty easy to use, but a few problems might trip you up the first few times you try it. Here are some common problems and their solutions.

✿ *My page takes a very long time to load.* ActiveX is pretty smart: if you use a control on your page, and that control needs some other components that you don't already have, it will helpfully go get the components you don't have. This can lead to unexpectedly long load times when you don't know you're missing any components. Unfortunately, there's not much to do about this, except to take comfort from the fact that after the new components are loaded you won't have to wait the next time.

- *There's a blank space where my control should be.* This is almost always the result of mistyping the CLASSID; as a result, Windows can't find the object it needs to load, so it won't display anything. Double-check the CLASSID against the ID provided by the control developers.

- *One or more of my tips don't display with the right icon.* The icon names are case-sensitive; you have to type them exactly as listed in the icon index on the CD.

- *One or more of my tips doesn't display right.* Make sure that you used # to separate each field in the tip definition and make sure that you have an icon, title, and text all defined.

Tool Tips

Throughout this session, you've been able to get the job done without special assistance from any tools. A good text editor is really all you need to add Java and ActiveX to your pages, but your tasks will be simplified with a few good tools.

Find a Good Java Toolset

It's very often handy to be able to run a Java applet on your machine without using a particular browser. This can help you isolate whether a problem your visitors report is because of the applet or the browser, and it gives you a good way to test new applets you're thinking about adding to your pages.

JavaSoft's JDK (**http://www.javasoft.com**) is free, but somewhat cryptic. Microsoft, Symantec, metrowerks, and others all make good-quality, inexpensive Java development tools; the $100 or so you spend on these tools can be money well-spent if you're going to do much Java work.

Use the ActiveX Control Pad

Microsoft makes an excellent, and free, tool called the ActiveX Control Pad; it's shown in Figure 7.11. It greatly eases the process of setting parameters for ActiveX controls; better still, it frees you from having to type in those finger-breaking, impossible-to-memorize CLASSID values.

The Control Pad won't help you find controls, but it will make it simpler and easier for you to include the controls you want to use.

Register Your Shareware

The ActiveX and Java worlds are not yet completely commercialized; many of the most popular—and useful—applets and controls are shareware. If you decide to use shareware objects on your pages, please pay for

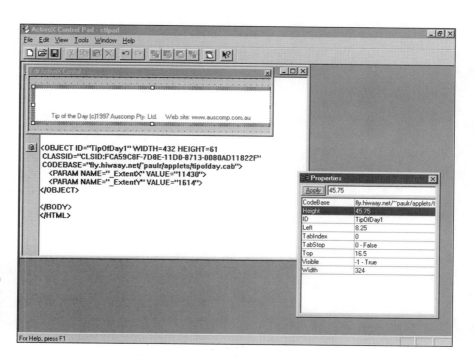

Figure 7.11

The ActiveX Control Pad makes adding ActiveX even easier.

them. This helps encourage the authors to continue development, and it gives other potential developers an incentive to write cool new objects in the future.

Wrap It Up!

In the previous session, you learned how to use animation, sound, and video. In this session, you learned something only a few Webmasters ever master: how to add dynamic content to your pages with ActiveX and Java. As you've seen, it's not nearly as difficult as it seems, and there are many worthwhile applets and controls just waiting for you to add them.

In the next session, you'll learn how to apply the finishing touches to your Web page, including how to make it more visible to search engines. See you there!

Applying the Finishing Touches

- Describing What's on Your Home Page
- Helping Search Engines Find You
- Adding Page Headers or Footers
- Accepting Advertising
- Exchanging Links with Other Sites
- Adding Password-Protected Pages

By now, you've learned how to jazz up your site with everything from simple design changes to ActiveX controls and Java applets. You might think there's nothing else to do, but there are a few finishing touches you can apply to your site to bring in more traffic and add a couple of cool features.

In this session, you'll learn how to tweak your pages so that search engines like Yahoo! and AltaVista can find your pages more easily. You'll also learn how to boost traffic to your site by exchanging links with other sites, and even how to accept ads from other sites!

Describing What's on Your Page

The Greek prefix *meta-* literally means "after." In common use, it means "something that describes itself"; you've probably heard of metalanguage (language describing or talking about language) and metamorphosis, but have you heard of *metadata*?

If not, don't worry—you use metadata every day even if you don't know it! Metadata tags provide a way for a document to tell about itself, perhaps by reporting its title or who wrote it. For example, the cover of this book is filled with metadata; it has a lot of little tags that describe the content of the book in various ways.

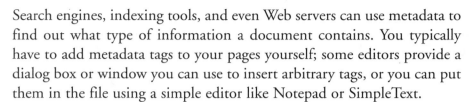

Search engines, indexing tools, and even Web servers can use metadata to find out what type of information a document contains. You typically have to add metadata tags to your pages yourself; some editors provide a dialog box or window you can use to insert arbitrary tags, or you can put them in the file using a simple editor like Notepad or SimpleText.

<META> tags are just like other HTML tags; they have two required attributes, CONTENT and NAME. For example,

```
<META NAME="Author" Content="Paul Robichaux">
```

tells any program or person who understands <META> tags that the value of the metadata entry named "Author" is "Paul Robichaux." The CONTENT value might just as easily say "Elvis Presley"; no one validates metadata to make sure that it's telling the truth!

Adding Metadata Tags to Your Pages

There's a little-known section of the HTTP protocol definition that says it's okay for a client to request just the <HEAD> of a document, and that servers should honor such requests.

You certainly might wonder why you'd ever *want* to fetch only the head of a document. The answer: <META> tags can live only in the <HEAD> container of the document. By getting only the document head—and the tags it contains—you can get the document title and description without having to download the whole page. This is a big win for search engines, indexers, and other types of automatic Webcrawlers that seek out and catalog information. The Web is so big that saving a few seconds on every page adds up quickly.

A simple example may help clear the air a bit. Check out this <HEAD> section from the home page for this book:

```
<HEAD>
     <META NAME="Author" Content="Paul Robichaux">
     <META HTTP-EQUIV="Content-Type" CONTENT="text/html;
          CHARSET=iso-8859-1">
```

```
<META NAME="Keywords" Content="web page design multimedia
     prima robichaux">
<META NAME="Description" Content="These web pages are a
     complement to
     _Jazz Up Your Web Site In A Weekend_.">
<TITLE>Jazz Up Your Web Site In A Weekend</TITLE>
</HEAD>
```

As you can see, there are four metadata tags, each of which describes some property of the document they're in. Some tags are self-explanatory; others are not. Let's examine each <META> tag in some detail, so that you'll know when to use them in *your* pages.

Understanding the Most Useful Metadata Tags

Because metadata describes the document it's in, there's no formal definition of which tags are legal and which aren't—anything goes. You're free to put any tag you want into a document, and Web servers and browsers are equally free to ignore it if they don't know what it means. With that in mind, let's look at five of the most commonly used tags.

All these tags follow the same format: the name attribute identifies the tag, and the content attribute provides a value for it. There are no restrictions on what you can put in the content attribute, but you should probably stick with plain text (although you can use non-English character sets with no problem).

The <AUTHOR> Tag

As you might expect, <META NAME="Author"> identifies the author of a page or set of pages. This tag is mostly useful for humans who might read the page; search engines all ignore it as of this writing. Don't let that discourage you from using it on your pages, though! One of the nicest feelings you'll get from the Internet is getting mail from someone complementing you on your pages.

The <KEYWORDS> Tag

Some search engines can use a list of keywords you provide for indexing. This has the advantage of letting you specify keywords for concepts that aren't on your pages. For example, if your page is all about vegetarian cooking, you can specify keywords like *meatless* and *meat-free* to help the engines match your contents to whatever search phrase the visitor types in.

To specify keywords, just put them in the CONTENT attribute, with spaces between them. Don't do anything special to separate phrases. For example, if your page is about the history of Limestone County, Alabama since the Civil War, you could provide key words like this:

```
<META NAME="Keywords" CONTENT="Limestone County Alabama postbellum
    history post-Civil War local history Athens">
```

Notice that all the keywords are treated equally; the search engine won't use punctuation when it searches, so you shouldn't use it either.

The <DESCRIPTION> Tag

When a search engine decides that your page matches the search terms it was given, it will usually return a chunk of the page's text. This text may or may not accurately reflect what the page is really about because the search engine has to make its best guess about which chunk to return. You can specify your own page description with the <DESCRIPTION> tag. If you do, the search engine can return your description instead of making one up.

Your description can be any size, although it's polite to keep it reasonably short. As with the keywords tag, it's best to stick to clean text because any HTML or formatting you include may not be displayed on the visitor's browser. Here's an example of a clear, useful description:

```
<META NAME="Description" CONTENT="These pages summarize the summer
    youth program at the 125th St YMCA, including hours, fees, and
    activities.">
```

TIP Make sure to include keywords and descriptions for your pages before registering them with search engines as discussed later in the session. If you do, the engines will be able to use your keywords and descriptions immediately.

The <SCRIPT> Tag

You may not see the <SCRIPT> tag used very often; its purpose is to notify browsers, servers, and indexers that a page contains some kind of scripting commands, including JavaScript or VBScript. Some indexers have problems with these commands, and it's often useful to know when a page contains scripts. Most page editors that let you insert scripting commands will automatically include this <META> tag for you, but sometimes you'll have to insert it yourself. The syntax is simple: just put the name of the scripting language you're using into the CONTENTS item.

The <STYLE> Tag

The <STYLE> tag is similar to the <SCRIPT> tag; it tells interested parties which style sheets a Web page uses. This allows a browser to go off and get any style sheets that it doesn't already have in its cache; otherwise, there would be no guarantee that the page would display as the author intended. Although <STYLE> isn't used much now, expect to see more of it as the CSS1 style sheet specification starts to take off.

Helping Search Engines Find You

Search engines like InfoSeek (shown in Figure 8.1) have done a great deal for the Internet. Before search engines became popular, the only way to find information was to either ask someone where to find it, or to bumble around looking for it. Now that InfoSeek, AltaVista, eXcite, and other engines have become popular, it's much easier to find what you're look-

Figure 8.1

InfoSeek provides a simple, fast way to search the entire Web.

ing for. However, you can make it easier for search engines to properly index your site, and display better summaries for visitors to boot. These engines use metadata to build their indexes of pages, so by salting your pages with the right kind of metadata you can improve your odds of being found.

How Search Engines Work

All search engines have one thing in common: they somehow get the text of Web pages, index them, and make the index searchable. The details of how each engine does its magic varies from engine to engine, but those aren't really important. What is important is understanding the indexing process that they use, so let's see how it works.

The engine starts by loading a Web page from its server. Because the page is HTML, the engine can pick it apart and make a list of links that appear

on the page. Each link is added to a *search list*, and the text on the page is added to the engine's index. When the whole page has been processed, the engine moves on to the next one.

The search list is constantly updated to keep track of which pages have been visited already and when. This keeps the engine from visiting pages over and over and lets the engine operators decide when to go back and revisit a page. The gap between visits can be anywhere from a day to two or three months, depending on how busy the engine is.

How are these visits scheduled? Like your local deli—first come, first served. When the engine finishes indexing a page, it goes to the next entry on the search list. New URLs that it wants to visit later are added to the end of the list. The longer the list gets, the longer the time span between visits from a particular engine.

When a new page appears on the Internet, the search engine won't know it's there unless one of two things happens. If another page already known to the server has a link to the new page, when the server revisits the old page it will pick up the new link and add it to the list. This means that the new page won't be included in the search engine's index until it gets to the original page again—and that might be a while! The second way is for the new page's owner to register the page directly with the search engine; that's the approach I recommend. Let's see how to do it.

Registering Manually

Each search engine has a slightly different form for submitting your pages. In general, though, they all want the URL of your main page, and some want your e-mail address, a list of keywords, or some other supporting information. The only real difference between the search engines' submittal process is the exact form you fill out; they're all suspiciously similar to each other. Table 8.1 lists the registration URLs of several popular search engines.

After you submit your URL, it will be added to the engine's search list. Some engines keep a separate list of new URLs, whereas others just tack

TABLE 8.1 REGISTRATION URLS FOR POPULAR SEARCH ENGINES

To register with . . .	go here . . .	with your . . .
AltaVista	`http://altavista.digital.com/cgi-bin/query?pg=tmpl&v=addurl.html`	URL
eXcite	`http://www.excite.com/Info/add-url.html`	URL, site location webmaster e-mail
InfoSeek	`http://www.infoseek.com/AddUrl?pg=DCaddurl.html&lk=noframes`	URL
Lycos	`http://www.lycos.com/addasite.html`	URL
Yahoo!	`http://add.yahoo.com/fast/add`	URL, category, title, geographic location

newly submitted entries on to the existing master list. There's no guarantee that a search engine will index your newly minted URL within any particular time frame; remember that if your pages have time-sensitive information like sports scores, political jokes, or information about the financial markets.

Registering with a Submittal Service

Instead of manually registering your page with each individual search engine, you can use a submittal service. These services do the legwork for you: you supply the URL of your page, and the service automatically submits it to many engines on your behalf.

As the number of search engines has grown over the last two or three years, so has the number of submittal services. Although a complete list is impossible, I'll mention a few of the best-known ones in case you want to consider using one:

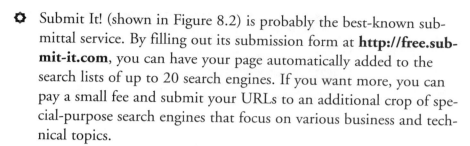

- Submit It! (shown in Figure 8.2) is probably the best-known submittal service. By filling out its submission form at **http://free.submit-it.com**, you can have your page automatically added to the search lists of up to 20 search engines. If you want more, you can pay a small fee and submit your URLs to an additional crop of special-purpose search engines that focus on various business and technical topics.

- ¡Register-It! (shown in Figure 8.3) offers several levels of registration service, ranging from a limited 16-engine free sample to a 100-engine package. They offer a 30-day money-back guarantee.

ON THE

CD

The CD includes SubmitBlaster, a Windows program that lets you quickly submit your site to many search engines. It's in `IBM\webtools\Submit`.

Are these services worth the money? Well, it depends. The majority of Internet users use just five search engines: Lycos, InfoSeek, AltaVista,

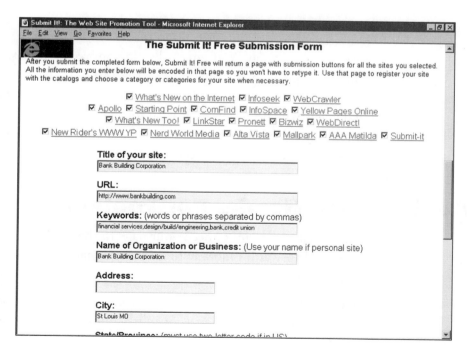

Figure 8.2

Submit It! offers an easy, free submission service.

Figure 8.3

¡Register-It! offers a 30-day money-back guarantee, as well as a limited free trial feature.

eXcite, and Yahoo!. You can easily add your pages to these four, and a few more, in less than an hour and save the $40-$100 fee. On the other hand, submittal services may include some of the specialized engines like Law-Crawler (which specializes in legal topics) that you might otherwise miss, and they *are* more convenient than bouncing from form to form, retyping the same URL over and over.

Adding Page Headers or Footers

Now that you've announced your page to the world, it's time to put your best foot forward. One way to do so is to make sure that your pages have a consistent appearance.

Consistency is one of the hallmarks of a well-designed site, and having basically the same headers (not to be confused with the <HEAD>) or foot-

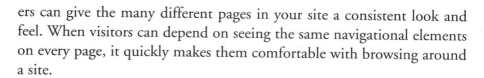

ers can give the many different pages in your site a consistent look and feel. When visitors can depend on seeing the same navigational elements on every page, it quickly makes them comfortable with browsing around a site.

The good news is that adding headers and footers is easier than you might think. There are two ways to add these elements; I'll talk about the easiest one first. Before that, though, how can you decide what should go in your headers or footers?

Knowing What to Add

You can add anything you want to your pages, and whatever you add can appear on every page on your site. Most headers and footers fall into two categories: navigational tools and identification. There are a few others: you often see page counters or "last updated on" timestamps used on the bottom of pages.

You might not want to add headers or footers to every page. For example, if your home page leads only to a small number of second-level pages, which then lead to other pages, you might want to put navigational tools only on the second-level pages. Check out Figure 8.4 for an example: a local gym's pages are structured like this, so I put headers and footers on the three pages in the middle, and then used a different set for the schedule pages (which link from `schedule.html`) and the facilities pages (linked from `facilities.html`). This preserves the look of each level in the tree while still providing consistency for the visitor.

Adding Navigational Tools

Probably the most common use of page headers and footers are navigational tools. You can provide navigation bars in a number of different ways: imagemaps, images within tables, and plain text are all easy to implement. Which one to use depends on what you're most comfortable with, and you can certainly use more than one. For example, Figure 8.5, taken from the Metrowerks Web site, has two navigation bars: the top

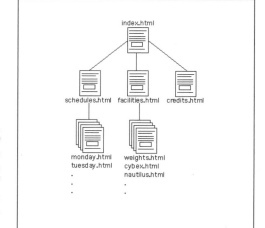

Figure 8.4

The home page has links to three pages; two of those three pages have links to other pages.

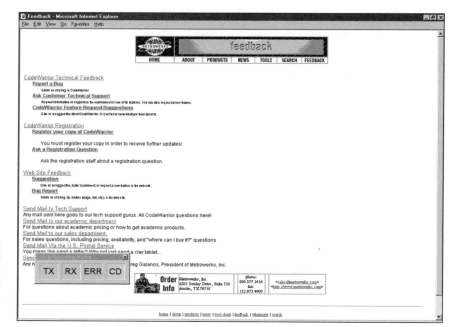

Figure 8.5

You can use more than one type of navigational aid on the same page.

one is an imagemap, whereas the bottom one is ordinary HTML. This ensures that visitors who aren't displaying images can still see the navigation links.

Adding Identity Elements

Marketing experts call a set of related pictures, logos, trademarks, and visual design an *identity*. For example, Microsoft, Apple, and IBM each spend millions of dollars every year to make sure that every electronic or paper document they produce for outside consumption uses the right logos, typestyles, and design elements so that the document is easy to identify as being theirs.

Some of these design elements make the transition to the Web very well. For example, Microsoft makes heavy use of a Web-based toolbar (shown in Figure 8.6) that appears atop almost all its pages. When you see it, it's a good clue that you're on a Microsoft page (especially because it features the Microsoft logo in the rightmost cell!).

Not surprisingly, many Web sites have their own identity. Most often, the Web identity matches the identity of the organization that owns the Web site; it's also common for personal or nonprofit Web sites to have a strong identity.

Figure 8.6

Microsoft's toolbar is a key part of its site identity.

If you think of each page on your Web site as a paper page, you can easily come up with identity elements that make sense for your site. Here are some ideas to help get you started:

- *Logos.* If you don't have one, design one! A small logo (no bigger than 96×64 or so) is a great way to "brand" each page. Put it in the upper left or upper right corner of the page.

- *Credits and copyright notices.* I don't recommend putting the entire set of credits or copyright notice on each page; people get tired of wading through that kind of stuff pretty quickly. Instead, have the last line on each page be a link to the credits and copyright page; you can also put a credits or copyright link in your navigation bar.

- *Contact information.* If your Web site exists to tell people about a real-world event, business, or happening, consider putting a short "how to contact us" section at the bottom of every page.

Manually Adding Headers or Footers

The low-tech solution for giving your pages a consistent header or footer is to add the code to each and every page you want to have it. This can be time-consuming and tedious, but it's not so bad if you only have a few pages.

TIP Some Web page editors offer support for templates and can apply consistent headers or footers across all pages with a click. FrontPage 97 has particularly good template support; check your editor to see whether it can help.

As I noted earlier, you might not need to put headers or footers on every page; think carefully about where to put these elements, and you may save yourself some work.

Automatically Adding Headers or Footers

Normally, when a Web server delivers a page, it doesn't interpret the HTML—it just shovels it over the network to whoever asked for it. This makes implementing a Web server somewhat easier, and it helps the server's performance because its duties are limited—at the cost of flexibility.

However, it didn't take long for some bright person to invent *server-parsed HTML* (also called *server-side includes,* or *SSI*). Here's how it works: the server reads an HTML file as it normally would, but instead of immediately sending it to the requester, the server looks through the file for commands it can execute and puts their output into the file before sending it out. SSI commands can do anything the Web server administrator allows; they can display the modification time for a file, run a program and put its output in the file. Alternatively, you can use an *include* command to put another HTML file in the middle of the requested file.

SSI Requirements

Before you can use SSI, there are a few hurdles to get over. First of all, not all Web servers support SSI (though Apache, Netscape's servers, WebStar, and Microsoft IIS—the most popular servers—all do). If your server doesn't support SSI, you're out of luck.

Your server administrator may also have turned off SSI for performance or security reasons. If SSI is enabled, you may only be able to use SSI files in certain directories on your server, and you may have to use a special extension on files that contain SSI commands (.shtml is the most commonly used extension for these files).

FIND IT ON ▶
THE WEB
NCSA invented SSI, and its pages at **http://hoohoo.ncsa.uiuc.edu/docs/tutorials/includes.html** are still a great tutorial.

Don't let these requirements scare you off, though; many administrators will be happy to turn on SSI if you ask them nicely. Even if they have commands turned off, you can often still use the include command to merge headers and footers into your pages.

Using SSI in Your Pages

SSI commands appear in your pages as comments. This may seem odd, but there's a good reason for it: it keeps the page's HTML legal in case the server doesn't parse the file before delivering it. HTML comment containers look like this:

```
<!— This is a comment. —>
```

Many editors automatically insert comments into files they generate, so you may already have seen them. SSI commands look like ordinary comments, except that there are commands between the comment marks. Anywhere a valid SSI command appears, the server will try to execute the command and put its output in place of the command. For example, this HTML

```
<h1>Here's a page</h1>
This document is located at &quot;<!—#echo DOCUMENT_URI —>&quot;
and was last modified at <!—#echo LAST_MODIFIED—>.<p>
```

will display the document's URL and modification time in place of the specified commands.

Using the #echo command

All #echo does is spit out the value of a predefined variable. The good news is that there are a number of variables you can use. Table 8.2 shows the most useful variables, and a more complete list can be found at **http://hoohoo.ncsa.uiuc.edu/cgi/env.html**.

If this all seems a little obscure, don't worry. A visit to the test script at **http://hoohoo.ncsa.uiuc.edu/cgi-bin/test-cgi** will probably help at this point; the script just spits out every variable it can, as shown in Figure 8.7, so that you can see what typical values look like.

Using the #include Command

The #include command allows the server to slip a copy of the file you specify into what it sends back to the client. For example, this simple file:

Variable Name	What's in It	Sample Value
DATE_GMT	current time in GMT format	Wed May 14 23:20:40
DATE_LOCAL	current time in whatever time zone the server is in	Wed May 14 19:20:55 CDT
DOCUMENT_NAME	filename of the current file	index.html
DOCUMENT_URI	full path to the current file	/users/paul/index.html
HTTP_REFERER	page visitor was on before your	http://hoohoo.ncsa. uiuc.edu/ cgi/examples.html
HTTP_USER_AGENT	browser the visitor's using	Lynx/2.6 libwww-FM/2.14
LAST_MODIFIED	last modification time/ date of file	Wed May 14 7:40:58PM

TABLE 8.2 A PARTIAL LIST OF VARIABLES YOU CAN USE WITH #ECHO

```
<HTML>
<BODY>
... some content ...
<!—#include virtual="/copyright.html">
</BODY>
</HTML>
```

doesn't look like much. When you combine it with the `copyright.html` file, this is the HTML the browser actually receives:

```
<HTML>
<BODY>
... some content ...
<hr>
<h6>©1997 <a href="mailto:paulr@hiwaay.net">Paul Robichaux</a>. All
    rights reserved.</h6>
</BODY>
</HTML>
```

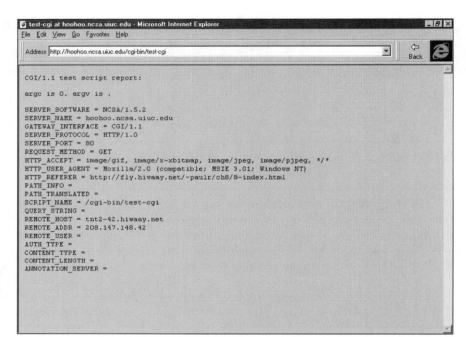

Figure 8.7

The NCSA test script shows you all the variables it can figure out.

You can put any HTML content into an include file, but it shouldn't be a complete file: don't use the <HTML> and <BODY> containers. Other than that, you're free to use images, tables, imagemaps, and any other content you want.

These includes are a great way to put a consistent disclaimer, copyright notice, logo, or navigational item on your pages. Instead of having to manually cut and paste the HTML into every single page on your site, you can just #include it, and all pages will use the same source file. The best part comes when it's time to change what you display—change one file and all pages that #include it will automatically get the changes! This is a huge improvement over manually fixing spelling mistakes or adding new text to every page on a large site.

The #include command can fetch its files in two ways. Which one you use depends on where the files you want to include are stored.

- ✪ `#include virtual="path"` tells the server to use the file specified by `path`. This path can be anywhere on your Web server, so that these are all legal paths that specify different files:

```
#include virtual="/shared/navbar.html"
#include virtual="/navbar.html"
#include virtual="~paul/navbar.html"
```

- ✪ `#include file="file"` also tells the server to use the specified file. The difference is that this file's path must be given relative to the current directory. For example, if your page is in `/usr/pages/joe/`, and you use this `#include` directive

```
#include file="common/footer.html"
```

the server will look in `/usr/pages/joe/common/footer.html` for the file.

In general, `#include virtual` is more versatile and easier to use because you can include any file anywhere on your server (assuming that you have permission to read it!).

Accepting Advertising

Think about the process of opening a new store. First, you have to find a place to have the store, and you have to buy fixtures, cabinets, furniture, and so on. After you've outfitted the store and laid in a stock of whatever it is you're selling, you'd probably advertise. Advertising is one of the finishing touches needed to get a new business off the ground—and it's the same way for Web sites.

Back in the "old days" of the Internet (that would be before around 1995!), commercial advertising on the Internet was strictly forbidden. The National Science Foundation's Acceptable Use Policy, or AUP, forbade "commercial" use of the net. It was generally considered all right to advertise your garage sale or used car, but real advertising was frowned upon.

ON THE

CD

Banner*Show is a cool application that makes it easy for you to add ad banners to your pages by using a small JavaScript program. It's on the CD in `IBM\Webtools\banner`. Of course, you can also use the KzmAdvertise applet discussed in Sunday morning's session; it's in `IBM\Webtools\kzmadver`.

Now that the Internet backbone is carried by commercial entities, advertising has become commonplace. Big media Web sites like those of the *New York Times*, CNN, and the *Wall Street Journal* have carried ads for a long time; but many smaller sites—even those run by individuals—are getting into the act.

CAUTION

Some Internet service providers will charge you much higher rates for a "business" account. One of the common tests to decide who's a business and who's not is whether the site accepts advertising. Make sure that your provider has a clearly stated policy to avoid any unpleasant billing surprises.

First of all, decide whether it makes sense for you to have ads. If your pages are describing your family genealogy and history, ads might not be worth the trouble. If, on the other hand, your pages talk about a commercial product or service, or even a hobby, ads might help defray your expenses and even let you turn a small profit.

How to Drum Up Business

After you've decided that ads are all right on your pages, the next step is to find someone who wants to advertise on your pages. The best advice I can give you is to be creative. Think of your target visitor audience (remember? you defined the ideal visitor way back in Friday evening's session); then think about who would like to advertise their products to that audience. There are some other things to keep in mind, though:

- *Be realistic.* Don't expect people to pay thousands of dollars for ad space on your pages. You probably shouldn't expect to get ad

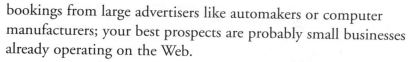

bookings from large advertisers like automakers or computer manufacturers; your best prospects are probably small businesses already operating on the Web.

○ *Be prepared.* Be ready to explain why ads on your pages make sense to the advertiser. Many businesses will ask for evidence of how much traffic your pages have, so be ready to show them access log summaries or other measures of how many visitors your pages get.

○ *Be flexible.* Web advertising isn't yet as structured as print, radio, and TV advertising. You may be offered services or goods instead of outright payment, and you will almost certainly find a few skeptics who want to try running ads for a short while to see whether they generate any increase in their business.

Joining an Advertising Co-Op

As an alternative to beating the bushes for advertising customers, you might consider joining an *advertising co-operative*, or *co-op* for short. These co-ops pay you a small fee (it usually tops around $0.01) for each unique visitor to your site who sees an ad. Although this isn't much, it can add up if you have a lot of traffic on your page, and there's not much you have to do.

The best-known co-op is Riddler's Commonwealth service. Although the details are too complex to explain here, the basic steps go like this:

1. Go to the Commonwealth page at **http://commonwealth.riddler .com/Commonwealth/join/member_signup.html**, where you'll find a ridiculously long license agreement. Read it; if you agree, proceed to the registration form.

2. Fill out the registration form (shown in Figure 8.8) and submit it. Commonwealth will process your application and send you a user-name and password via e-mail.

3. After you get your username and password, you can create a *portfo-lio* of your pages. This portfolio helps Commonwealth tie your

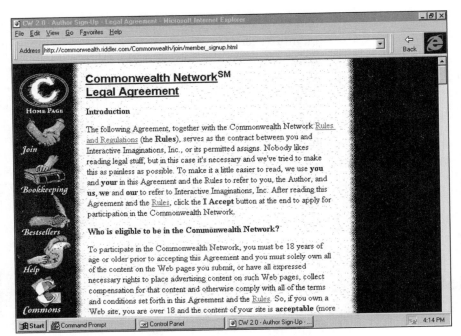

Figure 8.8

The Commonwealth registration form is awfully personal.

pages to a set of advertising statistics—that's how they calculate how much money they owe you.

4. Commonwealth will send you a block of HTML code for inclusion in your pages. This code will automatically fetch an ad from the Commonwealth server and display it; you don't have to keep any images on your site. You must place the HTML they send you at the top of each page you register in your portfolio, but the process after that is automatic.

Selling Stuff for Fun and Profit

Even if you don't want to put ads on your site, you can still make a buck by taking advantage of the newest trend in online retailing: *affiliate programs* that pay you a commission every time a visitor to your site orders a product from a particular vendor.

Sound too good to be true? Let's take a concrete example: computer books. If you join the Amazon Associates program and put a link to Amazon's catalog page for this book, every time someone uses your link to buy this book from Amazon, you get up to a 15% commission!

The Amazon Associates Program

Amazon (**http://www.amazon.com**) claims to be the world's largest bookstore, with more than 2.5 million books listed in their online catalog. Their Associates program pays a sliding commission, based on which books a visitor buys.

The program's fully detailed at **http://www.amazon.com/exec/obidos/ subst/partners/associates/associates. html**, but in a nutshell, here's how it works.

First, you join the program by filling out an application form. After you've been accepted, you put links from your pages to specific books in the catalog. For example, if you have a Web page dedicated to tournament bowling, you might have a "Books About Bowling" page that lists books about pro bowling. Each book on your page could have a link to the corresponding book page at Amazon.

When a visitor takes the link from your page to the book's page at Amazon, Amazon can tell where the visitor came from (your page, in this case), and they'll automatically credit your account if the visitor buys the book. The exact amount of credit depends on how much the book costs, what discount Amazon sells it for, and a number of other factors. In general, the commission ranges from 5% to 15%.

Amazon expects you to give visitors information about the book; they provide ordering and shipping, but their hope is that visitors will decide to buy books based on what your pages have to say about them. Their program is very attractive, especially if your pages describe some activity for which people are willing to buy books. Photography, gardening, and chess are just three possible examples.

TIP

For a terrific example of a profitable Amazon Associate site, check out **http://www.smartbooks.com**, which bills itself as the "source for information on books about the Internet."

The cbooks Express Partners' Program

cbooks (**http://www.cbooks.com**) focuses on technical and computer books; their Partners' Program is slightly different from Amazon's. cbooks pays a flat $10 fee for every *new* customer who goes from your site to theirs and places an order. Because the computer and technical books that cbooks sells tend to be more expensive than many titles in Amazon's catalog, the $10 fee can work out to be a 20% or 25% commission— certainly attractive!

Like the Amazon program, you start as a cbooks Partner by filling out an application form. After you're accepted, they'll send you the URL format you must use in links from your site; this format lets cbooks track arrivals at its site from yours, a necessary part of deciding how much to pay you.

Here's what their frequently asked questions list has to say about the program:

> We've designed our Partners Program to be simple and straightforward. You receive $10 for every new customer you send our way, no matter what book they buy, and no matter where they link to our site. You can point them to particular books that you've written, reviewed, or recommended, to a cbooks subject category showing all the latest books on a particular topic, or even to a cbooks Recommends reading list with frequently updated suggestions from our reviewers.

The TEC$Direct Program

If you'd rather link to a database of movies, software, and music, The Entertainment Connection (**http://econnection.com/TecDirect/ TecDirect.htm**) has a program targeted at you. In addition to popular

books, TEC sells movies on video and laserdisc, music on CD and cassette, and a variety of software.

Like the Amazon and cbooks program, you first have to fill out a short agreement to get access to TEC's database. After that's done, you can put a variety of links from your pages to items TEC sells. When visitors buy something you've referred them to, you get the credit.

TEC has a unique "URL generator" that lets you put in the title of the item you want to link to and select what the visitor sees (including a "buy this now!" icon) when entering and leaving your page. After you've made a choice, the generator spits out the URL you need to add to your page, greatly easing the process.

Exchanging Links with Other Sites

Now that you've invested so much time and creativity in building your site, wouldn't it be a shame if no one came to see it? Registering with search engines is a great way to make your site visible; in addition, there's another thing you can do to help promote your site, and it's cheap and easy to boot!

Besides the high-powered advertising schemes I just detailed, there's a kinder, gentler way to advertise your site: exchanging links with other Web sites. These exchanges can be formal or informal. For example, many Mac-oriented Web sites all exchange links—when you visit one of them, you can jump to any of the others with little effort.

If your pages are of interest to people who are already visiting other Web sites, it's a good idea to e-mail the Webmasters of those other sites and politely ask them to exchange links. Basically, you're saying "I'll put a link to your site on my pages if you'll do the same"—good, old-fashioned horse trading brought to the Internet!

There's also a high-tech, automated way to trade links: the LinkExchange, headquartered at **http://www.linkexchange.com**. Like the advertising ventures you read about earlier, the LinkExchange gives you a special bit of HTML that randomly picks a banner from their site. You paste the HTML block they supply onto each of your pages; here's what it looks like:

```
<a href="http://ad.linkexchange.com/X001019/gotoad.map"
    target="_top">
    <img width=440 height=40 border=1 ismap
        alt="Internet Link Exchange"
        src="http://ad.linkexchange.com/X001019/logoshowad?free">
</a>
```

If you want even more information on how to increase the number of visitors to your site, check out *Increase Your Web Traffic In a Weekend* by William Stanek (Prima Publishing: ISBN 0-7615-1194-6)

Like the commercially oriented ad banners you read about earlier, this HTML displays an image from the LinkExchange server on your page, without any extra work on your part. Unlike the others, the link and its ad are randomly selected from a pool of other LinkExchange participants. An example of what these ads look like is shown in Figure 8.9. Although there are a couple of short forms to fill out, Link Exchanging your site can be fun and will definitely help build awareness of your pages.

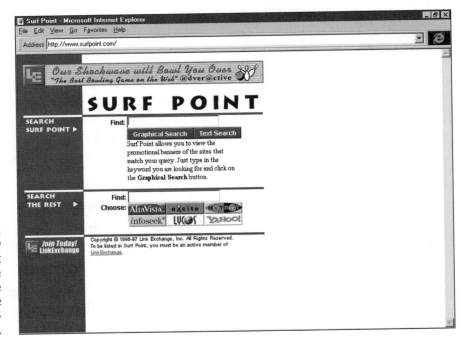

Figure 8.9

Pages that participate in the LinkExchange have banners with the distinctive blue-and-white icon.

Adding Password-Protected Pages

One of the Web's great strengths is that it makes it easy to distribute information to the whole world. Sometimes, though, you might not *want* to distribute your information everywhere. It's often useful, or even necessary, to lock away your pages and only give access to people who know the right password. For example, you might require a username and password before letting visitors look at drafts of your new book, or you might want to create a private area for officers of your garden club.

Now that you've finished building the content of your site, you can safely apply password protection to keep your private content private. Think of it like installing deadbolts in a newly built house—one of the last things that need to be done before the house is ready for occupancy.

NOTE It's not hard to add password protection to your pages if they're on a Unix server, but it helps if you're a little familiar with Unix. If you're not, you can always come back to this section later, or ask your Web server's administrator to help you.

Apache and NCSA HTTPd are the two most common Web servers in use today. These instructions will also work for Netscape's FastTrack and Enterprise servers. If you're using Microsoft's IIS or Personal Web Server, Star*Nine's WebStar, O'Reilly's WebSite, or another server, these instructions won't help you, but they should explain enough to help you tell your server administrator what you want.

Access Control Basics

Most Web servers have some way to restrict access to pages they serve: they can allow or deny connections from particular network addresses, or they can require the visitor to provide a username and password. You can combine the two if your server allows it.

The server administrator can use a file called `access.conf` to control whether individual users can specify access controls for their pages. This

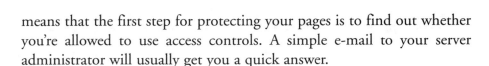

means that the first step for protecting your pages is to find out whether you're allowed to use access controls. A simple e-mail to your server administrator will usually get you a quick answer.

Assuming that the answer is yes, you can control access on a directory-by-directory basis. You do this by putting an access control file named .htaccess (don't forget the period on the front!) in each directory you want to regulate. The .htaccess file controls access to the directory it's in *and* all directories below it. For example, if you put a .htaccess file in /usr/paul/docs/drafts, it will govern access to that directory as well as files in the /usr/paul/docs/drafts/jazz/ and /usr/paul/docs/drafts/untitled/ directories.

The .htaccess file in turn points to a *password file*, which lists the users and groups that the server should use when granting access. Just because a name is in the password file doesn't mean it will be given access, but you can't give access to names that aren't in the password file.

Now that you know how access controls work, let's see how you build them.

Building the .htaccess File

The .htaccess file consists of two parts. The first part tells the server where the list of authorized users lives and how to tell who's authorized; the second describes exactly which types of access are allowed and which aren't.

Here's the first section of the .htaccess file from part of my Web site. Each item has a specific meaning to the server:

```
AuthUserFile /var/Lkr_data_/paulr/public_html/drafts/.htpasswd
AuthGroupFile /dev/null
AuthName Book Drafts
AuthType Basic
```

✿ AuthUserFile tells the server where the user password file is. You have to specify the complete Unix path to the file, or the server won't be able to find it.

○ **AuthGroupFile** tells the server where the group password file is. If you don't have one, use /dev/null (the Unix way of saying "don't use this file"); otherwise, give the full Unix path to the file.

○ **AuthName** specifies the *realm* for which access is being given. Most browsers will display a dialog box like the one shown in Figure 8.10, which shows the realm name. The realm is just a prompt for the human visitor—the software doesn't use it. Some browsers will label the realm as a "resource" or "area," but these terms all mean the same thing.

○ **AuthType** will usually be Basic. There are other types of authentication, but using them is outside the scope of this book.

The next section of the file actually specifies the access control restrictions. You build these restrictions with one or more *limit directives*, each of which contains a <LIMIT> container. Here's a pair of sample limit directives:

```
<Limit PUT>
order deny, allow
deny from all
allow from 206.151.234.*
allow from *.hiwaay.net
</Limit>
<Limit GET POST>
require user paul tim geneil tom brady bo jenny barb
</Limit>
```

Figure 8.10

IE's Authentication dialog box shows you what realm you're trying to get into so that you can figure out which username and password to use.

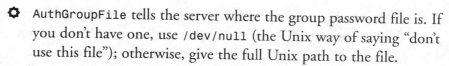

The first important part of <Limit> is the method specifier. You may remember that there are three basic HTTP methods: POST for sending form data, GET for retrieving pages and sending form data, and PUT for sending pages to a server. You can specify any or all of them in your limit directives; the limits in the directive will apply to whatever combination of methods you provide.

The next part of the limit directive is the Order keyword. You use this to tell the server what's important to you. Security restrictions come in two flavors: "deny everything except what I tell you," or "allow everything except what I tell you." The first is more secure, but the second's more flexible. Which one you use is up to you, but you have to provide an Order keyword to tell the server which approach you prefer.

Controlling Access By Network Address

The deny from and allow from keywords give you the tools to permit or deny connections from particular computers. You can specify one or more individual Internet addresses or a range of addresses. The server will interpret the directive shown earlier like this:

1. Obey deny directives first and then allow directives. This is the "everything is forbidden unless I say otherwise" approach; the server will apply any deny restrictions before it even thinks about any of the allow statements.

2. Deny all connections, no matter where they come from.

3. Allow connections from any computer whose network address starts with 206.151.234. The * wildcard tells the server that any value is acceptable. I could also have said allow from *.ljl.com.

4. Allow connections from anywhere in the hiwaay.net domain; this lets me check pages with the Lynx browser my Internet provider supplies.

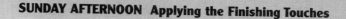
`allow from` and `deny from` will accept individual addresses or ranges of addresses specified with *, and you can use either TCP/IP addresses or DNS names. If you want to only allow visitors from your own Internet provider's network, you could either use their TCP/IP address range or the domain name.

Because you can specify which addresses to deny *and* which ones to allow, you can impose pretty much any type of restrictions you want. However, the order of your directives is important; if you use a limit directive like this:

```
order allow, deny
allow from all
deny from *.aol.com
```

it will promptly allow access to anyone because the `allow from all` directive comes before the `deny` directive.

Most public Web sites don't use address-based restrictions; they're more commonly found on intranets and extranets, where it's easy to specify who may and may not visit. Instead, most public sites use usernames and passwords for access control.

Controlling Access By Username and Password

You can make visitors supply a username and password to get access by using the `require user` keyword, which specifies a list of accounts that can be given access. Think of `require user` like the guest list at a fancy wedding reception: if your name's not on the list, you don't get in.

Remember the `AuthUserFile` statement from the previous section? It tells the server where your password file is. That password file looks something like this:

```
paul:y1ia3tjWkhCK2
tim:3aTqwT0kpTza0
geneil:urx6Ws4wMjP2q
```

. . . in other words, it's gobbledygook that only the server can decode. When the server sees a require user statement, it tells the browser to display the authentication dialog box shown earlier in Figure 8.10. When the user types in her name and password, the server can check them against the contents of the password file. If they match, access is granted.

In the case of my pages, the limit directive looks like this:

```
<Limit GET POST>
require user paul tim geneil tom brady bo jenny barb
</Limit>
```

This means that only people who know the password for one of these user accounts can reach the pages. But how did I get those passwords into the password file? Because the passwords are encoded, I don't have any way to figure out the right string to put in the file.

Fortunately, the HTTPd developers anticipated this problem and provided a program called htpasswd for building password files. htpasswd takes two arguments: the first is the path to the password file, and the second is the name of the user to add. When run, htpasswd will prompt you to enter the password for that new user account; then it will add it to the file. To add a password for a new user named Don to your password file in /home/mystuff/.htpasswd, you'd type

```
htpasswd /home/mystuff/.htpasswd don
```

The first time you use it, you also have to specify the -c flag, which tells htpasswd to create the file you specify, like this:

```
htpasswd -c /home/mystuff/.htpasswd me
```

After you enter the passwords for your users, you can build require user directives that specify any number of users—just separate them by spaces.

Controlling Access By Group

After you get more than a few users, though, you'll wonder why you can't just lump them into groups and control access on a group-by-group basis. The good news is that you can do exactly this! Instead of using `require user`, you use the very similar `require group` keyword, which takes a name of groups instead of individual users.

There are two key differences between group-based access and user-based access. First, you have to use `AuthGroupFile` to point to a group file. `AuthGroupFile` works just like `AuthUserFile`, but the file it points to looks slightly different. That file is the second difference; it contains group names, with each name followed by that group's members. Here's an example:

```
authors:paul brady bo jim vangie sean
editors:jenny vangie bo barb geneil christy tom
reviewers:tim vaughan pratt larry janie
```

The names in each group have to be defined in the file pointed to by `AuthUserFile`; the user and group definition files work together. You build the group file with any text editor. After it's built, you're free to use `require group` directives in your access controls. This directive will let editors and authors see pages, but not members of the `reviewers` group:

```
<Limit get>
require group editors authors
</Limit>
```

FIND IT ON THE WEB NCSA has an access control tutorial at **http://hoohoo.ncsa.uiuc.edu/docs/ tutorials/user.html**. There's also an excellent tutorial at **http://www.apacheweek .com/features/userauth**.

Wrap It Up!

Congratulations! In the preceding sessions, you've applied every conceivable kind of design trick to make your pages better-looking, faster-loading, and generally jazzier. With the material in this session, you can add the last few touches that really distinguish a site. Next, you'll see how some real-life sites were made over during the writing of this book and how the designers applied the principles you've just learned.

Fusing Everything Together

Real-World Web Sites

- ✪ Heavy Industry: LJL Enterprises, Inc.
- ✪ Nonprofit: Huntsville Area Rocketry Association
- ✪ Individual Page: Paul's Home Page

Throughout the book, you've learned how to improve your Web sites in a variety of ways. Now it's time to bring all the things you've learned together. The Web sites in this session are all real, live Web sites that were redesigned using the tips and tricks from this book. You might wonder why anyone would want to redesign a Web site they had already finished. In the case of the sites discussed here, there wasn't anything *wrong* with the existing sites, but all the Webmasters involved realized they could make their sites more effective, more memorable, and easier for visitors to use with a redesign.

Revamping your site also gives you an opportunity to examine the content of your site in accordance with the questions I posed in Friday evening's session. Not only can you redo the way your site looks; at the same time, you can renovate how it works and what it has to say to visitors.

For each of the sites in this session, you'll see a "before" and "after" comparison, and the Webmasters will tell you not only what they did, but why they did it. Cross-references to appropriate sessions in the book help point you in the right direction.

Heavy Industry: LJL Enterprises, Inc.

FIND IT ON ▶ THE WEB

LJL Enterprises is my employer; we make security software for safeguarding e-mail against tampering and eavesdropping. Our Web site is at **http://www.ljl.com**. (I say "we" and "our" because my day job is as a software designer for LJL.)

Background

Most visitors to our site are looking for information on securing their e-mail from intruders and snoops. These visitors are primarily looking for hard information on what our products are, how they work, and how they'll protect the visitor's valuable data. Typical visitors come in, find what they're looking for, and leave again.

A few visitors stumble across our site while searching for general information on privacy, security, or cryptography. Because our pages use all those words, we show up in Web search engine searches using those words, but we don't have any specific pages dedicated to those topics.

The content we wanted on the LJL Web site fell into six different categories. The categories came from what we do: we make and sell software. Most of these categories are applicable to any business:

- A *welcome page* with a message from our president and some brief information about the company's history and future.

- A *news page* with news about the company, our products, and the cryptography field in general; this is where we put product announcements and press releases.

- *Product information*, including screen shots, brochures (in Adobe Acrobat format), specification sheets, and demo versions.

- *General information* about LJL Enterprises (like what trade shows we'll be showing our products at), as well as information and links related to our main business: data security and cryptography.

- *Feedback forms* for users to tell us about problems with the software, ask questions before ordering our products, and make suggestions about our Web site.

- *Contact information* so people know how to reach us with questions, problems, suggestions, or—most important—orders!

Some of these categories overlap a bit; for example, contact information could go in its own category, or it could be lumped in with the company information.

Before . . .

The original LJL pages were grown like a pearl: one bit at a time. The original home page didn't have any links on it. As time passed and our product line grew, we expanded the pages bit by bit, but no one person was responsible for the overall design and appearance of the Web site, and it was updated infrequently.

The Old Home Page

The original home page is shown in Figure 9.1. As you can see, it uses a number of graphic elements—none of which match. In addition, there's no consistent use of styles, font size, text, or color, and the "bread and butter" links that we wanted customers to see were buried down at the bottom of the page.

The original home page also featured something that I warned against in the session on Java and ActiveX: a Java applet that doesn't do anything

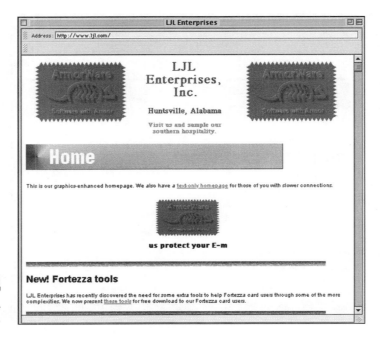

Figure 9.1

The original LJL home page.

useful! In our case, it drew a little animated envelope—cute the first time, but not so cute after an endless series of flying envelopes, which continued as long as you stayed on the home page.

Finally, the old pages (not just the home page) were static—after a visitor came to our pages, there wasn't anything to draw them back for future visits, unless they were just terminally curious.

The Old Products Page

Many customers who come to our site are looking for specific information about our products. The most frequent question our sales staff gets is whether ArmorMail supports a particular mail package, but our product information page (shown in Figure 9.2) didn't clearly show which mailers we supported.

Although this might sound like a problem with content, it's actually a weakness in the design too—the product index page didn't provide

Figure 9.2

The original LJL product information page.

a clear flow to show which products were supported. In addition, the design was dull; it didn't include any graphic elements to attract the visitor's attention once she hit the page.

. . . And After!

The new site contains the same basic content as the old site, but with a new and consistent design. The home page and all the pages linked from it use the same color scheme and background pattern, and pages have a shared design that helps the visitor feel at home with the site by making the pages look familiar.

The New Home Page

The new home page is shown in Figure 9.3 (in the figure, its table borders are turned on, though they're off in the real version). As you can see, this page is divided into three primary areas. The page header is built

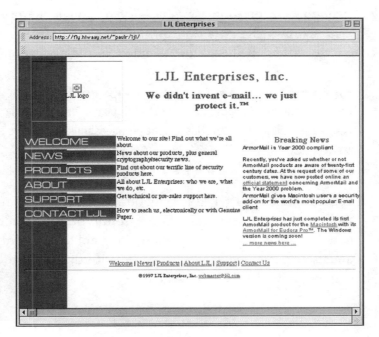

Figure 9.3

The new and improved home page depends on tables.

using a 2×1 table with a fixed width of 435 pixels. The width is fixed so that when the browser window is wider, the "LJL Enterprises" text cell doesn't wrap way past the edge of the rest of the page.

The primary content area for the home page is the big 8×3 table in the middle. This table has a fixed width of 512 pixels because we didn't want the sidelines to float and make the images in the leftmost column move around. Each of the table's rows has a fixed height of 25 pixels. Cell spacing is set to 0, and cell padding is set to only 1.

The first column contains navigation buttons; each button's an image that links to the appropriate page. The ugly blue border that gets added by default to linked images is turned off with BORDER="0". Next to each navigation button, there's a brief text description of where that button takes you. The buttons themselves all have <ALT> tags for browsers that aren't showing images.

The third column contains the "Breaking News" section, which is a 1×3 table nested within the primary table's right column. This table spans all eight rows of the primary table—even though the primary table only *needs* six rows, the extra two rows give the news table space to float without disturbing the height or alignment of the navigation buttons.

TIP

■ ■

The left column's images are all 336×50 pixels, but the table cells are sized to 168×25—half the real size. This lets the browser shrink them down to produce smoothly scaled text.

■ ■

For this redesign, I relied heavily on the material in Saturday morning's session on tables, which are the key to this design. In addition, you may find Saturday afternoon's session on graphics and images helpful to understand how the images are scaled with the WIDTH and HEIGHT attributes and how I chose color schemes.

The Products Page

The products page is the gateway to information on LJL's products. We wanted a page that would sum up the range of mail programs we support, without overwhelming visitors with details. Furthermore, we wanted to build a product index that would guide visitors to detailed information on the products they were interested in. The resulting page is shown (with table borders turned on) in Figure 9.4.

The banner image at the top of the page is the same image as was used in the home page's navigation bar, only this time it's shown at its full size. The background stripe border is the same, too, as is the page footer.

Because we want people to be able to jump to the product they're interested in, a table with a jump menu leads directly to the page for each individual product.

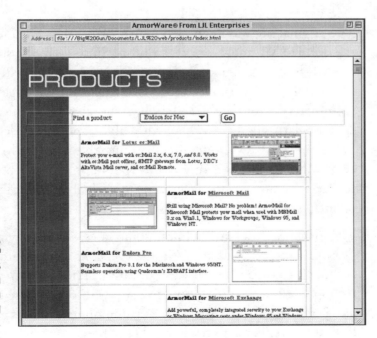

Figure 9.4

The new products page has screen shots arranged in an alternating table.

The real attraction on this page is the product information table. It uses six columns: the outermost left and right columns provide a margin for the page content, and the four columns sandwiched in the middle provide the content itself. Each product has its own row, with blank rows providing equal spacing between products.

The rows alternate from left to right. Even rows have a screen shot in the leftmost column, followed by a three-column span with descriptive text. Odd rows follow the opposite pattern: the descriptive text span comes first, followed by the screen shot. This back-and-forth layout provides a nicely balanced page, and the use of four columns for the central content makes it easy to assign proportional widths.

Like most of the other pages on this site, the product page's tables are fixed-width, as are the table's columns.

Tools and Tricks

The original site was assembled mostly by hand—when it was first done, the best HTML tools were text editors! Since then, the state of the art in HTML tools has thankfully improved. I did the site redesign on a Macintosh using two primary tools: Symantec's Visual Page HTML editor (commercial; around US $90), which has a great graphical interface and is particularly good at working with tables, and Pete Keleher's Alpha (US $25 shareware) text editor for tweaking the final HTML to get it just right. Alpha also has a very useful feature: it can search for and replace text across many files all at once—an invaluable aid for working on large or small sites.

The images were all drawn (or, in some cases, scanned) with Deneba's versatile Canvas 5.0 (Mac and Windows versions are each around US $300). Although Canvas is not as easy to learn as Photoshop, it combines Photoshop-like image editing functionality with object-based drawing tools, and it can import and export most common formats. As a nice bonus, it's less expensive. For converting batches of files at one time, I used Thorsten Lemke's GraphicConverter (US $40 shareware.)

Now on to the tricks I used while designing this site. As you've seen from the earlier figures, these pages make extensive use of tables for page layout, as discussed in Saturday morning's session. Tables provide the "scaffold" needed to provide a structure for each page. After you've built the scaffold, you can proceed with creating the building itself!

The product page shown earlier in Figure 9.4 uses a table whose cells are filled in an alternating pattern. This design is easy to build, since it's just a big table. Each product uses one cell for a screen shot and a span for the product information—the trick is to alternate which one comes first.

Nonprofit: Huntsville Area Rocketry Association

Huntsville, Alabama is nicknamed "The Rocket City" for good reason: it's home to NASA's Marshall Space Flight Center, the lead center for NASA's propulsion and rocketry programs. In addition, the US Army's Missile Command is there, as is the Space and Strategic Defense Command. Huntsville is filled with people who make their living as real rocket scientists, including engineers who have worked on the Mercury, Gemini, Apollo, and Space Shuttle programs for NASA and the Hellfire, Patriot, and TOW missiles for the Army.

FIND IT ON ▶ THE WEB   With all those rockets around, and given Huntsville's 50-year history of rocketry involvement, it's not too surprising that there's a local nonprofit group dedicated to the study, development, testing, and design of rockets: the Huntsville Area Rocketry Association, or HARA. Their site, created by Brian Day (**bday@hiwaay.net**), lives at **http://fly .hiwaay.net/~bday/hara/hara.htm**.

Background

FIND IT ON ▶ THE WEB   HARA was founded in 1979; it's a member chapter of the National Association of Rocketry (NAR; they have a super-cool Web site at **http://www.nar.org**). It has two purposes: to encourage students to pursue science-oriented careers and to promote high-power rocketry to the general population. These two missions mean that HARA's Web site has to be both informative and eye-catching; in addition, HARA and NAR members want to be able to use the Web site as a source to keep up with club happenings and scheduled events (as I write this, HARA has scheduled a rocket launch for less than ten days away!)

Before . . .

The existing site design features some rocket- and space-oriented images and themes, but none of them match, and the page design makes visitors scroll down a good ways to see what else is there.

The Old Home Page

The original home page is shown in Figure 9.5. The most prominent feature is the large (and cool-looking!) HARA logo, and the links on the page are strung out in a single column of italicized text.

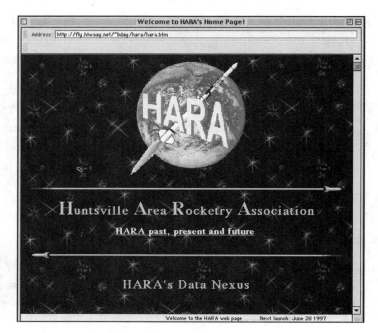

Figure 9.5

The original HARA home page is much taller than it is wide.

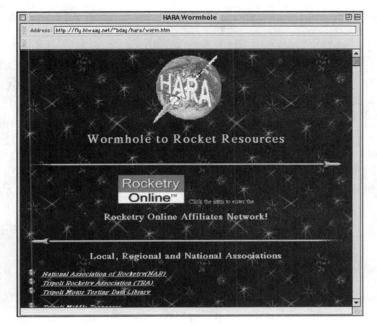

Figure 9.6

The list of rocket-related links is extensive, but its design is a little confusing.

The Old Links Page

The "Gateway To Rocketry" page (shown in Figure 9.6) is a great list of rocketry-related links, and HARA wanted to use it to draw people to its pages. The Frequently Asked Questions (FAQ) are of particular benefit to new visitors, but they're buried in the middle of the other links, and there's no order (alphabetical or otherwise) to the way the links are organized.

. . . And After!

The new HARA site contains exactly the same content as the old one, with different presentation. The new design focuses on clearly organizing the wealth of information on the site, so that visitors can more easily find it. In addition, the graphic design of the site has been simplified to make it easier to sort out what's on the pages.

The New Home Page

Figure 9.7 shows the revamped home page. It uses a large 5×11 table; the logo spans a big 3×9 chunk in the middle, and the list of links from the page has moved to the right-hand column. (It's worth mentioning yet again that, in the real version, table borders are turned off; this page looks funny with them on!) The table width is fixed to prevent resizing problems.

Instead of adding more table cells to create an indented list, Brian decided to use the non-breaking space trick to slightly indent the list of subcategories. By inserting three NBSP characters to create an indent, he was able to show the relationship between the items without using bullets or nesting tables. For example, the "HARA e-mail list" item's HTML looks like this:

```
<TD WIDTH="36%"><B>HARA e-mail list:</B><BR>
       <A
    HREF="http://fly.hiwaay.net/~bday/hara/email.htm">
        mailing list archives</A><BR>
       <A
    HREF="http://fly.hiwaay.net/~bday/hara/email.htm">
        subscription info</A>
</TD>
```

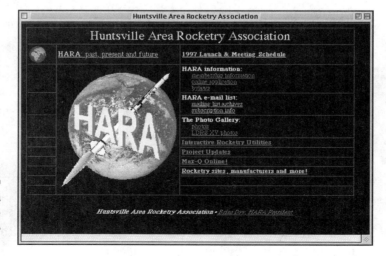

Figure 9.7

The new HARA home page puts the links and HARA logo side-by-side.

As a final touch, Brian chose new text colors to match the solid black background. Red is an attention-getting color that says "look at me"— perfect for unvisited links. Whenever labels are used, they're in bold and colored white, and visited links are gold.

The New Links Page

The new links page, shown in Figure 9.8, combines frames and tables to organize and structure the links so that visitors can find what they're looking for. The page is divided into three frames. The top frame, which doesn't ever change, has a link for the Rocketry Online link exchange. This logo frame isn't resizable. The right-hand frame on the bottom is the target frame for all the links in the left-hand frame; this makes it easy for visitors to skip from link to link without using the Back button in their browser.

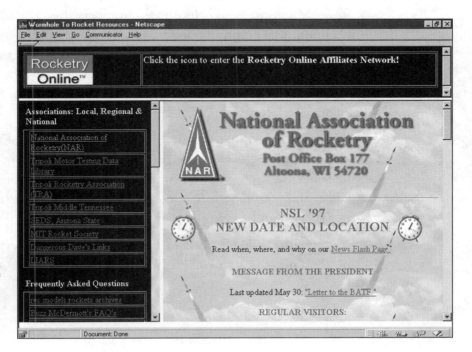

Figure 9.8

The new links page uses frames and tables together to organize the links.

The left-hand frame itself uses a series of tables to hold the links. Each category (FAQs, manufacturers, and so on) has its own two-column table. The category name is used as the table caption. In each table, the left-hand column's width is set to 3% of the table, and it's used as a spacer. The remaining column actually holds the link for that entry; Brian used the TARGET="content-right" attribute to make the links appear in the right-hand frame.

To make the frames look better, Brian did two things. First, he set the frame border color for each frameset to black (the same as the page background). In addition, he set the frame border to zero. Why do both? Not all browsers honor both attributes, so it's best to use both.

Tools and Tricks

Brian's background is as a Unix software developer, so he used the Unix-based *emacs* text editor to create his pages, and they were previewed using Microsoft and Netscape's browsers on Unix and Windows machines. The graphics came from a variety of editing and composition tools; some graphics came from the net, and their exact heritage is unknown. (However, Brian was careful to only use public-domain or shareware images; you should be similarly cautious to avoid infringing anyone else's copyright.)

Like most of the other sites in this session, Brian made heavy use of tables to control his pages' appearance. In addition, the links page takes advantage of frames (which you learned about on Saturday morning) to provide a simple-to-navigate index list that lets visitors keep track of where they've been and where else they can go.

Since the site redesign, Brian reports that visitor feedback has been uniformly positive, and members like the new look too!

Individual Page: Paul's Home Page

FIND IT ON ▶
THE WEB

Paul Stephanouk is a Webmaster from way back—he got his start on the Internet in 1989 and hasn't stopped since. Most recently, he's been working as a Web broadcaster, sort of a combination of a master of ceremonies, Webmaster, and network technician. He ran the Web site for the 1996 Democratic National Convention and the 1997 CountryFest Music Festival. When he's not broadcasting live events to thousands of people around the world, he's often spending time maintaining his own site, Paul Dot Com (**http://www.paul.com**).

Background

Paul Dot Com started as a typical Web home page; it had a few links and a little bit of biographical information about Paul. However, one day Paul had an idea: why not make his site a world-wide gathering place for people named Paul? Paul Dot Com was born! It features a registry of people named Paul, links to other Pauls' sites (including mine), and a wealth of Paul-oriented information.

Before . . .

The original site was built in bits and pieces, as Paul had time away from his other Web sites. Paul wanted to give the new site a fresh look, including a more consistent way for visitors to navigate. He also wanted to add more new content to attract Pauls and non-Pauls alike.

Paul's original home page is shown in Figure 9.9. It's a pretty impressive piece of work all by itself. The large "Paul Dot Com" logo on the left takes up one table section, and the short list of links on the right side takes up the remainder of the table.

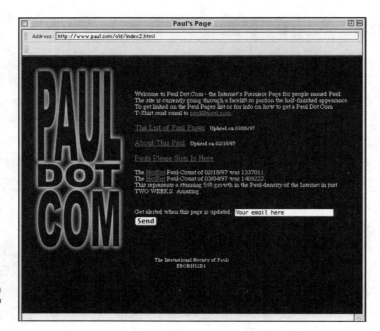

Figure 9.9

Paul's original page.

. . . And After!

Paul's new home page is shown in Figure 9.10. The page is now divided into two frames: the upper, nonresizable frame offers a navigation bar that remains visible no matter what content is in the lower frame, and the lower frame displays content thanks to the TARGET attribute.

The navigation map is worth a mention, too; it's built as a single GIF image, and Paul built a client-side image map (as discussed in Saturday afternoon's session on images) to turn it into a navigational tool.

Tools and Tricks

Paul used a variety of graphic and HTML tools to do his design. Most of the graphics were created in Adobe Photoshop and touched up with

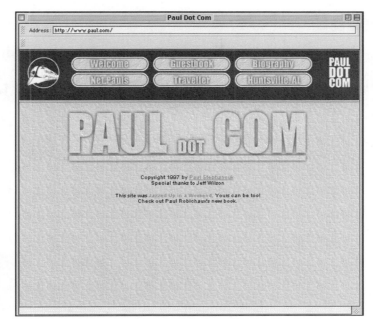

Figure 9.10

Paul's new page
features an
improved layout.

JASC's PaintShop Pro. Because Paul's job involves some travel, the pages
were edited with several tools, ranging in ease of use from the emacs Unix
text editor (not easy to use at all!) to Claris Home Page and the Windows
Notepad.

Like the HARA site, Paul's site takes great advantage of Saturday morning's sessions on tables and frames, as well as Saturday afternoon's session
on graphics.

Paul reports that traffic to his site has remained about the same—most
visitors find his site while searching for the name "Paul"—but that repeat
visitors have increased about 15% since the redesign hit.

Wrap It Up!

We've reached the end of the weekend, and you're ready to graduate—congratulations! The examples in this session should show you not only how other people have applied the lessons in this book, but how *you* can apply them to your own pages.

I hope that you've enjoyed learning how to jazz up your Web pages, and that you'll use your newfound Web superpowers only for Good.

What's on the CD?

The CD that accompanies this book contains example projects from the book, as well as a number of tools and utilities to assist you in "jazzing up" your current Web site and in creating exciting new content.

Running the CD

To make the CD more user friendly and take up less of your disk space no installation is required. This means that the only files transferred to your hard disk are the ones you choose to copy or install.

CAUTION

◆◆

This CD has been designed to run under Windows 95 and Windows NT. Please be advised that, although it will run under Windows 3.1, you may encounter unexpected problems.

◆◆

Windows 3.1

To run the CD:

1. Insert the CD in the CD-ROM drive.
2. From File Manager select File, Run to open the Run window.
3. In the Command Line text box type **D:\primacd.exe** (where D:\ is the CD-ROM drive).
4. Choose OK.

Windows 95

Because there is no installation routine, running the CD in Windows 95 is a breeze, especially if you have autorun enabled. Simply insert the CD in the CD-ROM drive, close the tray, and wait for the CD to load.

If you have disabled autorun, place the CD in the drive and follow these steps:

1. From the Start menu, select Run.
2. Type **D:\primacd.exe** (where D:\ is the CD-ROM drive).
3. Choose OK.

Macintosh

Although there is no user interface for the Macintosh, the CD is Macintosh compatible. You can find Mac compatible software in the directory labeled Macintosh.

The Prima User Interface

Prima's user interface is designed to make viewing and using the CD contents quick and easy. It contains four category/title buttons and four option buttons. Select a category/title button to display the available selection(s). Choose a title to see a description and the associated URL. After you've selected a title, click an option button to perform the desired action on that title.

Category/Title Buttons

The four category/title buttons are as follows:

- *Book Examples.* Example files and source code from *Jazz Up Your Web Site In a Weekend.*
- *HTML Tools.* An assortment of HTML editors and tools.
- *Multimedia.* Clip art, sound files, multimedia tools, and more.
- *Webtools.* Custom controls, Java applets, and animation tools to name a few.

Option Buttons

The Option buttons are as follows:

- *Explore.* Left-clicking this option in Windows 95 and NT allows you to view the folder containing the program files, using Windows Explorer. Right-clicking in Windows 3.x, 95, or NT brings up the Windows File Manager from which you can easily explore the CD.

- *Install.* If the selected title contains an install routine, selecting this option begins the installation process. If no installation is available, an appropriate message is displayed.

- *Information.* Click to open the Readme file associated with the highlighted title. If no Readme file is present, the help file will be opened.

- *Exit.* When you're finished and ready to move on, select exit.

- *Prev.* Takes you to the previous screen. Please note: this is not the last screen you viewed, but the screen that actually precedes the current one.

- *Next.* Takes you to the next screen.

The Software

This section gives you a brief description of some of the software you'll find on the CD. This is just a sampling. As you browse the CD, you will find much more.

- *1-4-All HTML Editor.* A 32-bit, tag based, shareware HTML editor for Windows 95 and NT4.

- *AusComp Graphics.* A selection of background images from Aus-Comp.

- *Animagic GIF.* A powerful animation tool that outputs GIF files that are 10 to 80 percent smaller than non-optimized GIFs.

- *Banner*Show.* Banner*Show lets you create slide show-like presentation of images and text on the World Wide Web page.
- *CoffeeCup HTML Editor.* This HTML editor comes with 100 animated GIFs, 20 JavaScripts, and 10 VBScripts.
- *DameWare Custom Controls.* An assortment of ten different ActiveX/OCX custom controls.
- *GoldWave.* A sound editor, player, recorder, and converter for Windows 95 and NT.
- *HTML Power Tools.* A collection of powerful HTML utilities, including a spell checker, syntax analyzer, rulebase editor, and more.
- *itsagif.* A handy utility for converting Macintosh PICT files and Windows BMP files to GIFs.
- *MapEdit.* A powerful, graphical editor for World Wide Web image maps.
- *RiadaCartel.* With RiadaCartel, you can insert moving LED signs into your Web pages to provide advertising, information, instructions, or even user interaction.
- *WebImage.* An image manipulation program used to enhance, optimize, and create graphics for the World Wide Web.
- *WinZip.* One of the most popular file compression utilities around.

APPENDIX B

Where to Get More Information

Even as good a book as this one can only start to scratch the surface of what you can do to improve your Web pages. This appendix is a list of resources for when you want to learn more; it includes pointers to sites that discuss Web browsers, HTML editors and converters, graphics editors and converters, Web art collections, and many different types of software tools.

This appendix is broken down into four sections:

○ *Enhancing Your Web Page: Graphics Tips and Tricks.* This section includes pointers to general graphics resources, as well as information on using interlaced/transparent GIFs, image sizing/scaling, bandwidth conservation, backgrounds, and Web art.

○ *Putting It Up on the Web: Placing, Maintaining, and Promoting Your Web Page.* When you have a final page ready to go, you're going to want to put it up on the Web. This section contains some pointers to resources that can help you place, maintain, and promote your Web page.

○ *Web Publishing Resource Materials.* This section gives you pointers to just about everything and anything you want to know about HTML and Web publishing, including HTML guides, tutorials, references, style guides, and more.

○ *Web Publishing Tool Chest: Programs and Utilities.* This section provides pointers to a slew of programs and utilities that can assist you in your Web publishing endeavors, including browsers, HTML editors, converters, templates, word processor add-ons, graphics editors and utilities, and more.

Some sections are further broken down into other categories. You'll notice that Mac and Windows programs are intermixed, too, instead of being separated.

There are a couple of things this appendix doesn't include. Programs included on the CD aren't listed here—you'll have to explore Appendix A, "What's On The CD?," to find out what's included. In addition, Web sites referenced in each session aren't duplicated here.

● ●

As you may have already learned, Web sites have a tendency to move, and disappear, with alarming frequency. As of spring 1997, all these sites were on the air and accessible; don't be alarmed (or surprised!) if they're unavailable when you go there. Where possible, I've included the site author's name too, so you can search for the topic *and* author name to find a page's new home.

● ●

Enhancing Your Web Page: Graphics Tips and Tricks

While learning basic HTML and planning and creating your first Web pages, you probably didn't have much time to get into the graphics end of it. The idea was to learn how to create your Web page first, and then learn how to graphically improve and enhance your Web page later. The following list of resources covers just about anything and everything you might graphically want to do with a Web page.

General Graphics Resources

If you're not already a graphics pro, Web graphics can be a little intimidating. These sites will help you spruce up, slim down, and pump up your site graphics with easy-to-use tips, tricks, and tools.

Creating High-Impact Documents by Netscape

http://home.netscape.com/assist/net_site
    s/impact_docs/index.html

Netscape's page on interlaced GIF images, JPEG images, image sizing, percentage autoscaling, and the percentage low/high resolution flip trick.

Jonathan E. Adair's Neat Tricks Page

http://keywest.csee.usf.edu:1111/adair/
    neat-tricks.html

An excellent rundown on interlaced GIF images, transparent GIF images, sizing your images, imagemaps, and browser dependence.

Inline Images Frequently Asked Questions by Brian Patrick Lee

http://galway.informatik.uni-kl.de/./
    comp/Mosaic/inline-images.html

An excellent overall treatment of inline image issues.

Graphics FAQ by the Aldridge Company

http://www.aldridge.com/faq_gra.html

Another FAQ that offers good information on GIFs, interlacing, miscellaneous graphic formats, and JPEGs.

DiP: A Guide to Digital Pictures & More

http://www.algonet.se/~dip/minimal1.htm

Links, tips, and tricks for Painter, PhotoShop, Kai's Power Tools and other graphics programs, plug-ins, and utilities.

Tom's Tips for Web Designers by Tom Karlo

http://the-tech.mit.edu/KPT/Toms/
    index.html

Tips on using Adobe Photoshop to create Web art.

Creating Interlaced and Transparent GIFs

An interlaced GIF is loaded in more than one pass, giving a "venetian blind" effect when viewed using a Web browser capable of viewing interlacing. A transparent GIF has a transparent background (not a background that is simply the same color of your browser's background). The following resources on the Web can guide you in creating interlaced and transparent GIFs for your Web pages.

The Transparent/Interlaced GIF Resource Page

http://dragon.jpl.nasa.gov/~adam/
    transparent.html
http://www.put.poznan.pl/hypertext/
    Internet/faq/t-gif/transparent.html

An excellent "clearing house" page for all manner of information on transparent and interlaced GIF graphics. Should be the first stop for anyone seeking information and guidance in these areas.

Creating Transparent Background Images by Kerry Keogan

http://www.magi.com/~kk/tbi2.html

An excellent step-by-step tutorial for using LView Pro 1.B to create transparent background images. Actually, you can use LView Pro to make any GIF image transparent, not just background images. For Windows users, LView Pro is the preferred tool for creating transparent images.

Transparent and Interlaced GIFs: How to Do It—Where to Get the Tools You Need by Bruce Morris

http://www.awa.com/nct/software/
    transgif.html

An article from NCT Web Magazine. Offers side-by-side interlaced and non-interlaced GIFs to demonstrate how they differ when loading.

Tutorials: Transparent GIFs by QuaLitty Design

http://www.qualitty.com/trans.html

Another step-by-step tutorial on using LView Pro to create transparent GIFs.

Moss' Transparent GIF Tutorial: Creating Transparent Gifs with LView Pro

http://lahs.losalamos.k12.nm.us/
    ~templetm/transtut.html

Yet another tutorial on using LView Pro to create transparent GIFs; but this one makes abundant use of screen shots and illustrations to illustrate the steps.

Transparent Background Images by the HTML Guru (Chuck Musciano)

http://members.aol.com/htmlguru/
    transparent_images.html

Treats creating transparent background images largely from a Unix perspective, but still applies to the Windows or DOS platforms.

The JPiG Project by Thomas Lindstrom and Ed Scott

http://www.algonet.se/~dip/jpig_1.htm

An interesting page on the quest for the nonexistent graphics format, the transparent JPEG format.

It discusses the possibilities of developing the JPiG graphics format, which would be a 24-bit JPEG format with soft-edge transparency (as opposed to hard-edge transparency, as is the case with transparent GIFs). The proposal is that this be implemented as a pair of plug-ins, one for Adobe Photoshop for creating the actual image, and the other for Netscape Navigator for viewing the image as an inline image on a Web page.

NOTE

See Creating High-Impact Documents in the "General Graphics Resources" section earlier in this appendix for additional information on creating interlaced and transparent GIFs.

Image Sizing and Scaling

Why worry about scaling and sizing images yourself when you can find tools and information to help you do it automatically?

Percentage Auto-Scaling by Netscape

http://home.netscape.com/assist/net_sites
    /impact_docs/auto-scaling.html

See Creating High-Impact Documents and Jonathan E. Adair's Neat Tricks Page in the "General Graphics Resources" section earlier in this appendix for information on image sizing and auto scaling.

See Creating High-Impact Documents in the "General Graphics Resources" section earlier in this appendix for information on how to do the "low/high resolution flip trick," an image sizing and scaling method that combines low- and high-resolution versions of the same banner graphic to create a "fade-in" effect, allowing a viewer to get a much quicker look at what a graphic contains, but with a slightly longer overall loading time.

Color Depth Optimization and Bandwidth Conservation

You can reduce the number of colors used to display a graphic to reduce the bandwidth, or size, of the graphic, which can significantly speed up loading of the graphic, often without significant loss of image quality.

The Bandwidth Conservation Society

http://www.infohiway.com/faster/
   index.html

Learn how to make your images load faster. Excellent information and tutorials on how to reduce the bit-depth (the number of colors in the palette) of GIF and JPEG graphics to reduce file size. Also offers information on creating background images that conserve bandwidth.

Backgrounds

Netscape introduced the capability to display background colors and images, but most other major graphical Web browsers have followed suit. The following resources can assist you in creating background colors and images for your Web pages.

Tutorials: Web Page Backgrounds by QuaLitty Design

http://www.qualitty.com/bgrnd.html

A rundown on background images, as well as assigning colors to backgrounds, text, and links.

The Background FAQ by Mark Koenen

http://www.sci.kun.nl/thalia/guide/
   color/faq.html

Everything, and I do mean everything, you might want to know about backgrounds.

Controlling Document Backgrounds by Netscape

http://home.netscape.com/assist/
   net_sites/bg/

Netscape's page on document backgrounds.

So You Want a Background, Huh? by Joe Burns

http://www.cs.bgsu.edu/~jburns/
   backgrnd.html

A good page on using background images and colors.

Making Seamless Backgrounds from Any Graphic by Thomas Karlo and Josh Hartmann

http://the-tech.mit.edu/KPT/Makeback/
   makeback.html

Advice on how to create "seamless" background graphics.

Web Art

Tons of Web art and other clip art is available for you to download and use in your Web pages. This section lists some pointers on where to find it.

GNNpress Clip Art

http://www.gnnhost.com/publish/clip-
   art/gnnclip.htm

A set of icons, bullets, rules, backgrounds, arrows, and other Web art that you can download and use in your Web pages.

Icons and Graphics by Julie A. Duncan

```
http://www.cameron.edu/~julie/creation/
    graphics.html
```

Bullets, balls, bars, buttons, and backgrounds.

Horizontal Rules/Bars by Craig Clark

```
http://www.psy.uwa.edu.au/iconshr.htm
```

Horizontal rules and bars adjusted to use a subset of the standard Windows 8-bit system palette.

Planet Earth Home Page: Images Section

```
http://www.nosc.mil/planet_earth/
    images.html
```

Tons of image links.

The Background Generator by Daniel Prust

```
http://east.isx.com/~dprust/Bax/
    index.html
```

A neat online utility that generates a background image that you create yourself. Requires a Java-capable browser, such as Netscape Navigator Gold for Windows 95.

Clip Art Brought to You by Deep Visions (formerly known as Sandra's Clip Art Server)

```
http://www.n-vision.com/panda/c/
```

An index to many, many clip art links. Includes links to many large clip art libraries and collections.

Barry's Clip Art Server

```
http://ns2.clever.net/~graphics/clip_art/
    clipart.html
```

Another omnibus clip art site.

Funet Collection (brought to you by Barry's Clip Art Server)

```
http://ns2.clever.net/~graphics/
    clip_art/funet.html
```

The whole Funet collection of clip and Web art from Finland. One of the biggest collections of clip art anywhere.

Rose's Backgrounds

```
http://www.wanderers.com/rose/
    backgrou.html
```

An A-to-Z index of links to background collections and libraries all over the Web.

The Virtual Image Archive by Brian Casey

```
http://imagiware.com/via.cgi
```

Lots of image links.

Gifs (alphabetically)

```
http://www.acm.uiuc.edu:80/rml/Gifs/
```

A good collection of GIFs.

Swedish University Network (SUNET) FTP Archive

```
ftp://ftp.sunet.se/pub/pictures/
```

A big FTP archive of clip art broken down into category directories.

The Image Server by Alan Messer

```
http://web.cs.city.ac.uk/archive/image/
    image.html
```

A collection of photos in various categories. No statement made about copyright, however; so if you want to use you might want to query first. Good photos, though.

Backgrounds and Textures

http://www.ncsa.uiuc.edu/SDG/Software/
   WinMosaic/Backgrnd/

An anonymous collection of some very nice background images.

The Clip Art Connection: Your Clip Art Treasure Chest by Eric Force

http://www.acy.digex.net/~infomart/
   clipart/

Loads and loads of image links.

Textures for HTML 3.0 Clients

http://www.baylor.edu/textures/

A collection of background textures.

MacDaddy's Background Sampler and Tutorial

http://flamestrike.hacks.arizona.edu/
   ~macdaddy/backgrounds.html

A tutorial on background colors and images, and a collection of more than 100 background images.

Dr. Zeus' Textures

http://www.best.com/~drzeus/Art/
   Textures/Textures.html

A small collection of somewhat surreal background textures.

Paul's More Backgrounds

http://www.niagara.com/~pmarquis/
   backgr.html

A collection of 161 backgrounds, including stone, wood, paper, marble, and more.

Paul's Ruled Lines and Bars

http://www.niagara.com/~pmarquis/
   free.html

A large collection of graphic rules and bars.

Paul's Directional Devices, Menu Bars, and Misc. Icons

http://www.niagara.com/~pmarquis/
   free2.html

Some more of Paul's stuff.

Laurie McCanna's Free Art Web Site

http://www.mccannas.com/

Tips, tricks, and Web art.

Ender Design: Realm Graphics

http://www.ender-design.com/rg/

Big collection of backgrounds, bullets, buttons, icons, and lines.

Public Domain Icons

http://www.eit.com/web/gopher.icons/
   gopher.html

Originally made for Mosaic for X, the first version of Mosaic.

The Backgrounds Archive by Tom Karlo and KPT Online

http://the-tech.mit.edu/KPT/bgs.html

An archive of seamless background images.

Putting It Up on the Web: Placing, Maintaining, Promoting, and Validating Your Web Page

After you create and graphically enhance your Web page, you're going to want to put it up on the Web. This involves finding a Web server to host your pages; then maintaining and promoting your Web pages after you put them up on the Web. Validating your Web page has two aspects: validating your HTML and validating your hypertext links (which have a habit of "going out" like lights on a Christmas tree). An additional but important concern, in the general area of putting materials up on the Web is copyright, ensuring that you both protect your own copyright while not infringing on the copyright of others.

Placing Your Web Page on a Server

After you create your Web page to your satisfaction, the first thing you need to do is find a server to host it. Here are some places to start looking.

Geocities.Com

`http://www.geocities.com/`

Totally free Web pages! Geocities is organized around a city metaphor: pick the city where you want your pages to "live" and off you go!

TowneSquare 2000

`http://townesquare.usr.com/`

USRobotics is best known for its modems, but it also offers free Web page hosting for its customers as part of its "TowneSquare 2000" project.

The Budget Web Host List

`http://www.callihan.com/budget/`

Steve Callihan's list of budget Web hosts, which is the online version of a list of affordable presence providers originally published in his article, "Web Site on a Budget," in the April 96 issue of *Internet World*.

The Budget Web Index by Alex Chapman

`http://budgetweb.com/budgetweb/`
`    index3.shtml`

Alex Chapman maintains this list, which surprisingly has minimal duplication of entries in Callihan's list.

The Free Pages Page by Peter da Silva

`http://starbase.neosoft.com/~peter/`
`    freepages.html`

Excellent review of several free providers, including information on what HTML editing tools the providers support and whether optional services are available for paying customers.

Web Presence Providers by Yahoo!

`http://www.yahoo.com/Business_and_Econo-`
`    my/Companies/Internet_Services/`
`    Web_Presence_Providers/`

The grandaddy of all presence provider lists—actually, several lists under this one heading.

Promoting Your Web Page

Just putting your page up on the Web isn't enough. You want people to notice it. A couple of the following services will register your Web page with all the major search engines and indexes. This list also includes some pointers to information on search engines and how to get your page to the top of the list, as well as on a link exchange service.

Submit It!

`http://www.submit-it.com/`

Allows you to submit your Web page to 15 different search engines and indexes by filling out just one form. Submit your Web page to Yahoo, Open Text, Infoseek, Webcrawler, Lycos, AltaVista, and others.

SubmitAll by the HOME TEAM

`http://www.hometeam.com/tools/`
   `submital.htm`

A service very similar to Submit It!

META Tagging for Search Engines by Alan and Lucy Richmond

`http://www.stars.com/Search/Meta.html`

Covers how to use the <META> tag to snag search engines. Invaluable information on how to get your page to the head of the list.

How Search Engines (Say They) Work by Danny Sullivan

`http://www.maxonline.com/webmasters/`
   `work.htm`

A good rundown on what the different search engines say about their own indexing criteria.

The Internet Link Exchange

`http://www.linkexchange.com/`

A free service in which you agree to display a revolving banner ad, and, in return, your banner ad is displayed on other participating Web pages. The number of times your banner ad is displayed is directly proportional to the number of banner ads

you display on your own Web page—the higher your number of hits, the more exposure you get.

Validating Your Web Page

Validating your Web page means two things: checking that your HTML is legal, and thus likely to display correctly on the browsers for which it is intended (for example, HTML 2.0 browsers, HTML 3.2 browsers, and so on), and checking that your links are alive and well.

HTML Validation Tools

`http://www.khoral.com/staff/neilb/`
   `weblint/validation.html`

Lists many links to validation services available on the Web.

Doctor HTML by Thomas Tongue and Imagiware

`http://www2.imagiware.com/RxHTML/`

Online service that will retrieve your Web page and run several tests on it, including for spelling errors, image bandwidth and syntax, document, table, and form structure, dead links, and command hierarchy. Site Doctor, a commercial service that allows you to validate a whole Web site is also available.

Web Law and Copyrights

Web Law FAQ by Oppedahl and Larson

`http://www.patents.com/weblaw.sht`

Excellent FAQ on legal issues related to use of information and materials on the Web. Discusses many gray areas.

10 Big Myths About Copyright Explained by Brad Templeton

http://www.clari.net/brad/copymyths.html

A good discussion of copyright issues on the Web.

The Mystery Behind the (c) by Christopher B. Skvarka

http://www.pitt.edu/%7Eskvarka/
  education/copyright/

Another good discussion of copyright issues on the Web.

Web Publishing Resource Materials

The following sections provide pointers to various kinds of Web publishing resource materials and other information available on the Web, including HTML reference materials (guides, tutorials, and references), style guides, general Web publishing information, templates, example Web pages, and the Microsoft-Netscape war.

HTML Guides, Tutorials, and References

This section lists guides, tutorials, and references, ranging from the simple to the more comprehensive, to help you more fully explore using HTML.

Demonstration of Basic and Advanced HTML Tags by Kristina Ross

http://www2.utep.edu/~kross/tutorial/

More of a demonstration of HTML than a how-to or tutorial. It provides, however, a good resource of example HTML from the simple to the advanced. Advanced areas covered include imagemaps, tables, and forms.

The Bare Bones Guide to HTML by Kevin Werbach

http://werbach.com/barebones/
  barebone_table.html

A good rundown in table form of HTML currently in use. As the title indicates, it's a "bare bones" guide. Not so much a how-to as a handy quick reference.

Hands-On HTML by @LearnSkills.com

http://www.learnskills.com/hohtml/
  hin_01.htm

Outline and materials for a course on HTML that you can actually sign up for and take. You don't have to sign up to use the materials though.

Hypertext Markup Language - 2.0 (Sept 22, 1995) by T. Berners-Lee and D. Connolly

http://www.w3.org/hypertext/WWW/MarkUp/
  html-spec/html-spec_toc.html

A comprehensive rundown of HTML 2.0 from the W3 Consortium. One of the coauthors is the godfather of HTML, himself, Tim Berners-Lee, often referred to as "the inventor of the Web"—the horse's mouth, in other words.

Crash Course on Writing Documents for the Web by Eamonn Sullivan

http://www.pcweek.com/eamonn/
  crash_course.html

Originally written as a quick and dirty guide for people in the PC Week Labs for creating Web pages on their server.

HTML Overview by Russ Jones

```
http://www.ora.com/gnn/bus/ora/features/
    html/index.html
```

As the title indicates, an overview, not an in-depth review, of HTML.

A Beginner's Guide to HTML by NCSA

```
http://www.ncsa.uiuc.edu/General/
    Internet/WWW/HTMLPrimer.html
```

NCSA is the home of Mosaic, the first widely distributed Windows & Mac Web browser—if it's not exactly the horse's mouth, it's at least one of its teeth. This is an excellent guide to HTML 2.0 with a couple extra HTML 3.0 tags thrown in.

HTML Quick Reference by Michael Grobe

```
http://kuhttp.cc.ukans.edu/lynx_help/
    HTML_quick.html
```

A fairly comprehensive but concise rundown on using HTML.

HyperText Markup Language Quick Reference by H. Churchyard

```
http://uts.cc.utexas.edu/~churchh/
    htmlqref.html
```

Another quick reference. Apart from the basic stuff, also includes information on reducing color depth and forms.

HTML, the Complete-ish Guide by Sunil Gupta

```
http://www.cis.ksu.edu/~jfy/
    html.reference.html
```

A fairly comprehensive, if brief, guide to HTML. Written as a guide for creating documents for X-Mosaic, but should apply across the board to other platforms.

Introduction to HTML by Peter Flynn

```
http://www.ucc.ie/~pflynn/books/
    ch7-8.html
```

An excerpt from the book, *The World Wide Web Handbook*, by Peter Flynn. Contains a good rundown on the ins and outs of HTML specifications, DTDs, and so on, as well as an introduction to HTML markup.

Introduction to HTML by Eric A. Meyer and Case Western Reserve University

```
http://www.cwru.edu/help/introHTML/
    toc.html
```

The most novel aspect of this site are the interactive quizzes that follow after each chapter—you get to select answers to multiple choice questions and then submit your answers for immediate feedback.

Intermediate HTML by Eric A. Meyer and Case Western Reserve University

```
http://www.cwru.edu/help/interHTML/
    toc.html
```

A continuation of Eric A. Meyer's Introduction to HTML, covering intermediate to more advanced HTML. Primary focus is on creating forms.

HTML Reference Manual by Sandia National Laboratories

```
http://www.sandia.gov/sci_compute/
    html_ref.html
```

A comprehensive online reference to HTML, past, present, and future. Note that the real goodies here, the descriptions of the HTML elements, are buried in the inconspicuous link, list of elements.

A Guide to HTML Commands by Richard Rutter

http://www.woodhill.co.uk/html/html.htm

A fairly complete A-to-Z HTML reference, covering almost all HTML tags.

Introduction to HTML by Ian Graham

http://www.utoronto.ca/webdocs/HTMLdocs/
    NewHTML/htmlindex.html

Excellent A-to-Z reference, from the author of the book, *The HTML Sourcebook*.

HTML EXAMPLE (Level 2.0) by Christian Sandvig

http://www.dcn.davis.ca.us/~csandvig/
    ip/example.htmluses

Uses a side-by-side approach, using tables, to show HTML code on the left and the results as they will appear in a browser on the right.

Compendium of HTML Syntax

http://www.winternet.com/%7Erlkelog/
    WIP/CompendHTML.html

The HyperText Markup Language: Netscape Version 2.02

http://www.best.com/%7Emcguirk/gavito/
    html-spec.html

A rundown on HTML up to Netscape 2.02.

HTML Reference by Microsoft

http://www.microsoft.com/workshop/author/
    newhtml/htmlr018.htm

Microsoft's rundown on the current state of HTML, including use of its own extensions. (Microsoft seems to want to keep moving this page around, or changing its name, without leaving any

forwarding address. Hopefully, this one will stay put. If it doesn't, then try its home page:

http://www.microsoft.com/workshop/author/
    newhtml/

W3Writer: A Basic HTML Tutorial by Gordon Hake

http://hake.com/gordon/w3-index.html

Basic tutorial on creating HTML documents.

HTML Style Guides

An HTML reference can tell you what HTML is and what it's supposed to do, but can't necessarily tell you how to use it to the best effect. To find out, listen to the sage advice of those who have been there before you.

What Is Good Hypertext Writing? by Jutta Degener

http://www.cs.tu-berlin.de/~jutta/ht/
    writing.html

An excellent common-sense style guide for writing good hypertext text.

How to Make Great WWW Pages! by Carlos L. McEvilly

http://www.c3.lanl.gov/~cim/webgreat/
    first.html

Contains an excellent collection of tips and just plain practical advice on how to make your page successful on the Web.

Composing Good HTML by Eric Tilton

http://www.cs.cmu.edu/~tilt/cgh/

An excellent style guide written by the one of the authors of *Web Weaving*, a book on HTML. Full of good practical advice.

The Ten Commandments of HTML by Sean Howard of Visionary Designs

http://www.visdesigns.com/design/
   commandments.html

Good common-sense pointers on using HTML.

Setting Up a Web Site by Anonymous

http://freethought.tamu.edu/~meta/
   setup-guide.html

A highly ironic, and funny, guide to doing all the right—I mean wrong—things in setting up your Web site.

The Hall of Shame by FLUX

http://www.meat.com/netscape_hos.html

Not really a style guide, but rather a gallery of bad style, and I mean really, really bad style. Worth checking out to see how not to do it.

Hints for Web Authors by Warren Steel

http://www.mcsr.olemiss.edu/~mudws/
   webhints.html

Good style guide that treats the subjects of Web authorship, portability, and Netscape 2.0.

Guide to Web Style by Sun Microsystems

http://www.sun.com/styleguide/

A style guide from one of the major players in the Web game.

Advice for HTML Authors by the HTML Writers Guild

http://ugweb.cs.ualberta.ca/~gerald/guil
   d/style.html

The result of a discussion on an HTML Writers Guild mailing list.

Style Guide for Online Hypertext by Tim Berners-Lee

http://www.w3.org/pub/WWW/Provider/Style
   /Overview.html

Wise words from the inventor of the Web.

HTML Bad Style Page by Tony Sanders

http://www.earth.com/bad-style/

Some HTML don'ts. A bit on the "purist" side, but has some good advice.

Web Style Manual by Patrick J. Lynch

http://info.med.yale.edu/caim/StyleManu-
   al_Top.HTML

The style guide used internally by the Yale Center for Advanced Instructional Media.

General Web Publishing Information

The HTML Writers Guild List of HTML Resources

http://www.hwg.org/resources/html/

A page to many more HTML links.

The Web Developer's Virtual Library

http://WWW.Stars.com/

Offers links to everything.

Bob Allison's Web Master's Home Page

http://gagme.wwa.com/%7Eboba/
   masters1.html

A compendium of resources and information on creating a Web presence.

Word Wide Web FAQ by Thomas Boutell

http://www.boutell.com/faq/

A compendium of all manner of information on the WWW, including Web publishing and authoring information.

WWW FAQ: What Newsgroups Discuss the Web? by Thomas Boutell

http://www.boutell.com/faq/ngroups.htm

Listing and discussion of Web publishing and authoring related newsgroups.

Search the AWEBS News archives

http://www.awebs.com/news_archive/

Allows you to do a search of archives of Web publishing and authoring oriented newsgroups. At time of writing, search included only current month, but plans are to include previous months, too.

Microsoft Internet Explorer Author's Guide and HTML Reference (Microsoft Site Builder Workshop)

http://www.microsoft.com/workshop/
  author/newhtml/

Microsoft's omnibus Web authoring site.

D.J. Quad's Ultimate HTML Site

http://www.quadzilla.com/

D.J. Quad's comprehensive Web site on all things HTML.

Web Page Templates

Web page templates can be handy as out-of-the-box solutions or as starting points for further elaboration. You can plug your own text into them or use them as guides for tagging your text.

Netscape Web Page Templates by Netscape

http://home.netscape.com/assist/net_sites
  /starter/samples/templates/index.html

Part of the Netscape Gold Rush Tool Chest. An excellent collection of templates covering a wide range of different kinds of Web pages.

Templates for Homepages by Christian Mogensen

http://www-pcd.stanford.edu/mogens/
  intro/templates.html

A selection of Web page templates, including plain, generic, and free-form pages, as well as resume and project description pages. These are pretty basic, at best starting points, not finished designs.

HTML Templates for Courses from the University of Maryland at College Park

http://www.inform.umd.edu:8080/EdRes/Fac-
  ulty_Resources_and_Support/template/

Includes templates for course descriptions and supplementary readings.

HTML 2.0 Templates by Jim Hurley

http://www.webcom.com/~hurleyj/
  article/templates.html

Includes a "standard head template" and a "standard trailer template," covering standardizing the header and address sections of your Web pages.

Web Page Templates by Lansing Community College

http://www.lansing.cc.mi.us/title3/
  sample.htm

A collection of Web page templates developed for use at Lansing Community College, including templates for List of Links, Divisional, Departmental,

Personal, Newsletter, Staff Directory, and Conference/Seminar Web page templates.

Advanced and Other HTML Features

The following resources can guide you in the implementation of many "advanced" HTML features, as well as other specific features of HTML that bear mentioning, including the Netscape and Microsoft extensions, HTML 3.2, character entities, tables, colors, forms, imagemaps, frames, GIF animations, CGI programming, Java, Shockwave, and RealAudio.

Netscape Extensions

Extensions to HTML 2.0 by Netscape

http://home.netscape.com/assist/
   net_sites/html_extensions.html

Word on the Netscape extensions to HTML 2.0 straight from the source.

Extensions to HTML 3.0 by Netscape

http://home.netscape.com/assist/
   net_sites/html_extensions_3.html

The How to Manual of Really Cool HTML

http://home.teclink.net/~rets/indy.html

Covers a number of things you can do using Netscape's extensions.

How Do They Do That with HTML? by Carl Tashian

http://www.nashville.net/%7Ecarl/html-
   guide/index.html

Covers many HTML tips and tricks, primarily using Netscape's extensions, including background and text colors, transparent and interlaced GIFs, font size and color changes, GIF animation, access counters, dynamic documents, browser detection, background sounds, frames, and tables.

HTML 3.0 and Netscape 3.0: How to Tame the Wild Mozilla by Webreference.com

http://webreference.com/html3andns/

A good discussion of Netscape HTML (NHTML) and its relation, and non-relation, to HTML. 3.0.

Mozilla DTD by Webtechs

http://www.webtechs.com/sgml/Mozilla/DTD
   -HOME.html

Microsoft Extensions

HTML Reference by Microsoft

http://www.microsoft.com/workshop/author
   /newhtml/local018.htm

Includes descriptions of all Microsoft's extensions to HTML, as well as a pretty complete rundown on the rest of HTML. (Note: Microsoft has a nasty habit of moving its reference pages around without providing forwarding links. Hopefully, this one will stay put.)

Microsoft IE DTD by Webtechs

http://www.webtechs.com/sgml/IE/DTD-
   HOME.html

HTML 3.2

HTML 3.2 is the latest specification for HTML, supplanting HTML 2.0 and superseding HTML 3.0. Want to know what it includes? Check out the following sites.

The W3 Consortium Announces HTML 3.2 by W3C (the World Wide Web Consortium)

```
http://www.w3.org/hypertext/WWW/
    MarkUp/Wilbur/pr7may96.html
```

The press release (May 7, 1996) announcing HTML 3.2. HTML 3.2 supersedes HTML 3.0, which wasn't ever released as a standard.

The Structure of HTML 3.2 Documents by W3C

```
http://www.w3.org/hypertext/WWW/MarkUp/
    Wilbur/features.html
```

The dope on HTML 3.2 directly from the committee that designed it.

HTML 3.2 DTD by W3C

```
http://www.w3.org/hypertext/WWW/MarkUp/
    Wilbur/HTML3.2.dtd
```

A Web site for those who want to get into the real nitty-gritty. May be too technical for some, however (DTDs are like that).

HyperText Markup Language v3.2 Reference

```
http://www.wvitcoe.wvnet.edu/~sbolt/
    html3/
```

W3C Activity: Hypertext Markup Language (HTML) by W3C

```
http://www.w3.org/pub/WWW/MarkUp/Activity
```

Answers questions about HTML 3.2 and current direction of the HTML standard.

Character Entities and the ISO-8859-1 Character Set

The extended, or special, characters that you can use in Web pages are defined by the ISO-8859-1 character set, also sometimes called the ISO-Latin1 character set. Using these characters properly can be tricky, but it's the key to writing pages in languages other than English.

Pointers to Information About ISO-8859 by A. J. Flavell

```
http://ppewww.ph.gla.ac.uk/~flavell/
    iso8859/iso8859-pointers.html
```

Excellent rundown on issues involved with ISO-8859 character set.

Character Code Coverage - Browser Report by A. J. Flavell

```
http://ppewww.ph.gla.ac.uk/~flavell/
    iso8859/browser-report.html
```

Reports on support among browsers for ISO 8859-1 characters.

8-bit ASCII Codes (for ISO-Latin1 character set) by W3C

```
http://www.w3.org/pub/WWW/MarkUp/
    Wilbur/latin1.gif
```

Provides a table of all ASCII numeric codes and corresponding displayable characters for the ISO-Latin1 character set.

ISO Latin1 Text Entities

```
http://info.arc.com/docs/lynx/
    lynx_help/ISO_LATIN1_test.html
```

Lets you see how your Web browser displays named character entities in the ISO Latin1 character set.

ISO Latin1 Character Codes

http://www.pact.srf.ac.uk/~nathan/
   chars.html

A listing of both named character entities and ASCII character codes.

W3Writer: HTML Special Characters by Gordon Hake

http://hake.com/gordon/w3-spec.html

An excerpt from the HTML 2.0 specification edited and simplified for beginners.

ISO8859-1 Table by Martin Ramsch

http://ecsdg.lu.se/iso8859-1.html

ISO 8859-1 National Character Set FAQ by Michael K. Gschwind

ftp://rtfm.mit.edu/pub/usenet/
   news.answers/internationalization/
   iso-8859-1-charset

Discusses how to use European (Latin American) national character sets on Unix-based systems and the Internet.

Tables

The following resources are tutorials and references on including tables in your Web pages.

HTML Table Tutorial by Urban A. LeJeune

http://www.charm.net/~lejeune/tables.html

An excellent tutorial on creating tables; focuses on Netscape Navigator.

NCSA Mosaic(tm) Tables Tutorial

http://www.ncsa.uiuc.edu/SDG/Software/Mo
   saic/Tables/tutorial.html

NCSA's tutorial on tables.

TableMaker by Sam Choukri

http://www.missouri.edu/~c588349/table-
   maker.html

A neat online utility that allows you to enter your table data into a form, and then it creates the HTML table for you.

The Table Sampler by Hagan Heller

http://www.netscape.com/people/hagan/htm
   l/tables1.html

A "by example" tables tutorial.

So You Want a Table, Huh? by Joe Burns

http://www.cs.bgsu.edu/~jburns/table.html

Another Joe Burns "So You Want..." page, this one on creating tables.

Setting Colors

You can set the color of the background of your Web page, as well as for foreground text and links, including regular links, already visited links, and activated links (links on which you have pressed down the mouse button but not yet released it). You also can use the COLOR attribute of the <FONT> tag to assign different colors to sections of text within a Web page. Originally introduced by Netscape, many other Web browsers now support these capabilities.

Colors by InfiNet

http://www.infi.net/wwwimages/
    colorindex.html

An excellent resource for information on setting colors for your backgrounds, text, and links. Includes a listing of colors and their hex codes that you can click on to see what they are going to look like.

Hypertext Handbook: Color Chart by Multimedia Productions

http://world.std.com/~ldjackso/
    5colors.htm

Extensive display of full range of colors and their hex codes. Organizes colors into different shades and hues of reds, oranges, yellows, greens, blues, indigos, and violets.

The Hex Color Guide

http://www.cranfield.ac.uk/docs/hex/

Includes a table of hex codes for different colors.

Weber "Color" Chart by Ray Weber

http://felix.scvnet.com:80/~weber/
    colorweb.html

A chart of hex values displayed in their resulting colors.

RGB Hex Triplet Color Chart by Doug Jacobson

http://www.phoenix.net/%7Ejacobson/
    rgb.html

An excellent chart of hex codes and their corresponding colors. Chart is a GIF file that can be downloaded (in Netscape Navigator, click on it with the right mouse button).

X11 Based RGB Color Table

http://nickel.as.arizona.edu:8080/
    cgi-bin/color_table.pl

Allows you to submit an X11 color name and then returns results of matching colors in a RGB database. A search for "red" returned 26 different matches, form "indiared" to "violetred4." Color names are displayed in their corresponding colors, along with their hex codes. A great resource.

The Color Specifier for Netscape by HYPE Electazine

http://www.users.interport.net/
    ~giant/COLOR/hype_color.html

Lists the names of colors and their ASCII and Hex RGB values, with a link from each color name to a page using it as a background color. Actually, this will specify colors for any browser capable of viewing background, text, or font colors, not just Netscape (Netscape did introduce this, however, so . . .).

ColorMaker by Sam Choukri

http://www.missouri.edu/~c588349/
    colormaker.html

From the same source as the TableMaker utility. Lets you point and click to specify colors for the background, text, and links and then specify a Web page; then shows you the new colors applied to the page.

Decimal<—>HEX Converter

http://www.sci.kun.nl/thalia/guide/
    color/dec-hex.html

Entering decimal values for Red, Green, and Blue will return corresponding hex numbers. Entering hex values will return corresponding decimal numbers.

Victor Engel's No Dither Netscape Color Palette

http://www.onr.com/user/lights/
   netcol.html

Discusses strategies and provides color chart for getting best color display results, especially in Netscape Navigator.

The Joy of Hex (Get Hexed!) by Pequod

http://www.stardot.com/%7Elukeseem/
   hexed.html

This is a handy form-based online utility that allows you to enter RGB decimal values (0-255) for background, text, link, and visited link colors and then see your results displayed in the colors you have specified, along with the RGB hex codes you need to insert in your Web page to get the same effect.

Forms

Forms are an advanced feature of HTML 2.0. They can be used to create customer response or order forms, for instance.

Introduction to Web Forms by the Information Technology Division Emory University

http://www.cc.emory.edu/INFODESK/MM/FORMS

Assumes a good working knowledge of Unix (being able to copy files, change the permissions on files, use a text editor, and so on).

A Tour of HTML Forms and CGI Scripts by Sanford Morton

http://www.halcyon.com/sanford/
   cgi-tour.html

Assumes some familiarity with the Perl programming language.

Carlos' FORMS Tutorial by Carlos Peros

http://robot0.ge.uiuc.edu/~carlosp/
   cs317/ft.1.html

Aimed more at the beginning to intermediate user.

HTML Forms for Feedback by Bill Jenkins

http://www.englib.cornell.edu/
   instruction/www/email-forms-class.html

A good tutorial on forms aimed at the beginning to intermediate user.

HTML Forms Examples by Michael Grobe

http://kuhttp.cc.ukans.edu/cwis/people/
   Michael.Grobe/examples.html

A set of forms examples.

Mosaic for X version 2.0 Fill-Out Form Support by NCSA

http://www.ncsa.uiuc.edu/SDG/Software/
   Mosaic/Docs/fill-outforms/
   overview.html

Written relative to Mosaic for X, but should apply to other browsers that support forms.

HTML forms refresher course

http://www.itp.tsoa.nyu.edu/~student/
   jamie/help/cgi-perl/forms.html

Uses a table to give side-by-side illustrations of specific form examples and their HTML coding.

HTML Forms Table by Curt Robbins

http://ftp.clark.net/pub/cargui/
   formchrt.html

A handy table-based quick reference to forms tags and their attributes.

HTML Form-Testing Home Page by Glenn Trewitt of Digital Equipment Corporation

```
http://www.research.digital.com/nsl/
   formtest/home.html
```

Allows you to test different browsers for their forms compatibility. Your test then becomes part of the overall test results, which are updated every 15 minutes and reviewable online.

So, You Want a Form, Huh? by Joe Burns

```
http://www.cs.bgsu.edu/~jburns/forms.html
```

Another Joe Burns contribution, this time on creating forms.

Imagemaps

You can use imagemaps to define an image to act like a menu, on which you can click in different areas of the image to activate different hypertext links.

NCSA Imagemap Tutorial

```
http://hoohoo.ncsa.uiuc.edu/docs/
   tutorials/imagemapping.html
```

A step-by-step tutorial for creating imagemaps.

Imagemap Help Page by Steve Rogers for Hiway Techologies

```
http://www.hway.net/ihip/
```

A good resource for information on imagemaps.

Constructing an Imagemap for Your Home Page by Mark Rasmussen

```
http://www.et.byu.edu/resources/
   imagemap.html
```

Good basic information on constructing imagemaps.

Clickable Imagemaps by Russ Jones

```
http://www.ora.com/gnn/bus/ora/
   features/miis/index.html
```

A concise explanation of how imagemaps work, excerpted from the book, *Managing Internet Information Services.*

Creating Clickable Images in CNC Web Pages

```
http://www.cris.com/help/web/
   clickimage.html
```

Targets the beginning to intermediate user.

So You Want an Imagemap, Huh? by Joe Burns

```
http://www.cs.bgsu.edu/~jburns/
   imagemap.html
```

Excellent tutorial aimed at the non-techie. An NBNSOFT Content Award Winner.

Implementing Client-Side Imagemaps by Spyglass

```
http://www.spyglass.com/techspec/
   tutorial/img_maps.html
```

Step-by-step instructions on how to create client-side imagemaps.

Frames

Netscape originally introduced frames, but Microsoft has since supported them, too. Frames enable you to divide the browser window into "frames," with different Web pages active in each frame.

Frames: An Introduction by Netscape

```
http://home.netscape.com/assist/
   net_sites/frames.html
```

Netscape's own rundown on the feature it introduced.

Netscape Frames by Charlton Rose

http://sharky.nomius.com/frames/menu.htm

A great page on using frames. Makes effective use of graphic illustrations.

FrameShop! by Sam Choukri

http://www.missouri.edu/~c588349/
    frameshop/index.html

From the same source as TableMaker and Color-Maker. An interesting online utility that enables you to enter information for main frames and sub-frames into forms. It then automatically creates the codes for the frames for you. It can create up to three main frames and up to three subframes for each main frame.

Introduction to Frames by Webspinners

http://www.spunwebs.com/sites2c/
    frmtutor.html

An excellent tutorial on creating frames, as well as three templates.

Framing the Web by Webreference.com (Dan Brown)

http://www.webreference.com/dev/frames/

Another good rundown on creating frames. Includes a cheat sheet.

GIF Animation

The GIF89a standard for GIF images allows for the creation of animated GIF files—an image file containing several separate images that are displayed rapidly in turn. Here are some pointers to where you can find out more.

Wilson's GIF Animation Tutorial by Wilson Chan Wai Shing

http://www.comp.polyu.edu.hk/%7Ec4075231
    /gif.html

Everything you want to know about GIF animation.

Samiel's GIF Animation Page

http://www.fastlane.net/~samiel/
    anim.shtml

Another good page on GIF animations.

GIF Animation on the WWW by Royal E. Frazier

http://www.reiworld.com/royalef/
    gifanim.htm

Lots of stuff on GIF animations. Includes a tutorial. Also includes the 1st Internet Gallery of GIF Animation.

Counters and Statistics

So You Want a Counter, Huh? by Joe Burns

http://www.cs.bgsu.edu/~jburns/
    counter.html

Another in Joe Burns' excellent series.

WebCounter

http://www.digits.com/

A source for free counters, as well as information and guidance on using counters.

Internet Audit Bureau

http://www.internet-audit.com/

A sponsor-provided free service that will compile usage statistics for you on your page or pages.

So, Why Can't We Find Out Exactly How Many People Are Hitting Our Web Site? by Organic Online Services

http://www.organic.com/Home/Services/
traffic-analysis.html

Some caveats on Web statistics.

CGI and Perl Programming

The Common Gateway Interface by NCSA

http://hoohoo.ncsa.uiuc.edu/cgi/

An authoritative description of what CGI is, how it works, and what you can do with it.

Decoding FORMs with CGI by NCSA

http://hoohoo.ncsa.uiuc.edu/cgi/
forms.html

Aimed at advanced users.

CGI Tutorial by Nik Silver

http://agora.leeds.ac.uk/Perl/
Cgi/start.html

Assumes knowledge of the Perl programming language.

Perl Tutorial by Nik Silver

http://agora.leeds.ac.uk/Perl/start.html

Just the thing if you don't already know enough Perl to use his CGI Tutorial.

Java and JavaScript

Brewing Java: A Tutorial by Elliotte Rusty Harold

http://sunsite.unc.edu/javafaq/
javatutorial.html

An excellent tutorial on using Java.

Beyond Java: Distributed Objects on the Web by Eamonn Sullivan

http://www.pcweek.com/navigator/1218/nav1
218.html

JavaScript Outpost

http://intergalactinet.com/javascript/

A compilation of links to Web pages on JavaScript.

Introduction to JavaScript by Stefan Koch

http://rummelplatz.uni-mannheim.de/
%7Eskoch/js/script.htm

A comprehensive JavaScript tutorial.

Java Technology Update from Personal Computer Magazine

http://www.vnu.co.uk/bc/pcm/603java.htm

A good discussion of Java and its potential, as well as its drawbacks. Has an interesting section on "Java's rival and friends," including discussion of the Java positions, pro or con, of Macromedia, Silicon Graphics, Borland, Microsoft, Netscape, IBM/Lotus, and Symantec.

The Java Developers Kit by JavaSoft

http://java.sun.com/products/JDK/
1.0.2/index.html

Besides letting you download the latest version of the Java Developers Kit, offers lots of information online about Java.

JavaScript Tutorial: Intermediate Level by Intergalactinet

http://intergalactinet.com/javascript/JSI
ntTutor.html

Multimedia

Shockwave by MacroMedia

`http://www.macromedia.com/`

Shockwave is a set of plug-in authoring tools for Authorware, Director, and Freehand and a Netscape plug-in that allows display of streaming animation. You can download the software at this site.

RealAudio: Audio on Demand for the Internet by Progressive Networks

`http://www.realaudio.com/`

Includes two products, RealAudio Play and Real AudioServer. Enables playing and delivering of on-demand streaming audio. You can download the software at this site. Requires a 16-bit sound card. Works with numerous Web browsers.

Miscellaneous Advanced and Other HTML

Advanced HTML programming by Sky Coyote

`http://www.intergalact.com/hp/part2/
   part2.html`

Rundowns on imagemaps, forms, and CGI.

Hypertext links in HTML by Murray Maloney (SoftQuad)

`http://www.sq.com/papers/
   Relationships.html`

Discusses use of the REL and REV attributes of the LINK and A (Anchor) tags.

A Proposed Convention for Embedding Metadata in HTML by Stuart Weibel

`http://www.oclc.org:5047/~weibel/
   html-meta.html`

Discusses a proposed convention for including metadata using the <META> tag in HTML documents.

General Web Resources

This section lists useful Web-related resources that can help Web publishers.

Glossaries

Guide to Web Terminology by Information Innovation

`http://www.euro.net/innovation/
   Web_Word_Base/Dictionary.html`

A good glossary of Web terms, with links.

Hypertext Handbook: Glossary of Terms by Multimedia Productions

`http://world.std.com/~ldjackso/hthb5.htm`

A list of links to definitions.

The Websurfer's Handbook: The Web-to-English Dictionary by The Asylum

`http://asylum.cid.com/handbook/
   handbook.html`

A funny compilation of hip Web slang—impress your friends and coworkers!

Online Magazines

This section lists some online magazines that target Web developers and publishers.

Web Developer Magazine

`http://www.webdeveloper.com/`

By the publishers of *Internet World*. You can do a keyword search of articles from back issues.

WebMaster Magazine: The Executive Resource for Doing Business on the Net

`http://www.cio.com/WebMaster/wmhome.html`

Case studies, interviews, how-to strategies, and new products and services. Aimed at IT executives, senior managers, and corporate Webmasters, with the slant definitely on doing business, making money, but a good information source for anyone wanting to make an impact on the Web.

WEBsmith: the How-To Magazine for Technicians of the World Wide Web

`http://www.smithing.com/`

A resource for Web-related developers.

Web Professionals' Digest

`http://www.littleblue.com/webpro/`

The Web Developer's Journal

`http://nctweb.com/nct/software/`
`    eleclead.html`

Web Tools Review

`http://www-swiss.ai.mit.edu/wtr/`

An online journal for Web developers.

Web Success

`http://www.kdcol.com/~ray/index.html`

An online magazine that focuses on Web marketing and resources to promote commerce on the Internet.

Web Site Promotion Newsletter

`http://www.meh.com/meh/about.html`

Reports monthly on methods and resources for publicizing Web sites.

WWWiz Magazine

`http://wwwiz.com/`

Read the latest issue, browse through back issues, or read late-breaking news.

Web Week Magazine

`http://www.webweek.com/`

Read the premier weekly magazine for all matters Web related. Back issues are also available for browsing.

TechWeb: The Technology Information Source

`http://techweb.cmp.com/`

WebTechniques: Solutions for Internet and Web Developers

`http://www.webtechniques.com/`

The Spider's Web

`http://www.incontext.com/spidweb/`
`    index.htm`

Aimed at Web developers and designers.

Navigate! The Online Magazine for Netscape Users

http://www.netscapepress.com/zine/

Off the Net

http://home.mcom.com/assist/net_sites/
  off_the_net.html

Another Netscape-originated online publication.

Netscape World

http://www.ntscpwld.com/

Another Netscape-oriented online publication, but this one isn't by Netscape.

World Wide Web Journal by O'Reilly/W3C

http://www.w3.org/pub/WWW/Journal/

The journal of the World Wide Web Consortium, published by O'Reilly and Associates. Not the full version of the journal, which is available only through subscription, but contains excerpts.

Internet/Web History and Statistics

Internet Statistics: Web Growth, Internet Growth by Matthew Gray

http://www.mit.edu/people/mkgray/net/

Internet Facts by Parallax Webdesign

http://www.echonyc.com/~parallax/
  interfacts.html

Statistics on size/growth and demographics of the Net.

Internet statistics by Vincent O'Keefe

http://webnet.mednet.gu.se/computer/
  internet-statistics.txt

Internet Stats and History by Mike Bray

http://www.oir.ucf.edu/~mike/
  statistics.html

A page of links to many other Web pages on statistics and history of the Net.

Internet Evolution (GIF graph) by A.M. Rutkowski and the Internet Society

ftp://ftp.isoc.org/isoc/charts/
  history-gifs/timeline.gif

Project 2000 by Hoffman, Novak, and Kalsbeek

http://www2000.ogsm.vanderbilt.edu/
  baseline/internet.demos
  .july9.1996.html

Report on Internet and Web use in the U.S.

Hobbes' Internet Timeline by Robert H. Zakon

http://info.isoc.org/guest/zakon/
  Internet/History/HIT.html

A Brief History of the Internet and Related Networks by Robert H. Zakon

http://info.isoc.org/guest/zakon/
  Internet/History/Brief_History
  _of_the_Internet

Short History of the Internet
by Bruce Sterling

```
http://info.isoc.org/guest/zakon/
    Internet/History/Short_History
    _of_the_Internet
```

A Timeline of Network History
by Stan Kulikowski II

```
http://info.isoc.org/guest/zakon/
    Internet/History/Timeline_of
    _Network_History
```

Internet Statistics—Estimated
by Internet Solutions

```
http://www.netree.com/netbin/
    internetstats
```

CyberStats
by FAS CyberStrategy Project

```
http://www.fas.org/cp/netstats.htm
```

Web Publishing Tool Chest: Programs and Utilities

Many of the links in previous sections are just for learning, but the items in *this* section point to tools, tools, and more tools.

Software Collections

I put these collections first because they have so much cool stuff, and they're all well-organized, so it's easy to find things.

TUCOWS: The Ultimate Collection of Winsock Software
by Scott A. Swedorski

```
http://tucows.com/index.html
```

The place to go to find anything and everything in Internet software, including browsers, HTML editors, graphics editors, and much, much, more. An absolute must for anyone's bookmark list or hotlist. Don't let the name fool you—it includes Mac programs, too!

Stroud's CWSApps List

```
http://www.cwsapps.com/cwsa.html
```

Another omnibus site where you can find just about any Web or Net-related software program or utility.

Randy's Windows 95 Resource Center

```
http://206.151.75.235/html.tools.html
```

This one focuses on Windows 95 software.

Web Browsers

Don't already have a Web browser? Thinking of switching? Want to assemble a collection of Web browsers you can use to check your pages? The following are pointers to general information on Web browsers, as well as where you can find and download many Windows Web browsers.

Picking the Perfect Web Browser
by C/NET

```
http://www.cnet.com/Content/Reviews/
    Compare/Browsers/
```

Includes reviews of 28 browsers for Windows, Macintosh, and OS/2.

BrowserCaps: A Catalog of the HTML Support Provided by Different Web Browsers by David Ornstein

http://objarts.com/bc/

These are survey results on how different browsers handle HTML. You can participate, submitting your browser to the test.

BrowserWatch

http://www.browserwatch.com/

Offers breaking news in the browser and plug-ins industry.

Web Browser Test Page

http://www.uky.edu/~magree00/TestPage.html

Tests your browser's capability to display GIFs and JPEGs, as well as tests for MPEG, QuickTime, WAV, and AU players.

HTML Editors, Add-Ons, Converters, and Templates

Here are software tools to help you create and edit your HTML files, including HTML editors, word processing add-ons, converters, and templates.

HTML Editors

After you learn some HTML, you might want to try out one or more of these HTML editors to make your HTML coding life easier.

WebWarrior by Timothy Paustian

http://facstaff.uwisc.edu/paustian/
    webwarrior/index.html

Cool Macintosh HTML editor, with syntax coloring, full drag-and-drop, and complete scriptability. Freeware.

Alpha by Pete Keleher

http://www.cs.umd.edu/faculty/keleher/
    alpha.html

Powerful text editor programmable in Tcl or Apple-Script; includes customized templates for HTML, Perl, Java, and other Web-oriented languages. It's so good I used it (along with Visual Page) to create the HTML in this book!

Visual Page by Symantec

http://www.symantec.com

Very powerful WYSIWYG HTML editor for Macintosh. Includes site management features and excellent Java support. $99 or so retail. My best recommendation: I used it for this book.

HoTMetaL by SoftQuad

http://www.sq.com/products/hotmetal/
    hm-ftp.htm

HoTMetaL Free Free Version 2.0 is a noncommercial evaluation version for Windows 3.1 available for download. The price for the commercial version, HoTMetaL Pro 3.0, is $159 U.S. and $199 Canadian.

HotDog by Sausage Software

http://www.sausage.com/

Demonstration copies of 16-bit Standard and Pro Versions and 32-bit Standard and Professional Versions (written specifically for Windows 95) are available for download. Evaluation periods are for 14 or 30 days, after which the software will stop working, but you can e-mail for an extension of the trial period. Prices for the registered versions are $29.95 for HotDog Standard 2 (Win 3.1), $39.95 for HotDog Standard 32-Bit (Win 95), $99.95 for HotDog Professional 2 (Win 3.1), and $99.95 for HotDog Pro 32-Bit (Win 95).

HTMLed
by Internet Software Technologies

`http://www.ist.ca/htmled/`

Both a 16-bit version for Windows 3.1 and a 32-bit version for Windows 95 or Windows NT are available for download. The registered version is $29 U.S. and $35 Canadian.

HTML Assistant Pro 2 for Windows
by Brooklyn North Software Works

`http://www.brooknorth.com/`

A freeware version is available for download. The registered version is $99.95 U.S. and $139 Canadian.

<Live Markup>
by My Software Company

`http://www.mediatec.com/`

The 16-bit version is available for download for a 14-day free evaluation, after which the software will stop working. Registered versions (16-bit and 32-bit) are $49. The 32-bit version is for both Windows 95 and NT.

Web Weaver by McWeb Software

`http://www.tiac.net/users/mmm/`
`    webweav.html`

This is the evaluation version. The registered version is $12.

Web Wizard: The Duke of URL by
ARTA Software Group

`http://www.halcyon.com/artamedia/`
`    webwizard/`

Both the 16-bit and 32-bit (Win 95/NT) are available for download. No pricing information mentioned.

Webber by Cerebral Systems
Development Corp.

`http://www.csdcorp.com/webber.htm`

Evaluation version is available for downloading. Registered version is $30 U.S. and $40 Canadian. Versions are for Windows 3.1.

HTML NotePad by Cranial Software

`http://www.cranial.com/software/htmlnote/`

Shareware version available for download. Registration is £24 or U.S. $45.

Aardvark Pro by Functional Business
Systems of Australia

`http://www.fbs.aust.com/aardvark.html`

Two versions are available for download—a free version and a shareware version. Registration of the shareware version is $59 U.S. and $89 Australian.

Arachnid by Tim Long

`http://rhwww.richuish.ac.uk/resource.htm`

No pricing information mentioned.

EdWin by Michael Sutton

`http://www.vantek.net/pages/msutton/edwin`
`    .htm`

16-bit noncommercial download version is available. Registration cost is $35 for 16-bit and 32-bit (Win 95/NT) versions.

Gomer HTML Editor
by Stoopid Software

`http://clever.net/gomer/`

Registration is $15.

HTML Handler by Jonathan Reinberg

http://happypuppy.com/digitale/hthand.html

Freeware. Both 16-bit and 32-bit (Win 95) versions are available for download.

HTML Easy! Pro by Joe Lin (Basic Concept Studio)

http://www.trytel.com/~milkylin/

Both English and Chinese language versions are available for download. No pricing information mentioned.

Kenn Nesbitt's WebEdit

http://www.nesbitt.com/

Both 16-bit and 32-bit (Win 95/NT) 30-day trial versions are available for download. Registration is $39.95 for both 16-bit Personal/Education version and 32-bit Standard edition, and $79.95 for 16-bit Commercial version and 32-bit Professional version.

WebPen by Informatik Inc.

http://www.execpc.com/~infothek/
  webpen.html

Both the Standard and Pro versions (both Win 3.1) are available for download. Registration is $19 for the Standard version and $39 for the Pro version. Standard version includes an offline browser and an OLE-link to MS-Word spellchecker. The Pro version includes WinCopy screen capture, GifWeb transparent GIFs tool, and Hotspots Imagemaps tool.

TC-Director by Tashcom Software

http://pages.linkstar.com/tashcom-soft-
  ware/index.html

Both 16-bit and 32-bit versions are available for download. Registration is $25 for 16-bit version and $30 for 32-bit version.

WebMania by Q&D Software Development

http://www.q-d.com/

Supports creation of frames, forms, and client-side imagemaps. A download version is available. Registration is $34.95 for WebMania Standard and $49.95 for WebMania Pro.

DerekWare HTML Author

http://shell.masterpiece.com/derek/
  derekware/

Free Windows 95 HTML editor that supports HTML 2.0 and Internet Explorer extensions.

HTML Builder by FLFSoft

http://www.execpc.com/~flfsoft/
  HTMLBuilder.html

$30. A 32-bit HTML Editor (Windows 3.1 requires Win32s).

WinHTML by Gulf Coast Software

http://www.gcsoftware.com/winhtml.html

16-bit and 32-bit versions available. $25/49.

InContext Spider

http://www.incontext.com/products/
  spider1.html

$79. 30-day evaluation version is available (expires after 30 days).

Web Ed for Windows

http://www.ozemail.com.au/~kread/
  webed.html

Free.

The Web Media Publisher

http://www.wbmedia.com/publisher/

$30. A 32-bit HTML editor. Includes FTP upload and internal Web browser. Evaluation version available for download.

Microsoft FrontPage

http://www.microsoft.com/frontpage/

$149. $109 for users of Microsoft Office for Windows 95 applications. No demo or beta version available for download.

CMed

http://www.iap.net.au/~cmathes/

A 32-bit HTML editor for Windows 95/NT. Supports HTML 2.0 and 3.0, Netscape and Microsoft extensions. CMed is shareware. A 30-day evaluation version available for download. Registration is $25 (U.S.) and $30 (AU).

WebThing by Paul Lutus

http://www.arachnoid.com/lutusp/
   webthing.htm

A Windows 95 HTML editor that supports drag-and-drop conversion of word processing files, tables, outlines, and so on, to HTML. Supports frames and JavaScript. This software is described as being "Careware." The author doesn't want money, but a demonstration of "care," such as stopping whining for a week. Otherwise, WebThing can be freely copied and distributed.

Add-Ons to Productivity Software

If you want to use your favorite word processor or spreadsheet for editing HTML files, here are some add-on HTML editors for various office productivity software.

Internet Assistant for Microsoft Word for Windows

http://www.microsoft.com/msword/
   internet/ia/default.htm

Internet Assistant is available for free from Microsoft in both 16-bit (Win 3.1) and 32-bit (Win 95) versions, plus a version for the Macintosh version of Word.

Internet Assistant for Microsoft Excel

http://www.microsoft.com/excel/
   Internet/IA/

Microsoft built HTML exporting into Excel 97, but for previous versions (including the Mac Excel 5.0), go here to get an Excel add-in which exports Excel tables into HTML.

Internet Assistant for Microsoft PowerPoint

http://www.microsoft.com/powerpoint/
   Internet/IA/default.htm

If you're using PowerPoint 95 (Windows only), you can grab this Assistant to convert your presentations to HTML for use on the Web.

HTML Author for Microsoft Word for Windows 6.0

http://www.salford.ac.uk/iti/gsc/
   htmlauth/summary.html

Does not work with Microsoft Word for Windows 7.0 (Win 95), but a 32-bit version is projected for the future. Registration is 28 pounds sterling, with other currencies acceptable provided you add 10% to your local equivalent based on the exchange rate at the time of posting.

Internet Publisher for WordPerfect 6.1 for Windows

```
http://www.wpmag.com/Windows/1996/
   apr/WPIPZIP.EXE
http://www.schaft.com/ftp/HTML_Stuff/
   wpipzip.exe
ftp://ftp.esva.net/pub/win31/wpipzip.exe
```

Since Novell sold WordPerfect to Corel, Novell has dropped the Web page for Internet Publisher. However, you can still download Internet Publisher (free) at any of the three preceding addresses.

HTML Converters and Templates

Converters are handy if you have a bunch of files you want to convert to HTML. Templates are used in Word for Windows to create HTML files from your word processing files.

ANT_HTML.DOT

```
http://mcia.com/ant/antdesc.htm
```

A document template for Microsoft Word 6.0. Works in Word for Windows, NT, and 95 (and Word for Macintosh), and international versions of Word 6.0 and above. Includes support for HTML 2.0 plus the Netscape extensions. Has a customizable toolbar for user-added tags. Includes a WYSIWYG previewer. A demo version is available for download. Registration is $39, plus an additional $3 if you're in Texas.

CU_HTML.DOT by Anton Lam

```
http://www.cuhk.hk/csc/cu_html/
   cu_html.htm
```

A document template for Microsoft Word for Windows 6.0 and 2.0. WYSIWYG creation of HTML files inside Word. There is no registration fee. Software is provided without warranty or support.

GT_HTML.DOT by the Georgia Tech Research Institute

```
http://www.gatech.edu/word_html/
```

From my alma mater, provides what it terms a "psuedo-WYSIWYG authoring environment" for creating HTML files in Word 6.0 (Windows or Macintosh). It should also work with Word for Windows 95 and Word 97, but no absolute promises are given. A version also is available for Word for Windows 2.0. Freeware.

Wp2Html

```
http://www.res.bbsrc.ac.uk/wp2html/
```

Conversion/template package for WordPerfect. Converts WordPerfect files to HTML. Runs stand-alone and is designed for the batch conversion of multiple existing WP documents. Can convert tables, text, styles, and most formatting codes. Can handle equations and figures, subject to the limitations of HTML (Netscape). Evaluation kit, which is an earlier version of the software and works with WordPerfect 5.1 or 5.2 files, is available for download. Registration is 5 UK pounds.

WPTOHTML 2.0 by Hunter Monroe

```
http://www.lib.ox.ac.uk/~hunter/
   wptohtml.htm
```

Conversion/template package for WordPerfect for DOS. Versions available for 5.1 and 6.0. Can also be used with WordPerfect 5.2/6.0/6.0a for Windows, as well as any other version of WordPerfect that can use the same printer drivers and style files. Supports conversion of special characters and equations to transparent inline images (.XBM format). Freeware.

WPTOHTML 1.0 by Hunter Monroe

```
http://www.coast.net/SimTel/msdos/
  wordperf.html
```

Download WPT51d10.ZIP for 5.1 version and WPT60D10.ZIP for 6.0 version. Older version than 2.0, but supports conversion of tables of contents, cross-references, indexes, endnotes, and WP 6.0 hypertext links to HTML hypertext links. Available for WordPerfect 5.1 and 6.0 for DOS. Freeware.

EasyHelp/Web by Eon Solutions Ltd.

```
http://www.eon-solutions.com/easyhelp/
  easyhelp.htm
```

Converts Word for Windows documents to either Windows Help files or HTML files. Two versions are available for download, one for Word 6/7/NT (which includes both 16-bit and 32-bit versions) and the other for Word for Windows 2.0. Required version 3.10.505 (extended) or later of the Microsoft Help Compiler if you want to compile Help files. Registration is $140.

AmiWeb by Steve Belleguelle

```
http://www.cs.nott.ac.uk/%7Esbx/
  amiweb.html
```

This is a combination of macros, stylesheets, and a converter program for creating HTML files from Ami-Pro for Windows. (Note: Ami-Pro has since become Word Pro, and it is not specified whether this package will work with the Word Pro versions.) AmiWeb supports the creation of tables. See also the set of macros, FORMS.ZIP, by Ashley Bass, available at the same site for creating forms using AmiWeb. Although it is not specifically stated, this appears to be freeware. No pricing information is mentioned.

Advantage HTML-ASCII Converter

```
http://www.demon.co.uk/advantage/files.htm
```
Shareware that strips HTML codes.

DBF to HTML Converter by Ronald A. "Andy" Hoskinson

```
http://www.demon.co.uk/advantage/
  files.htm
```

$20. Shareware. Converts dBase/XBase files into HTML.

ForeFront ForeHTML

```
http://www.ff.com/pages/forehtm.htm
```

$169. WinHelp to HTML converter. Windows 3.1 and Windows 95 versions available. Demo versions available for download (demo versions limit you to 10 topics).

WebWorks Publisher by Quadralay

```
http://www.quadralay.com/Publisher/
```

$895. Calls itself the premier FrameMaker-to-HTML converter. 30-day evaluation versions available for download (Windows 3.1 requires Win32s).

KEYview: The Universal Viewer by FTP Software

```
http://www.ftp.com/mkt_info/keyv2.html
```

Works as a file viewer and converter. Can convert multiple different formats to HTML. Also functions as a Netscape plug-in for viewing multiple file formats on the Web. 30-day evaluation version available for download. Cost: $49.95.

RTFtoHTML by Chris Hector

```
http://www.w3.org/pub/WWW/Tools/rtfto-
  html-3.0.html
```

The latest version of RTFtoHTML (3.0), incorporating RTFtoWEB features. Converts between RTF (Rich Text Format) and HTML. Supports tables, Netscape and Microsoft extensions, splitting long documents into smaller files. Supports coversion from RTF export from Microsoft Word,

WordPerfect, Next, Claris Works, Framemaker, and any other word processor capable of exporting RTF files. Shareware. Price not mentioned (other than its being "small").

WebMaker by Harlequin

http://www.harlequin.com/webmaker/

Converts between FrameMaker and HTML. Offers customizable conversion of text, graphics, tables, and equations. Evaluation version available for download. Evaluation version is not time-restricted. The only feature limitation is that you can only create up to five separate HTML pages from any one FrameMaker document. Registration is $99.

Automated Page Creators, Site Managers, and Web Authoring Suites

Do you think you might need more than just an HTML editor to help manage your HTML files? Planning on setting up a large Web site? For an "industrial strength" solution, check out the following pointers to automated page creators, site managers, and Web authoring suites.

Web Publisher 1.1 by SkiSoft

http://www.skisoft.com/skisoft/

An automated Web page production tool. Allows you to seamlessly convert and enhance documents with from Word, WordPerfect, AmiPro, and FrameMaker into Web pages. Automatically converts images to GIFs, builds tables, builds tables of contents with links to headings, converts numbered and bulleted lists, and places signatures, mailto URLs, and corporate images/logos into your documents. Includes batch conversion of multiple documents. A free 30-day trial version is available for download. This is a fully functional version, not a demo or limited-function version. Registration is $495 for the Standard Edition and $990 for the Professional Edition (which includes the Long Document Utility, which can take a long document and break it up into HTML subpages).

QuickSite by Deltapoint

http://secure.deltapoint.com/qs/

A Web site development and management system. Requires no HTML coding. Automatically establishes all links to your pages. It is project- and database-oriented. Supports embedding of forms. Transfers finished files to your site via FTP. A 30-day evaluation version is available for download. Registration is $79 (Internet: Unlock Code Only) and $99 (Retail: Box, Manuals, and Disk).

HTML Transit by InfoAccess

http://www.infoaccess.com/

Automates production of HTML electronic publications. Allows direct import of native formats of most major world processors and most graphic formats. Automatic generation of table of contents and index hypertext links, linked navigation icons. Handles HTML 2.0, 3.0, and browser-specific extensions. An evaluation version is available for download, but will stop working after 15 days. However, if you order before the 15 days are up, you can save $100 off the purchase price (you must, however, fill out the download form in full). The registered version is $495 but has a 30-day no-risk guarantee.

WorldDoc by SPI Inc.

http://www.spii.com/

Allows point-and-click creation of Web pages without having to learn HTML. A trial version is available for download, but is time-limited to 15 days. Registration is $49.

Dr. Web's Internet ListKeeper

http://www.drweb.com/lkeeper/

Designed for the user who knows absolutely nothing about the Internet but wants to maintain a frequently changing Web page. It automatically generates Web pages and then, at the click of a button, FTPs them to your server. Provides default styles or can be customized for custom Web pages. A 30-day demo version is available for download. Registration is $49.

Internet Creator:
The Web Site Builder

http://www.forman.com/ic3/ic3.htm

$189. 15-day trial version available for download. Build and maintain unlimited number of Web sites with no need to learn HTML.

Macromedia Backstage Designer Plus

http://www.macromedia.com/software/
  backstage/index.html

$79. 30-day trial version of Backstage Designer (not Plus) is available for download. Word processing-like HTML editing, automates plugging in Shockwave and Java applets, professional image editing. Project-level management system and site maintenance tool.

8Legs Web Studio
by Foghorn Software

http://www.fogsoft.com/~fogsoft/index.htm

Integrated project management and Web editing application. Fourteen-day evaluation version for Wndows 95/NT is available for download—it stops working after the evaluation period is over, but you can temporarily extend the evaluation period via e-mail. Registration is $59.

Corel Web.Designer

http://www.provantage.com/PR_10372.HTM

$99. Retail only. Suite of tools comprises complete HTML authoring package for Web page creation; includes 7,500+ Internet-ready clip art images. Offers: WYSIWYG HTML authoring; 120+ professionally designed templates; graphics/text file conversion; effortless publishing of existing documents to the Web; much more. No HTML knowledge required.

LinkStar Site Launcher

http://www.linkstar.com/linkstar/
  bin/tools

Free. Available in 16-bit and 32-bit versions. First create your Web page; then post and promote it with LinkStar Site Launcher.

Dummy by Sausage Software

http://www.sausage.com.au/dummy.htm

HTML editing for dummies (or the non-technically gifted). Provides step-by-step guide to Web page creation using pregenerated style templates. Supports Netscape Navigator tags. Fully functional version for Windows 95 available for download. Registration is $25.

4W Publisher
by Information Analytics

http://www.4w.com/4wpublisher/index.html

A database tool for developing and storing Web pages. Current version is a 16-bit version, but a 32-bit version is promised soon. A demo version is available for download, but is limited to five database records. Registration is $250.

SiteMan by GreyScale Systems

http://www.morning.asn.au/siteman/
  index.html

An offline site management tool that will check links, analyze HTML files, do global search/replace, and find orphans in multiple-directory Web sites. Available in three versions, SiteMan 2 for Windows 3.1 (for single directory Web sites), and SiteMan 3-16 for Windows 3.1 and SiteMan 3-32 for Windows 95/NT (both for multiple-directory Web sites). Site-Man 2 is $30 (AUS$35), and SiteMan 3 is $50 (AUS$60). A free trial version is available for download.

CyberSpyder Link Test by Aphrodite's Software

http://www.cyberspyder.com/cslnkts1.html

$25. Shareware. Checks the links of your Web site to see whether they are still good.

Graphic Editors, Viewers, and Converters

WebPainter from Totally Hip Software

http://www.totallyhip.com

WebPainter is a cool, fast paint program specially designed for creating Web images. It's available for Win95, WinNT, and the Mac; its demo version is full-featured but will only save three animated frames.

LView Pro by MMedia Research Corp.

http://world.std.com/~mmedia/lviewp.html

A 16-bit version is available for Windows 3.1 (Ver. 1.B), and a 32-bit version is available for Windows 95, Windows NT 3.51, and Windows 3.1 w/Win32s. In addition to other image-editing features, LView Pro's main claim to fame is its capability for easily creating transparent GIFs. A must-have for any Web publisher. Registration is $30.

PaintShop Pro by JASC, Inc.

http://www.jasc.com/pspdl.html

It is available in two versions, a 16-bit version for Windows 3.1 and a 32-bit version for Windows 95/NT. Supports more than 30 image formats. Also supports Adobe Photoshop plug-ins. This is a full-featured paint program. Also a must-have for any Web publisher. Registration is $69, and $99 for the PaintShop Pro Power Pack, which also includes Kai's Power Tool's SE CD-ROM.

GraphicConverter by Thorsten Lemke

http://www.lemkesoft.com

Macintosh graphics tool that supports more than 40 formats, ranging from GIF, JPEG, and PNG to Atari 8-bit images and Photoshop files. Easily handles transparent images and palette reduction. Registered version does batch conversions. US$30.

GIF Construction Set for Windows by Alchemy Mindworks

http://www.mindworkshop.com/alchemy/gif-
  con.html

Can create transparent GIFs and GIF animation files, as well as add nondestructive text to images. It is available in a 16-bit version for Windows 3.1 and a 32-bit version for Windows 95.

GIFmation by BoxTop Software

http://www.boxtopsoft.com

GIFmation is an extremely elegant Mac-only tool for creating animated GIFs. It's hard to describe until you use it, but once you do you'll be hooked.

Graphic Workshop for Windows by Alchemy Mindworks

http://www.mindworkshop.com/alchemy/
   gww.html

From the makers of the GIF Construction Set. Converts files between a wide range of differnt file firmats, including file formats from Ventura Publisher, Paintbrush, PageMaker, Word, WordPerfect, CorelDraw!, Deluxe Paint, and more. It can also reverse, rotate, flip, crop, and scale images, as well as dither color images into halftones, dither color images, reduce color depth, and manipulate and adjust color, contrast, brightness, sharpness, softness, and such. Can be run in batch mode for converting multiple files. It's available in two versions, a 16-bit version for Windows 3.1 and a 32-bit version for Windows 95. Registration is $40.

VuePrint by Hamrick Software

http://www.hamrick.com/

An image viewer for Windows that claims to use a special form of color dithering to produce high-quality pictures. It can also view UUEncoded images and MIME/Base 64 images. It is available in two versions, a 16-bit version for Windows 3.1 and a 32-bit version for Windows 95, Windows NT, and Windows 3.1 w/Win32s (available for download at the site). Registration is $40.

WebImage by Group42

http://www.group42.com/webimage.htm

Allows you to define and view transparent GIFs, create and edit imagemaps (including client side, NCSA, or CERN compliant map files), interlace GIF and PNG images, as well as a broad assortment of other operations, including image optimization and color depth reduction. Also allows you to apply a variety of "Web effects" to images, including buttonizing images, adding borders and text, creating button bars, and embossing tiled backgrounds. Supports a wide range of different file formats. Can decode and encode UUEncoded files. Two versions are available, a 16-bit version for Windows 3.1 and a 32-bit version for Windows 95, Windows NT, and Windows 3.1 w/Win32s. Demo versions are available for download that you can test out for ten days (it isn't specified whether they actually stop working at that time, but I would assume so). Two versions are available. Registration is $39.95.

GraphX Viewer by Group42

http://www.group42.com/graphx.htm

A graphics viewer for Windows 3.1 from the makers of WebImage. Allows you to view and convert a wide range of different image formats, including BMP, FAX G3/G4, GIF, JPEG, PCX, PNG, SunRaster, TARGA, TIFF, and XWD. Also can export to PostScript. Can also encode and decode UUEncoded files. Can also cut and paste, crop, color reduce, resize, rotate, and mirror images, as well as adjust brightness, contrast, sharpness, gamma, and so on. GraphX Viewer is provided as freeware for private, noncommercial use. For commercial use (such as using it at work), registration is $29.95.

PolyView Graphics Viewer/Converter by Polybytes

http://198.207.242.3/authors/polybytes/
   default.html

A graphics viewer, conversion, and printing utility for Windows 95 or NT. It uses multithreading to allow, for instance, reading and writing of muliple image files at the same time. It includes image appearance manipulation, copy and paste, and DDE execution capabilities. Registration is $20.

GIFTOOL by Home Page, Inc.

http://www.homepages.com/tools/

An MS-DOS utility that does interlacing and transparency, batch conversion of multiple images, and more. It is also available for various Unix platforms. Home Page, Inc., is a Web authoring consulting firm and, because no pricing information is given for GIFTOOL, my assumption is that it is free.

Painter 4 by Fractal Design

http://www.fractal.com/

Apart from a wide range of other high-end paint features, also includes the capability to create interlaced and transparent GIFs and imagemaps. It is available in versions for Window 3.1 and Windows 95. A demo version is available for download, but for Windows 95 only (that's a switch—usually it's the other way around). It is a biggy though—more than 8 MB. It contains all the features of the regular program except the capability to save, print, paint across a network, and work with frame-by-frame animation. All the Natural-Media tools are available for your use. No time-limit is mentioned for the demo version. Registration is $549 (includes CD-ROM).

VuGrafix by Informatik, Inc.

http://www.execpc.com/~infothek/
    vugrafix.html

Can view ten different graphics formats, including GIF, TIFF, JPEG, WMF, WPG, BMP, PCX, and DCX. Can view thumbnails and slide shows. Features include rotation, scaling, inversion, color adjustments, mirroring, and copy and paste. Registration is $19.

3DEnvMap by Thanassis Tsiodras

http://manolito.image.ece.ntua.gr/
    ~ttsiod/

A 3D renderer from Greece. Requires WinG, which you can find at http://manolito.image.ece.ntua.gr/~ttsiod/wing10.zip

PhotoImpact GIF/JPEG SmartSaver by ULead Systems

http://ulead.iready.com/

A plug-in program for the 32-bit versions of Adobe PhotoShop and Ulead PhotoImpact. PaintShop Pro also can use PhotoShop plug-ins, but you'll have to test it out to see whether it works. It allows dynamic WYSIWYG optimization of JPEG and GIF images to get the best balance possible between image size and quality. Non-Ulead PhotoImpact users can us the software for a 30-day trial period only (although it doesn't say whether the software actually stops working, I suspect that would be the case).

Dr. Jack's HTMLView

http://www.drjack.com/htmlview/welc2.htm

$10. Nine-day evaluation period. Available in 16-bit and 32-bit versions. An image browser that allows you to batch view graphic files, even in different directories.

TC-Image by Tashcom Software

http://www.linkstar.com/page/
    tashcom-software/tc-image.html

Lets you view, crop, grab, and print images. Registration is $20.

Miscellaneous Web Publishing Tools

Many hard-to-categorize tools come in very handy when you're publishing Web pages.

Imagemap Utilities

These are programs that can help automate the process of creating clickable imagemaps.

Map This

`http://www.ecaetc.ohio-state.edu/tc/mt/`

A freeware imagemap utility written to run under Windows 95 or NT, or Windows 3.1 w/Win32s (available for download). Also supports client-side imagemaps.

MapEdit by Boutell.Com, Inc.

`http://www.boutell.com/mapedit/`

Available in 16-bit (Windows 3.1) and 32-bit (Windows 95/NT) versions. Includes support for client-side imagemaps, as well as support for frames and toolbars. An evaluation copy is available that is good for 30 days, plus a 10-day grace period. My assumption is that the software stops working at the end of the evaluation and grace periods. At any rate, it is stated that you need to register the software before the evaluation period (and grace period) expires. Registration is $25.

Forms Utilities

Forms can add interactivity to your Web pages, but many shy away from them because they are difficult to set up, require CGI script support, and so forth. And after you've set up a form, you have to extract the form responses from the rest of your e-mail before you can read them, as well as organize and keep track of them. It would be nice if there was something available to automate all this, and there is.

WebForms by Q&D Software Development

`http://www.q-d.com/`

From the makers of the HTML editor, WebMania. Allows creation of forms to accept orders for products, conduct surveys, and so on. The program comes in two modules, WebForms Forms Generator and WebForms Response Reader. The first creates the forms. The second reads the responses from any WebForms form. If you are using a standard POP3 mail server, it will dial directly into your mailbox and download all your forms responses, automatically separating them from other e-mail, importing them into the WebForms database. WebForms comes in two version. Registration of WebForms Standard is $21.95. Registration of WebForms Professional is $34.95.

Tables Utilities

So you have some data that you want to display as a table, but the idea of handcoding it with Table tags is just too daunting. No problem. Here are a couple utilities that can covert data from Excel or a table from Word for Windows 6.0 into an HTML table.

XL2HTML.XLS by Jordan Evans

`http://rs712b.gsfc.nasa.gov/704/`
`    dgd/xl2html.html`

This is a Visual Basic macro for Microsoft Excel. It can be used with Excel 5.0 for Windows or Macintosh, as well as Excel 7.0 for Windows 95. It allows you to specify a range of cells and convert them to an HTML table. This is unsupported freeware.

hcTableToHtml by Yuri M. Lesiuk

`http://www.w3.org/hypertext/WWW/Tools/`
`    hcTableToHtml.html`

This is a freeware WinWord 6.0 table to HTML converter.

Frames Utilities

The use of frames is proliferating rapidly on the Web. Want to get into the act? No problem. Here's a utility to make it all easy.

Frame-It by GME Systems

```
http://www.iinet.net.au/~bwh/
   frame-it1.html
```

Uses a point-and-click interface to generate frames. Both Windows 3.1 and Windows 95 versions are available. Registraton is $15.

Color Utilities

Hate hex? Do you find that finding just the right colors for your Web page is an unnecessarily difficult process? No problem. Here are some utilities that you can use to find just the right combination of colors for your Web page.

HTML Color Scheme Designer by Wolf Spider Web Architects

```
http://www.sound.net/%7Ewolfs/htmlcsd/
```

Allows you to easily test text, link, and background color combinations. When you find the combination you want, you can copy the complete tag line to the Clipboard for pasting into your HTML file. A Beta version is available for download. No pricing information is mentioned.

Colour Buster by Tashcom Software

```
http://www.linkstar.com/page/tashcom-
   software/index.html
```

By the makers of TC-Director HTML Editor. It does color to hex code conversions. Click on the color and Buster calculates the right hex code to insert in your HTML file. This is freeware.

Color Machine

```
http://ucunix.san.uc.edu/~hamilte/
   colors.html
```

Free. Small utility that automates insertion of hex color codes.

Color Picker for HTML by Vector Development

```
http://www.cjnetworks.com/~vecdev/vec-
   tor/
```

Freeware. Another utility for inserting color hex codes.

FTP and Telnet Software

When you get around to putting your Web pages up on the Web, as well as maintaining your Web pages after they're up on a server, you're going to need a way to do it.

FTP Software

FTP software allows you to remotely (from your own computer) maintain and update your Web pages on a Web server.

WS_FTP by Junod Software

```
http://www.csra.net/junodj/default.htm
```

After you get around to wanting to put your Web page or pages up on the Web, you'll need a way to do it. It is available in both a 16-bit version (Windows 3.1 and a 32-bit version (Windows 95/NT). Registered versions are available for $37 from Ipswitch at **http://www.ipswitch.com/pd_wsftp.html**.

Fetch

http://www.dartmouth.edu/pages/softdev/
    fetch.html

Easy-to-use, full-featured Mac FTP client. $25 shareware. Full support for Internet Config.

Anarchie

http://www.share.com/peterlewis/

Nifty multiwindow Mac FTP client. $10 shareware. Can do Archie & MacSearch lookups. Full support for Internet Config.

CuteFTP by Alex Kunadze

http://www.cuteftp.com/

This is another FTP client that you can use to upload files to or download files from the Net. Registration is $30.

Integrated Internet FTP
by Kent D. Behrens

http://www.aquila.com/kent.behrens/
$25.

Telnet Software

Telnet software allows you to log onto a server (a Unix Web server, for instance) where you have an account and then run its software to update and maintain your Web pages. You might prefer using a Telnet client to update your pages on the Web, or your Web host may not provide FTP access.

NetTerm for Windows
by IntraSoft International, Inc.

http://starbase.neosoft.com/~zkrr01/

NetTerm includes a Telnet client and more. It is available in both 16-bit and 32-bit versions. Registration is $20.

Trumpet Telnet
by Trumpet Software International

http://www.trumpet.com.au/

Software, however, is not available for download from Trumpet's site. Download (ftp) it from ftp://papa.indstate.edu/winsock-l/tel-net/trmptel.zip. This is freeware.

NiftyTelnet

http://andrew2.andrew.cmu.edu/dist/
    niftytelnet.html

Small, fast, rock-solid Mac telnet client. 68K and PowerPC versions. Freeware.

Net and Web Automation Tools

Auto WinNet Version 2.0

http://www.webcom.com/autownet/

Automates FTP, Web browsing, e-mail, and USENET News. FTP automation allows you to download files by the truckload, hammering at busy sites until they open, or scheduling downloads for late at night. If you want to vacuum stuff off the net, this is the tool to do it with. WWW automation allows downloading of Web pages while you sleep and then viewing them offline. Downloads Web pages and all associated files. E-mail automation allows mailing list management. Send announcements, newsletters, and more, to hundreds of recipients. USENET News automation allows reading and editing of posts offline. The evaluation version only includes the FTP capabilities. This is not the easiest programs in the world to figure out how to use, but if you need to download a bunch of files off the net, there's nothing else like it. Registration is $49.

Web Whacker by Forefront

`http://www.ffg.com/whacker.html`

Allows automatic downloading (or "whacking") of Web pages, complete Web sites, including text and images, for offline browsing. Whacked Web pages are relinked on your local hard drive. Free trial versions are available for Macintosh, Windows 3.1, and Windows 95. Registration is $49.95.

Browser Buddy by Softbots

`http://www.softbots.com/bb_home.htm`

Calls itself a "prefetching agent." Helps you organize your URLs and automates downloading of Web site files so that they can be viewed offline from your local hard drive. Thirty-day evaluation versions are available for both Windows 3.1 and Windows 95. Registration is $39.

URL Grabber 95

`http://www.brooknorth.com/grabr95.html`

This doesn't grab the whole page, just the URL. Great for grabbing URLs you want to include in your Web pages. Freeware version available—limits the number of URLs that can be saved before restarting. Registration is $19.95.

Miscellaneous Software

These are programs and utilities of general use to Web publishers.

Antivirus Scanners

Although downloading software from company sites or from major software collections is generally not a risk, pulling stuff down from an FTP directory that anybody can post to might expose you to the risk of catching a virus. Here are a couple antivirus programs that can give you some protection.

Thunderbyte Antivirus

`http://www.thunderbyte.com`

Both Windows 3.1 and Windows 95 versions available. Can be downloaded from **http://tucows.phx .cox.com/files/tbavw701.zip**.

McAfee VirusScan for Windows

`http://www.mcafee.com/`

Both Windows 3.1 and Windows 95 versions available. Can be downloaded from **http://tucows.phx. cox.com/files/wsc-22fe.zip**.

McAfee VirusScan for Macintosh

```
ftp://ftp.amug.org/pub/amug/
   bbs-in-a-box/files/util/m/
   mcafee-virusscan-1.0.1.sit.hqx
```

The Mac version of McAfee's popular virus scanning tools.

Disinfectant

```
ftp://ftp.amug.org/pub/amug/
   bbs-in-a-box/files/util/d/
   disinfectant-3.6.sit.hqx
```

The extremely popular freeware Macintosh antivirus program.

File Viewers and Managers

The material that goes into a Web page doesn't necessarily come from only one source, but might include files in different word processing, spreadsheet, database, and graphics formats. It would be nice if there was one utility that would let you view all these. Well, there is.

Drag and View by Canyon Software

http://www.canyonsw.com/

A multipurpose file viewer for Windows that can view files and display them as they will appear in their native applications, across a broad spectrum of different file types, such as word processing, spreadsheet, database, archive, and bitmapped and vector graphic files. Versions are available for Windows 3.1 and Windows 3.1. Registration is $35.

File Compressors/ Decompressors and Decoders

Most software programs and graphics collections that you can download from the Web are compressed to conserve space and download times. After you download something, you need to be able to uncompress it. The following utilities should cover all the bases.

WinZip by Nico Mak Computing, Inc.

http://www.winzip.com/

If you are going to download ZIP, TAR, or virtually any other compressed file from the Web, you need WinZip. An evaluation version is available for

download. Register the software to get rid of the nag screens. A 16-bit version (Windows 3.1) and a 32-bit version (Windows 95/NT) are available. Registration is $29.

Stuffit Expander

http://www.aladdinsys.com

If you're using a Mac, you'll encounter Stuffit files (they usually end in .sit.) Stuffit Expander is a free decompressor for Stuffit, ZIP, TAR, ARC, and CompactPro files; you can also register a $15 upgrade that makes the decompressor PowerMac-native.

Stuffit Expander for Windows

http://www.aladdinsys.com

Aladdin makes the wildly popular Stuffit and Stuffit Deluxe compression tools for the Mac; Stuffit Expander for Windows lets you open and share "stuffed" files on your Windows machine.

Wincode

http://tucows.phx.cox.com/files/
    wc271b16.zip

Encodes and decodes UUEncoded files.

Getting Sound and Video into Your Computer

I n Saturday evening's session, you learned how to use sound, video, and MIDI music on your Web pages. Before you can use these multimedia features, though, you must *have* some sound files, music files, or video clips to use on your pages.

This appendix will gently introduce you to the often-puzzling world of capturing sound and video with your computer. A complete treatment of this topic could—and does—fill an entire book, so I'll just cover the basics; but at the end of each section, I'll provide pointers and references to places where you can learn more.

◆◆

Be very careful about using other people's music, video, or sounds on your Web pages. Copyright law can be complicated, but—in general—it's safe to assume that every CD, videotape, and MIDI file in your collection is copyrighted by *somebody*. Always get permission before using someone else's works on your page, even if you're only using a very short snippet. Not only is it a polite thing to do, but it's also the law.

◆◆

All About Sound

Sound travels through the air as a series of waves. Each wave is a pressure disturbance. The impact of these waves against your eardrums jiggles the sensitive bones of your inner ear, and voila! you hear Mozart, or Metallica, or Mojo Nixon. Of course, you're used to seeing cassette players, CD players, car radios, and other electronic gizmos that turn electrical signals into sound waves—but let's talk about the opposite process, converting sound into electrical signals, for a minute.

Sound waves are *analog*; that means that they're made up of smooth, continuous changes from one value to another. The graceful curve of an ocean wave is a classic example of analog data: each point on the wave flows smoothly into the next, with no gaps or disconnections.

Computers are digital, though; they represent things as discrete values, like a series of steps. The smooth motion of a sine wave, to a computer, is really a jagged-looking series of stairsteps: each step represents a value that the computer can directly represent as a string of 1s and 0s. Values in between are lost.

The process of converting analog data—like sound—to digital form is called *sampling*. The theories that underlie sampling are much too detailed (and boring!) to talk about here; suffice to say the quality of a digital copy of an analog source increases as you take more samples and grab more data with each sample.

Sound Basics

To grab sounds from the outside world, computers use sampling hardware built into sound cards or, sometimes, directly onto a computer's motherboard. This hardware takes sound from some outside source, samples it, and stores the resulting stream of digital data as a sound file.

 NOTE   To save space, I'll just say "sound cards," but what I mean is "sound cards or built-in sound hardware like that found on machines from Apple, Intergraph, and Dell."

Sound cards usually have two sets of connectors on them. One is a *line-level input*—that's where you plug in the CD player, cassette deck, or microphone that's providing the sound. It's called a line-level input because it's designed to work with the small electrical signals that most audio devices produce. Non-line-level inputs would require a *preamplifier* (or *preamp*) to boost the signals enough for the sound card to "hear" them. The second set of connectors is the sound output, where you connect your stereo, speakers, or headphones so that you can hear the sound card's output.

Most sound cards also include *sound synthesis* capability, meaning that they can make new sounds (not just play back recorded ones). Sound synthesis is what game programmers use to play explosions, music, and sound effects in their games; it can also be used to play MIDI music or even synthesized speech, with the right software.

Some PC sound cards, notably the well-known SoundBlaster family from CreativeLabs, also include a CD-ROM interface. One card thus gives you sound recording, sound playback, and access to CD audio, as well as CD-ROMs. A few of these sound cards (including most Macs) can directly grab digital audio from an audio CD and save it in digital form on the computer—invaluable for capturing sound effects or small snippets of music from a favorite CD.

The *sampling rate* and *sample size* that a sound card support determine how good the recorded sounds will sound. The sampling rate is a measure of how many times per second the card can grab a sample of sound. Audio CDs, and most sound cards, sample 44,100 times per second, or 44.1 kiloherts (KHz). Many cards can also use lower sampling rates, which trade reduced quality for smaller file sizes. The most common sampling rates are 22.5KHz, 11.25KHz, 8KHz (the rate used by the Bell System's telephone gear), and 4KHz.

The sample size is a measure of how much data the card grabs for each sample. The bigger the sample size, the more room there is to measure subtle changes in sound: a 16-bit card registers 256 times as many sound levels as an 8-bit card. You'll see cards with "32" and "64" in their names; these numbers refer to the number of musical notes the card can play at one time, *not* the number of bits in a sample.

Choosing Sound Hardware

Let me start with the easy part: if you're using a Mac, you're stuck with the Apple sound hardware built into it. (Actually, there are some high-end Mac sound cards meant for professional recording, but if you need one of those you're already way beyond what I can teach you.) All Macs can handle at least 8-bit, 22.5KHz recording; all Power Macintosh models can handle 44.1KHz, 16-bit recording.

For PCs, the situation varies widely. A number of computer-chip vendors make sound synthesizer chips, and these chips are used both in plug-in sound cards like the popular SoundBlaster series from Creative Labs and on the motherboard of computers from Dell, Intergraph, Micron, and many other vendors. That means that the first step in choosing sound hardware for your PC is to figure out whether your PC already has sound hardware built into it! Of course, many other vendors include plug-in sound cards as part of the package you get when you buy their brand of computer. Before spending money on an add-on card, make sure that you don't already have one in your machine.

Assuming that you do need to add a sound card, here's what to look for:

- Don't buy a card unless it's SoundBlaster compatible, period. There are very few incompatible cards on the market, but if you buy one, some of the sound software you want to use may not work. (I use, and recommend, genuine SoundBlaster cards just because I know they'll work, but there are many other good brands available.)

- 16-bit cards sound much better than 8-bit cards, and there's usually very little price difference. Many manufacturers have a "value" package that includes just the sound card and a "premium" package that includes the card and some software—you can often save money by sticking with the basic package.

- The capability for a card to play several musical notes at once is called *polyphony*. When playing MIDI music, polyphony lets the card play several instruments' worth of music at once, just like a band would. Sixteen-voice (or 16-note, whichever you prefer) polyphony is the minimum I'd consider; 32- or 64-voice polyphony will be useful if you plan to play, or record, lots of MIDI scores. Many games can take advantage of extra polyphony when playing background music and sound effects.

- Many cards integrate a controller for an IDE CD-ROM drive. You may or may not need this capability, so look for it when buying if it's important.

- Advanced cards use something called *wavetable synthesis* to make their sounds. Instead of using a mathematical model of what a piano sounds like, for example, wavetable cards use an actual (but very small) snippet of a real piano and manipulate it to play piano notes. Although they're more expensive, wavetable cards offer vastly superior sound quality for music. Some cards offer an expansion slot that you can use to plug in an add-on wavetable module in the future; these cards are a good way for you to get started with audio before upgrading to wavetable audio.

You'll notice that I didn't say anything about choosing a card for recording sound! That's because, for all practical purposes, the cards are all the same—you plug in a microphone or line-level source (like a CD player or cassette recorder), and you record. The sampling rate and sample size of the card you buy will determine how good your recordings sound—for maximum quality, make sure that the card you choose can handle 44.1Khz stereo at 16 bits. (However, remember that for most Web use, 22Khz mono at 8 bits is a better compromise between sound quality and download time.)

Recording Sounds with Win95

Windows 95 (and Windows NT 4.0) includes a simple sound recorder called (what else?) Sound Recorder. You can launch it from the Start menu; it's in Programs, Accessories, Multimedia. In this section, you'll learn how to use it to record sounds, and I'll give you a brief tour of Cool Edit, an excellent shareware sound editor.

Choosing a Sound Source

Before you start recording audio, you must tell Windows 95 what audio source to use for input. You do this with the Audio Properties dialog box, which you can open in several ways:

✿ Choose the Audio tab in the Multimedia control panel (choose Start, Settings, Control Panels; then double-click Multimedia).

✿ Right-click on the speaker icon on the taskbar.

✿ Use the Edit, Audio Properties command in Sound Recorder.

Whichever route you choose, you'll see the dialog box shown in Figure C.1. We're mostly interested in the controls inside the Recording group here, although you can adjust playback properties here too. Here's what the Recording controls do:

✪ The Volume slider controls how much the sound card will amplify the incoming signal before recording it. You'll probably have to experiment with this setting to find the value that makes your recordings sound best; you may have to adjust it when switching from microphone to line-level inputs.

✪ The Preferred device drop-down list shows all the audio devices that Windows 95 can see; whichever you select will be used as the recording source. If the drop-down says (None), that likely means that Windows 95 can't find either your sound card or the driver for it; to fix this, consult your sound card's documentation.

✪ You can choose the recording quality with the Preferred quality drop-down list. There are three available qualities: CD quality is 44.1Khz, stereo, 16-bit; radio quality is 22Khz, mono, 8-bit, and telephone quality is 11Khz, mono, 8-bit. If you're feeling adventurous, you can use the Customize button to create your own quality settings.

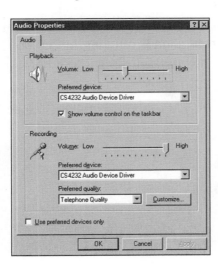

Figure C.1

Use the Recording group of the Audio Properties dialog box to select a recording source and quality.

Recording Sounds with Sound Recorder

After you've chosen a sound source, you're ready to launch Sound Recorder and start grabbing some sounds for your Web pages. The Sound Recorder window is shown in Figure C.2. As you can see, it only has a few controls, and they look like the standard VCR/CD player/cassette player controls you're used to seeing.

The displays right under the menu bar show you how long the current sound is, where the insertion point is located, and what the current sound (whether recording or playing) looks like. Immediately beneath these displays is a slider that allows you to jump to any part of the recorded sound. As you drag the slider, the Position and waveform displays change to show exactly where you are in the sound sample. Finally, the five buttons at the bottom of the Sound Recorder window are the actual controls that allow you to record and play back your sounds.

When you open Sound Recorder, it's ready to record—just click the Record button (which is the only one active when you're recording a new sound) and start recording! As it records, you'll see a visual display of the sound, and the Position, Length, and slider will all update so that you can tell how much sound you've recorded.

The waveform display of the sound makes it easier for you to tell where the sounds begin, end, and change—so it's easier for you to delete portions of a sound. Because recorded sounds can take up lots of space, it's wise to economize and clip out any unneeded silences or spaces in the sound.

When you're finished recording, you can use the fast-forward and rewind buttons (or the slider) to go to any point in the sound. This feature lets

Figure C.2

Sound Recorder offers a simple, no-frills tool for recording Windows sounds.

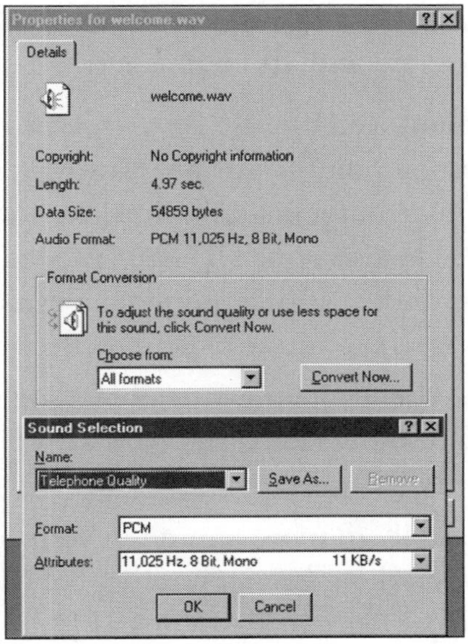

Figure C.3

The Sound
Properties dialog
box lets you
convert sounds
to another
sampling rate.

you start playing at a particular point; it also lets you jump to any place in the sound and record over the rest of the sound from that point forward.

When you're finished recording, use the File, Save command to save your sound; it'll be saved as a standard .WAV file. If you recorded it with one quality setting and want to save it as another, you can use the File, Properties command, which will display the Sound Properties dialog box shown in Figure C.3. If you click the Convert Now button, you'll see a dialog box that allows you to choose a sound quality for the file. You can also use the Change button in the Save or Save As dialog boxes to convert the sound when you save it.

Editing Sounds with Sound Recorder

After you've recorded a sound, you can use Sound Recorder to apply some simple transformations to it, including inserting and mixing sounds, changing their volume, and adding echo.

The Edit menu lets you copy and paste sounds just like any other type of data. Here's what you can do with its commands:

- When pasting a sound, you can use Paste Insert to add the sound at the current insertion point—just like pasting text into Notepad, the stuff after the insertion point will slide over to the right to accommodate the new insertion. The Paste Mix command mixes the pasted sound into the existing sound; you can use this command to add voice-overs to music or sound effect tracks.

- If you want to insert an entire file instead of a sound from the Clipboard, you can use Insert File and Mix with File to insert or mix an entire sound file.

- When you use the slider to move around in your sound file, you can quickly erase everything before, or after, the current position with the Delete Before Current Position and Delete After Current Position commands.

The Effects menu offers some basic special effects. Even though they're simple, they can still come in handy. Here's what you can do:

- The Increase Volume and Decrease Volume commands change the volume of your sound mathematically. Think of these commands like a magnifying glass—if you have a scratchy or "noisy" sound, you can make it louder or softer, but you'll also make the noise louder or softer too.

- The Increase Speed and Decrease Speed commands change the playback speed by stretching the sound out (to decrease the speed) or mashing it into a shorter time (to speed it up). The sound's pitch will change when you change its speed, so don't be surprised if the results sound funny.

- Add Echo adds a booming echo effect, making the sound reverberate when it's played back. (Most radio stations do this with their DJ's voices to make them sound better!) There's no "remove echo" command, though.

⚙ <u>R</u>everse takes the existing sound and reverses it—just the thing for making, or finding, hidden messages in your sounds!

Getting Acquainted with Cool Edit

What if you want to really get down and dirty with your sounds? Sound Recorder is free and easy to use, but it only scratches the surface of the cool things you can do to recorded sounds. Enter Cool Edit 96, from Syntrillium Software. It has a broad array of cool features, including the capability to distort, amplify, and tweak sounds; insert TouchTone™ sounds, random noise, or periods of silence; and provides a really cool spectrum display that shows your sound's peaks and valleys.

ON THE

CD

The CD also includes GoldWave, an equally well-written sound editing package. It's in `IBM\Multimed\goldwave`.

FIND IT ON ▶
THE WEB

You can get Cool Edit 96 from a number of Web sites, including DOWNLOAD.COM (**http://www.download.com**) and Syntrillium, the manufacturer (**http://www .syntrillium.com**). The demo version lets you use any two sets of features at a time; the full version is US $50, and the Lite version is US $25.

The Cool Edit window (with a sample of "Virtuality" from Rush's *Test For Echo* CD) is shown in Figure C.4. Because the sample is a stereo sound, two sound channels are shown in the window: the left channel is on the top, and the right channel is on the bottom. The window is jam-packed with information and controls: the toolbar at the top of the window gives you access to most of Cool Edit's functions, and the CD player controls at the bottom let you record sound from audio CDs.

Recording a sound with Cool Edit is pretty easy; here's all you need to do.

1. Launch Cool Edit and use the <u>F</u>ile, <u>N</u>ew command; you'll see the New Waveform dialog box shown in Figure C.5. Choose the sampling rate, sample size, and stereo/mono settings you want to use; then click OK.

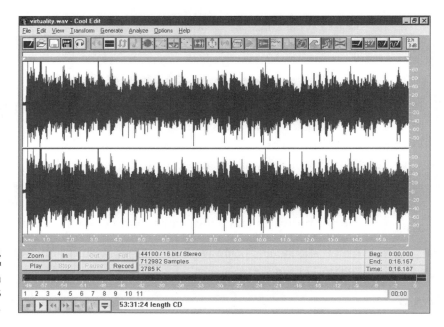

Figure C.4

Cool Edit is like a Ginsu knife: it has a zillion uses.

Figure C.5

The New Waveform dialog box lets you specify quality settings for your new sound.

2. Use the commands in the View menu to customize what you see; you can see one or both stereo channels, and you can choose to see either a spectral or waveform view of your sound when you record it. The spectral view shows which frequencies make up the sound, whereas the waveform view shows the actual pattern of the sound wave.

In addition, you can tweak the horizontal and vertical scales used to draw the sound's data. Finally, you can show or hide the CD player controls.

3. Click Record to start recording. If you want to record sound from a CD, show the CD player controls with View, CD Player; then click the track number you want to record before clicking Record. After you start recording, Cool Edit will update the main window to show you how much you've recorded, how much more recording space you have, and what the recorded sound looks like.

4. When you're finished recording. click Stop; then use the File, Save command to save your sound file to disk. After it's saved, you're ready to start editing it.

Editing Sounds with Cool Edit

Cool Edit offers too many editing features to discuss here—it's worthy of a small book all by itself. However, I'll hit the high points so that you can get an idea for what you can do with it.

Selecting sounds is simple: just click and drag in the waveform or spectrum views to select a snippet of sound, or use the Edit, Select Entire Wave command. The selection will be highlighted so that you can see what you'll be editing. Most of Cool Edit's commands apply to the whole sound when nothing is selected or the selection when something is.

The Edit menu offers commands for cutting, copying, and pasting snippets of sound from within Cool Edit or the Windows Clipboard. You can mix-paste a sound like in Sound Recorder; you can also adjust the sampling rate with the Adjust Sample Rate command—handy for changing the playback speed until you get just the sound you want.

The Transform menu is the real heart of Cool Edit's prowess; it offers a wide array of sound effects and filters that you can use to modify your original sounds. Here's a small sample (no pun intended):

- The Invert, Reverse, and Silence commands let you flip, reverse, or mute the selected sound portion.

- The Amplitude submenu lets you amplify or mute the volume level of any part of the sound. You can also change the relative loudness of individual channels or the overall shape of the waveform.

- The Delay Effects submenu gives you access to a whole bag of nifty tricks: you can add echo or reverberation to a sound (including using preset settings like "large occupied concert hall" or "shower"), or you can add a delay and flange effects.

- The Filters submenu lets you apply filters that screen out certain parts of the sound. This is helpful when removing vocals from a musical track or filtering out background noise, though it takes some experimentation to find the best filter values.

- Noise reduction is an audio engineer's way of saying "clean up all the junk sounds," and Cool Edit's noise reduction features allow you to do just that.

- The Special submenu provides a truly odd feature, the Brainwave Synchronizer. I can't do it justice—you'll have to try it for yourself.

- The Time/Pitch submenu lets you "stretch" a sound so it takes longer to play, while keeping its original pitch. This is a great way to figure out what the lyrics to that song *really* say because you can slow down the track without making its pitch drop to James Earl Jones territory.

One of the best things about Cool Edit is that it has full undo support, even on very large audio files. You can experiment to your heart's content and undo any operation whose result doesn't meet your expectations. Have fun!

Recording Sounds with the Mac

Apple includes a simple utility called (what else?) SimpleSound with the MacOS system software. In this section, you'll learn how to use Simple-Sound to capture sounds; you can also use sound-editing software like Macromedia's SoundEdit 16 to capture, edit, and add special effects to your sound files.

Choosing a Sound Source

The first step in recording sounds with your Mac is to tell the computer where to get the sound. You basically have three choices, though some

Macs may have more (like computers with TV tuner cards installed), and others may have fewer:

⚙ The microphone jack on the back of the Mac lets you plug in line-level sources like CD players, cassette decks, microphones, and audio-out cables from VCRs.

⚙ The AV connector (that funny-looking square connector) lets you use a monitor with built-in speakers and microphone, like Apple's 1710AV.

⚙ The internal or external CD drives can be used to capture digital audio directly from CD *if* your drive's an Apple drive.

You tell the computer which source to use with the Monitors and Sound control panel, which is shown in Figure C.6. The three icons across the top control what's shown in the rest of the window. We're interested in sounds, so click the Sound button, and you'll see the window shown in Figure C.6.

For recording sound, the interesting stuff is in the Sound Input group. The drop-down menu in that group lists the sound input sources available on your machine. Use the menu to select the sound input device you want to use.

The Listen check box controls whether sound coming from the selected source is also sent to the computer's speakers. If you've been listening to

Figure C.6

The Monitors & Sound control panel is the nerve center for sound input on the Mac.

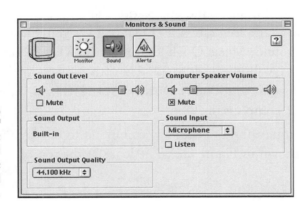

audio CDs on your computer, the Listen box is probably already checked. If you're recording directly from a microphone, you should turn off the check box. If you're recording from a cassette, CD, videotape, or other source, leave the Listen box checked so that you can hear what the computer is recording.

TIP There's plenty of online help for the Monitors & Sounds control panel: use the Mac help menu (it may be labeled Help, or it may look like a lightbulb in the menu bar). From the Finder, choose Help; then use the Topics list to open the Sound topic.

Recording Sounds with SimpleSound

The easiest way to record sounds is to use the SimpleSound application, which comes as part of the MacOS system software. It usually lives in the Apple menu, though you may have moved it elsewhere. When you launch SimpleSound, you'll see a window listing the current alert (or "beep") sounds installed on your machine. Recording a new sound only takes four easy steps:

1. Make sure that the input source in the Monitors & Sound control panel is set to the source you want to use. If you're using an audio- or videotape or CD, make sure that it's cued to where you want to start recording.

2. Open the SimpleSound application. Then use its Sound menu to choose a sampling rate: CD Quality gives you 44.1KHz 16-bit stereo sound; Music Quality gives you 22KHz 8-bit mono sound; Speech Quality records at 22KHz with 8-bit mono samples and 3:1 compression; and Phone Quality uses 22KHz, 8-bit mono samples and 6:1 compression.

3. Use SimpleSound's File, New command to display the Record window, shown in Figure C.7. The icons at the top of the window

Figure C.7

The Record window uses familiar controls to control the recording

control the recording and playback process, and the thermometer at the bottom shows how much sound your computer can hold at the currently selected quality level.

4. Click Record to start recording. While recording, you can use the Pause and Stop controls. When you finish recording, click Stop, and you can replay the new sound with the Play button or save it with the Save button.

Recording Music from CD

One of the coolest features of QuickTime is its capability to directly capture sound from an audio CD and turn it into a QuickTime movie. Ordinarily, when you record sounds from an audio CD, the CD player converts the digital data from the CD into analog audio signals, and the sound card turns the analog signals fed to it back into digital data. The QuickTime method grabs digital data directly from CD, preserving its sound quality.

Any program that uses QuickTime can take advantage of this feature. MoviePlayer, included with the standard QuickTime package that's part of the MacOS, lets you quickly convert audio CD tracks with a few simple steps:

1. Open the MoviePlayer application (it's usually in the Apple Extras folder.) Choose the File, Import command. When the standard file open dialog box appears, navigate over to the audio CD you want to use and select the track you want to import; then click Convert.

2. QuickTime will ask you where to save the converted file. It will add Movie to the end of the track name; for example, if you're

converting track 8 on an audio CD, QuickTime will suggest "Track 8 Movie" as the name for the saved file.

If you just want to grab the entire track, click Save, and Quick-Time will start importing the track. By default, it will use 22KHz, 8-bit, mono samples.

3. If you want to change the recording options, or record only a portion of the track, click Options, and you'll see the dialog box shown in Figure C.8.

4. Use the Settings group to control the sampling rate and size to use for the recorded file. Use the Start and End controls in the Audio Selection group to record a section of the track; you can either type in the start and end times or drag the little boxes at the ends of the gray bar at the bottom of the group. If you don't know where you want to start and stop, use the Play button to play the track and watch the index pointer (the little gray rectangle with the pointy top), which will indicate how much time has elapsed during playback.

When you've set everything the way you want it, click OK, and QuickTime will record the track and save it in the file you specified.

Figure C.8

The QuickTime import options dialog box gives you control over how you convert audio CD data to QuickTime movies.

That's all there is to it—you now have a digital version of an audio CD track that you can mix, edit, and sample to your heart's content. Please remember, though, to respect the original creator's copyright in your reuse of his or her work!

Converting Sounds

After you've recorded a Mac-format sound (whether from CD or not), you may still need to convert it to another format for use on the Web. QuickTime sound files and .AU files are the two most common formats, and SimpleSound can't produce either—but Norman Franke's freeware SoundApp can!

FIND IT ON ▶
THE WEB
The latest version of SoundApp is available from the author's page at
http://www-cs-students.stanford.edu/~franke/SoundApp/.

SoundApp is frighteningly complete. It can convert between Mac, DOS, Unix, Windows, and Amiga sound formats; and it supports MPEG audio, MOD files, and other esoteric formats as well. Its claim to fame is its versatility; fortunately, the author has included a shortcut for converting files to the most commonly used format: Sun's .AU format.

You convert files with SoundApp's File, Convert command, which brings up the imposing-looking dialog box shown in Figure C.9. Although you can use the pop-up menus beneath the file list to come up with your own conversion settings, the fastest way to go from any file type to a plain .AU file is to use the pop-up menu directly beneath the Open button. When you click on it, you'll see a list of predefined conversion settings—just choose WWW .au from the list, and SoundApp will automatically transform your file into the correct format for use on the Web.

Of course, you can also use the options in the Convert menu to choose your own custom conversion format. When you're satisfied that the format you've chosen will work well for your visitors, you can use the Convert, Edit Settings command to add your settings to the pop-up list discussed earlier.

Figure C.9

SoundApp's conversion dialog box gives you many conversion options.

Where to Learn More

An introduction like this only scratches the surface, but it should get you started. When you want to learn more, there are a number of good information sources available to help you move on:

- Rich Grace's book *The Sound and Music Workshop* (Sybex; ISBN 0782118011) is a thorough and engaging guide to capturing sound and music on your PC; it has great MIDI coverage.

- Helmstetter and Simpson's *Web Developer's Guide to Sound & Music* (Coriolis Press; ISBN 1883577950) has excellent advice on how to do "real" audio work, including how to hire voice talent and how to find, and use, professional recording studios.

- The *rec.music.makers.synth* Usenet newsgroup is dedicated to making music with all kinds of analog and digital synthesizers.

- Guido Van Rossum maintains an extensive list of frequently asked questions (FAQs) about audio formats at **ftp://ftp.cwi.nl/pub/audio/**.

- The HITSQUAD home page (**http://www.hitsquad.com/**) has an extensive collection of Windows and Macintosh sound utilities, as well as a good collection of music-related books.

All About Video

We're all used to seeing moving video on television, to the point where it doesn't seem impressive to most people—but getting CNN, PBS, or *Homicide* from the studio to your television actually requires a lot of complex equipment and technology.

Video cameras capture images and turn them into analog voltages: the exact mechanism varies (expensive network-quality cameras do it one way, inexpensive consumer camcorders another), but they all share this common function. After the analog signal has been generated, it can be broadcast over the air or recorded on videotape. Most videotape recorders use analog signaling, just like a cassette tape.

Electronics in your VCR or television receive the broadcast or videotape signal and turn it back into the right analog format for your television to display. In the US, that format's called *NTSC*; it consists of 30 frames per second (fps), each with separate red, green, and blue color components. Television images can have rich color ranges because their signals are analog.

Video Capture Basics

Video capture is the process of taking these analog NTSC signals and sampling them to turn them into digital data that your computer can use. Some computers, like Apple's Power Macintosh 7300 and 8600, have video capture hardware built in; most computers, though, require add-on cards or peripherals to capture video.

Speaking of capturing video: there are really two types of capture you'll see mentioned. The first is *full-motion* capture, and it's what most people think of when they think of video capture. Full-motion capture means that the card and software can capture frames in rapid sequence to produce a digital clip where the images move. *Still* capture is the second method; it's used by products that grab one frame at a time. Think of the difference between a disco strobe light and a camera flash: they both produce bright flashes of light that freeze motion, but the strobe light keeps flashing in a rapid pattern, so people appear to keep moving between flashes.

There are four characteristics to examine when choosing a full-motion video capture card:

- The *frame rate,* measured in frames per second, or fps, indicates how many images a capture card can grab. Because NTSC video sends 30 fps, a capture card that can grab 30 fps can keep up with broadcast or taped video without losing any frames.

- Because TV signals are analog, part of the capture process is mapping the video into pixels on the screen—like tracing the *Mona Lisa* onto graph paper. The *frame size* tells you how big each captured frame will be. Bigger frames take longer to capture and more space to store, but they provide more "graph paper" to put the image on, so the resulting image looks better. Frame sizes tend to be fractions of the standard 640×480 VGA screen: 160×120, 320×240, 480×320, and 640×480 are the most common sizes.

- The *color depth* tells you how many colors each frame will have. 8-bit color (256 colors) is common, but 16-bit and 32-bit color (65,536 and 16.7 million colors, respectively) are becoming more common, and they produce better-looking images.

- The *compression methods* that the card and software support dictate how big the final movies will be, as well as how fast they can grab frames. Cards that can compress images using their own onboard hardware can grab more frames faster than cards that use software compression. Cards that support JPEG or Motion-JPEG compression offer good compression at a reasonable cost; cards with MPEG compression tend to be more expensive but produce better-looking video.

Choosing Video Hardware

By and large, the determining factor in what video capture hardware you buy will be how much you want to spend. Even inexpensive capture units like the $200 Snappy from Minolta produce usable results, and a $500 card like the Avid Cinema or miro DC-10 can produce video that would be the envy of many small-town TV stations.

When choosing a video card, examine the four factors listed earlier. For most Web use, you won't want movies bigger than 320×240 in 16-bit color, but if you also want to take your edited videos and print them onto videotape, the extra size and color depth will be worthwhile.

Another key factor is what software comes with the card. Most low-end cards include simple applications that can capture video but not edit it. Midrange cards often include tools, like ulead's Media Studio or Adobe Premiere, that let you add special effects, MIDI soundtracks, titles, and other nifty video tricks. Professional systems, like the ones from Radius, come with sophisticated editing, dubbing, and re-recording software that will let you do anything ABC, NBC, CBS, or HBO can do in their production studios.

Here's a quick rundown of the most popular low- and mid-range cards, with some current street prices. Bear in mind that the market for these gizmos is changing fast, so you should comparison-shop before buying one:

- ✿ Avid makes professional video equipment used by the major networks and Hollywood studios; they also make a cool Macintosh-based video capture unit called Cinema (**http://www.avidcinema.com**). Cinema captures 320×240 in 16-bit color at 30 fps, but it can output at 640×480 for recording videotapes. The included software makes it extremely easy to record, edit, and tweak video; you'll read more about it in a bit.

- ✿ Creative Labs (**http://www.creativelabs.com**) is best-known for its line of SoundBlaster sound cards. It also makes a still capture rig called the VideoBlaster WebCam. It's optimized for putting still images on Web pages; as you'll see later in the session, it does an excellent job.

- ✿ miro (**http://www.miro.com**) makes a number of cards, ranging from the inexpensive DC-10 (around US $400; captures 8-bit color 30fps at 320×240) to the DC-20 and DC-30 (US $625 and US $900, respectively; captures 60fps at 640×480 in 16-bit color). All miro cards use PCI slots, and they make versions for the PC and the Macintosh.

☼ Most of Truevision's (**http://www.truevision.com**) products are targeted at video professionals with big bucks to spend; the Bravado 500, though, is a capable card that can handle 640×480 at 30fps for around US$600.

☼ US Robotics makes the Bigpicture (**http://www.usr.com/ home&office/bigpicture/**), a nifty integrated system that combines a 33.6Kbps modem, a video capture card, and videoconferencing software. It's featured in more detail in the section "Capturing Video with the USRobotics Bigpicture" later in this appendix.

NOTE TV tuner cards are becoming popular; these cards take a video signal from a cable box, antenna, or VCR and let you watch TV in a window on your monitor. A few TV tuner cards let you capture still images, but none that I know of can capture moving video—don't confuse them with video capture cards.

Capturing Video with the USRobotics Bigpicture

USRobotics bills its Bigpicture as "All-in-one Video Fun"—and they're not exaggerating! Bigpicture requires a Windows 95 machine with a 75MHz or faster Pentium and at least 16M of RAM. There are three versions: one includes only the video capture card; one includes the card and a neat little baseball-size color video camera; and the top-of-the-line model adds a 33.6Kbps "video modem." USR promises that the video modem is upgradable to its ×2 56Kbps technology, but the upgrade isn't done as I write this.

There's more to Bigpicture than the hardware: it also includes software for capturing and editing video (Asymetrix VideoProducer), distorting and generally fooling around with it (Kai's Power Goo), and holding videoconferences over the Internet (VDOLive) or between you and another Bigpicture user (RapidComm).

Installing the Hardware and Software

The Bigpicture can seem like an imposing bundle of gear: the complete "video kit" package has two cards that go inside your PC and the external camera, plus a batch of cables and connectors. The manual provides complete, well-illustrated instructions, so even if you're not a hardware guru you'll still be able to install and use Bigpicture. The basic steps are as follows:

1. Use Windows 95 to uninstall any modems you already have installed.

2. Turn off the computer and open its case.

3. Install the USR video modem card in a vacant ISA slot (the manual tells you how to tell PCI and ISA slots apart).

4. Install the Bigpicture video capture card in a vacant PCI slot.

5. Put the case back on your PC and connect the camera, modem, and phone cables.

6. Turn on your PC and start Windows 95. When the New Hardware Detected dialog box appears, put the USR software CD into your CD-ROM drive and use the Browse button to find the appropriate drivers on the CD. When you click OK, Windows 95 will install the drivers for the Bigpicture modem and video card and then restart itself.

That's it! The manual covers the same six steps in about 25 pages, but their explanation actually provides enough detail for even beginning computer users. The process is painless.

USR has bundled all the Bigpicture software into a single installer. You can choose which individual components you want to install; the default is to install all the following:

- Digital Video Producer (DVP, from Asymmetrix, **http://www .asymetrix.com**) is a video capture and editing program; we'll talk more about it in a moment.

- Kai's Power GOO (from MetaTools, **http://www.metatools.com**) is a really cool image-warping program. Words can't do it justice— it lets you pull images like taffy, stretch and warp them, and do just about anything else you can imagine.

- RapidComm is a combination phone, speakerphone, videophone, answering machine, and fax machine. You can videoconference with other BigPicture users (or anyone else with a videophone that uses the H.324 standard), but not across the Internet.

- VDOLive (from VDO Corporation, **http://www.vdo.com**) is a streaming video player that you can use by itself or with a Web browser.

- VDOPhone (also from VDO Corporation) is an Internet video-conferencing tool that allows you to make and receive videophone calls with other VDOPhone users across the Internet.

- Bigpicture is an application launcher that gives you a floating window for quick access to all the other components listed here.

Although the added software is really cool, the only components I'm going to talk about here are the two parts of the DVP package: DVP Capture and DVP itself. The two of them together give you an easy-to-use setup for grabbing and editing video for use on your Web pages.

Capturing Video with DVP Capture

DVP Capture is pretty easy to use, especially for capturing video that you want to put on the Web. When you first open it, you'll see a window like the one shown in Figure C.10 (except that your window won't have me in it!). The icons across the top of the window are DVP Capture's tool-

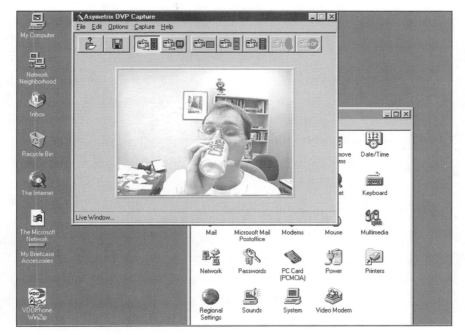

Figure C.10

DVP Capture shows you a live preview of what it sees through your camera.

bar; the rest of the window is devoted to a preview area that shows you what DVP Capture "sees" from your video source. If you have a camera connected, it will show you whatever the camera sees. If you have a VCR connected, it'll show you whatever output the VCR is producing.

The first step to successful video capture is to tell DVP Capture what settings to use when capturing. Doing so actually involves several different dialog boxes; let's see what steps are required.

NOTE Asymetrix notes that video capture is "demanding on your system." They recommend that you defragment the hard disk you're using to record video onto and that you capture to drives that aren't using Stacker or DoubleSpace. In addition, run as few other programs as possible while capturing for maximum video quality.

1. Set a file name for the captured video using the File, Set Capture File command. This tells DVP Capture where you want the video to go; it doesn't save anything there until you start capturing.

2. Allocate some space for the capture file with the File, Allocate File Space command. This command lets DVP Capture reserve a block of space to write the video in; that way, it doesn't have to pause when writing the video to disk. DVP Capture will always use as much space as you allocate, and it will take more if your video takes up more than the reserved space.

3. Decide whether you want to capture audio along with your video. If not, skip to the next step. Otherwise, open the Set Audio Format dialog box with the Options, Audio Format menu command; then select a sample size and frequency for the captured sound. Click OK to close the dialog box after you've made your choices. (Hint: the default of 8-bit, 11kHz mono is fine for most uses.)

4. Open the Video Format dialog box (see Figure C.11) with the Options, Video Format command. The drop-down list and buttons in the Image Dimensions group control how large an image DVP Capture will capture. The exact contents of this group depend on your video card; usually you'll see choices for 640×480, 320×240, and 160×120 in the pulldown. The 1/4, 1/2, and Full buttons refer to a standard 640×480 VGA window. The Image Format drop-down list lets you change what color type DVP Capture uses; you shouldn't need to change it.

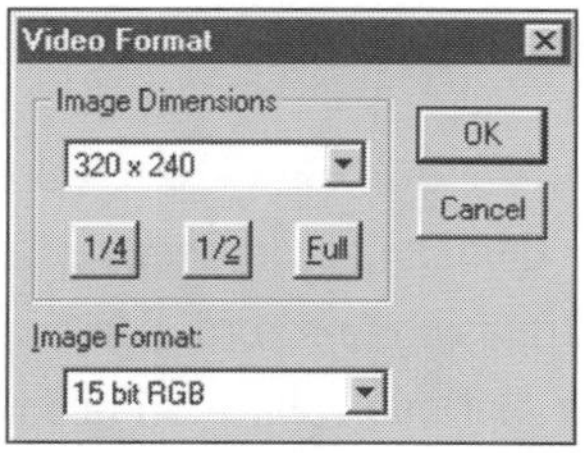

Figure C.11

The Video Format dialog box lets you specify a capture frame size and format.

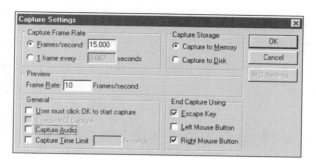

Figure C.12

The Capture
Settings dialog box
gives you control
over how the
capture proceeds.

5. Open the Capture Settings dialog box (shown in Figure C.12) by
using the Capture, Settings command. This dialog box lets you
control how you start and stop the capture, what happens during
the capture, and how many frames per second your capture will
include. The controls are all self-explanatory, so I won't go into
detail here.

6. You can change the video compression method used with the
Options, Compression command. DVP Capture only knows how
to record AVI files, for which the default compressor is Intel's
Indeo. Indeo (installed as part of Windows 95 and Windows NT)
does a good all-around job, so you don't need to adjust the compression settings unless you want to see what effect they have on
the size of the captured file. However, if you buy other video software, or install Apple's free QuickTime, you'll see that other com-
pressors besides Indeo are available.

After you've completed these steps, you're ready to actually capture video.
You can capture video three ways. The first, single-frame mode, grabs one
frame every time you click the capture button. Think of this like clicking
the shutter button on a camera: one click produces one picture. To capture just one frame, use the Capture, Single Frame command.

The second, frame mode, grabs a sequence of individual frames and saves
them as individual files. Like single-frame mode, DVP Capture will capture a frame every time you click the button; this is like the motor drive

mode on many cameras that keeps taking pictures as long as you hold down the button. To use frame mode, use the <u>C</u>apture, <u>F</u>rames command.

The third mode captures a sequence of individual frames and saves them as a movie. You can trigger this capture mode with the <u>C</u>apture, <u>V</u>ideo command.

In all three cases, DVP Capture will write the captured files to the file you set in step 1 earlier; you can then open the file in DVP to edit it, or use another editing tool. Of course, you can just take the saved AVI file and put it on your Web site without further processing; in many cases, the clip you record in DVP Capture will be ready to use without any extra work on your part.

NOTE If you have a VCR, laserdisc player, or other source that supports Microsoft's Media Control Interface (MCI) standard, you can control it from within DVP Capture and DVP, but explaining MCI is beyond this appendix—if you have the equipment, odds are excellent you already know how to use it.

Editing Video with DVP

There's good news and bad news about DVP. The bad news is that it's a complicated program to learn (see Figure C.13!), and space limitations prevent me from explaining how to use it in any detail. The *good* news is that Asymetrix has spent considerable effort to make DVP easy to use, and the DVP package includes good documentation and a Startup Advisor that guides you through assembling your first video.

The basic process for using DVP, or any other video editing software, is this:

1. Create a storyboard that lays out the story your video is trying to tell. You can do this with pen and paper, a word processor, or your favorite outlining tool—the point is to come up with a set of images that will tell your story.

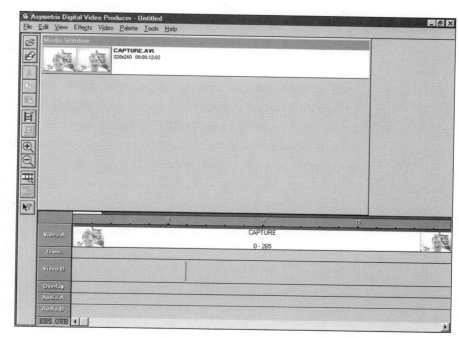

Figure C.13

DVP looks imposing at first, but it's simple to use when you learn what the windows are for.

2. Shoot or find video that helps tell the story you outlined in your storyboard. Use DVP Capture or another capture tool to get it into your computer.

3. Use DVP to cut and paste segments from each video clip into a master timeline, which puts your video sequence in a time-based order. Building a timeline is like sorting photos for a photo album by the date they were taken, except that you can use any order you want.

4. Use DVP to add special effects, transitions, and title overlays.

5. Add voice-overs, soundtracks, or audio that enhances the video sequence.

6. Save the completed masterpiece and print it to videotape or put it on your Web site.

Capturing Video with Avid's Cinema

Avid made its fortune by making professional video capture and editing systems. If you've seen *Jurassic Park* or CNN, you've see their equipment in action. Avid's first foray into the home market is their Cinema card, a full-motion video capture and compression card that works in conjunction with the built-in (or add-on) video digitizing hardware in Apple's line of Power Macintosh and Performa computers. The video digitizer grabs frames from the outside world, and the Cinema card compresses them with Motion-JPEG and converts them into a 30fps stream of 320×240 frames.

To use Cinema, you need a PCI-based Performa or PowerMac with at least 16M of RAM and video input hardware. If you have a Performa 6200, 6300, 6400, or 6500, you can add the Apple Video System to grab the video for Cinema; if you have a Power Macintosh 7500, 7600, 8500, 8600, 9500, or 9600, you can use the built-in video digitizer.

If your Mac supports S-Video input, Cinema can use it. Regardless of whether it does, it can produce S-Video output, plus it can "print to videotape" in either NTSC (the TV format used throughout North America) or PAL (the format used in most of Europe, except France).

FIND IT ON ▶   Avid maintains a whole Web site dedicated to the Cinema card and software combo at
THE WEB   **http://www.avidcinema.com**.

What really makes Cinema cool, though, is the included software. It uses a storyboard metaphor to help you organize your video clips and put them in the sequence you want the finished product you have. Cinema also lets you apply video effects via drag-and-drop, and it includes special features for adding captions, credits, and other finishing-touches features. There's a wealth of tips, tricks, and general hand-holding that makes it easy to make good-looking videos, even if you're a camcorder klutz.

Installing the Hardware and Software

Cinema comes in a surprisingly small box. When you open it, you'll find a single PCI card, plus a bewildering array of cables, two nicely printed manuals, and two CDs. One of the manuals is completely dedicated to explaining how to install the Cinema card in every type of Mac that can use it, but here's a brief summary for the impatient:

1. Turn off the computer and open its case.

2. Find the PCI slot nearest the Digital Audio/Video (DAV) slot on your motherboard. (The manual has several diagrams illustrating the DAV slot's exact position for each kind of Mac.) Put the Cinema card in it.

3. Connect the appropriate ribbon cable between the DAV slot and the DAV connector on the Cinema board.

4. Close your computer, plug it in, and boot it.

5. While it's booting, hook up the two sets of color-coded audio/video cables: one set goes from your camcorder or VCR to the video input of your Mac, and the other goes from the video output of your Mac to whatever you're recording the final video on. There are separate audio cables in case you want to bring in music or do a voice-over.

6. Insert the Avid Cinema CD into your Mac and run the standard Apple installer. Cinema will install itself, then you'll have to reboot.

Getting Started with Cinema

When you launch the Cinema application, the first thing you'll see is Cinema's initial welcome screen, shown in Figure C.14. This window allows you to do one of three things:

✿ The Plan New Movie button helps you make a new movie using one of Cinema's *storyboards*. A storyboard is nothing more than a list of what scenes you want your final movie to have. One of Cinema's unique features is that it comes with a number of predefined storyboards, including "Our Baby," "Christmas," "Wedding," "Field Trip," "Sales Training," and "Family Reunion."

✿ The Edit Existing Tape button is for those (like me!) who are too impatient to use a storyboard and just want to start editing video.

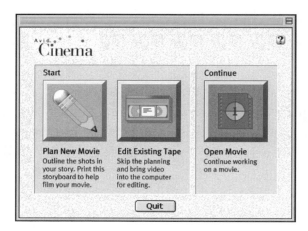

Figure C.14

Cinema's startup window gives you three choices.

You might still want to edit your video even if it already tells a story; for example, you can add voice-overs, special effects, and titles to an existing piece of video.

✪ The Open Movie button lets you reopen a previously saved movie and edit it some more.

Let's begin by clicking the Make New Movie button. When you do, Cinema asks you to choose a storyboard from four categories: Home, School, Office, and Other. As you navigate between categories, the list of available storyboards changes. When you find the one you want, click the Open button. Cinema asks you to specify where you want to save the movie files.

After you've done that, Cinema opens up its main window. As you can see in Figure C.15, Cinema uses a tab metaphor to separate different parts of the movie-making cycle. You can jump from tab to tab at any time. The first tab, Storyboard, shows a scrolling list of scenes in the storyboard.

You can edit the title, description, or length fields by clicking them, and you can rearrange scenes by dragging them around the list. The New Shot button in the upper corner of the storyboard tab lets you add new shots, too. When you're finished editing the storyboard, Avid recommends that

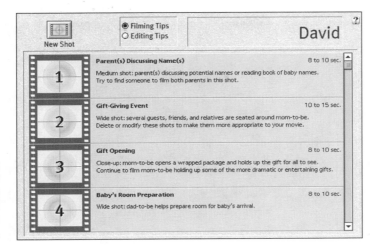

Figure C.15

Cinema's windows use a series of numbered tabs to help you navigate.

you print a copy of your storyboard with the File, Print command so that you'll have it handy when you're actually shooting the video.

Capturing Video with Cinema

TIP If you click the Edit Existing Tape button in Cinema's startup window, it will bring you directly to the Bring Video In tab, but you can always go back later and add a storyboard if you want.

The Bring Video In tab is where you actually digitize video from your VCR or camcorder. The tab itself is shown in Figure C.16; it's divided into several sections:

- The video source is displayed in the large area on the left. Right above it, Cinema tells you how much more video you can record based on your available disk space.

- The recording controls in the upper-left portion of the window show you the audio levels, let you mute audio, and most important—tell Cinema when to start and stop recording.

Figure C.16

The Bring Video In tab lets you organize and store your video clips.

- ☼ The storyboard scene list is in the lower-right corner. It shows all the scenes from the current storyboard. You can drag them to reorder them, or add new shots with the New Shot button. When you click on a scene, Cinema highlights it, and any video you record will go to that scene.

- ☼ The gray area at the bottom of the window is the Video Track; it shows where each scene's clip is located. You'll use the Video Track much more when you get around to actually editing the movie.

When you're ready to capture the video for a storyboard, here's what you'll need to do:

1. Open the Cinema application; then open or create your movie. Rearrange the storyboard until you're happy with it.

2. If you don't already have it, shoot video of your event according to the storyboard.

3. Go to the Bring Video In tab and select a scene from the story-board scene list. Cue your VCR or camcorder to the appropriate

position; then use the Record and Stop buttons in Cinema to record the video for that scene. (Avid recommends that you capture an extra three seconds at the start and end of each scene so that you can add special effects later.)

As you add each scene's video, you'll see the scenes appear on the Video Track.

4. Save your movie—you're ready to edit!

Editing Video with Cinema

Cinema's Edit Movie tab is shown in Figure C.17. Unlike its predecessors, it has a second row of tabs: Viewer, Effects, Titles, Sound, and Library. These tabs give you some insight into how Cinema views the editing process. A complete description of how you use all of Cinema's capabilities would fill a whole book, so I'll give you a quick rundown on the overall process so you can judge whether Cinema would work for you.

The Viewer, also shown in Figure C.17, shows you two things: a video image of the current clip (with a movie controller that you can use to

Figure C.17

The Edit Movie tab is where you put together your scenes and add special effects, audio, and music.

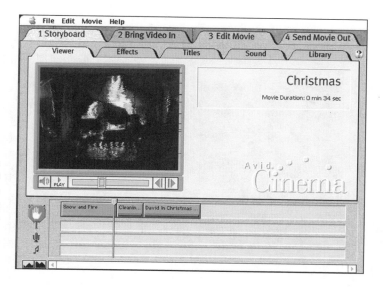

start, stop, and play the clip) and an expanded set of tracks. The Video Track you first saw in the Bring Video In tab has been joined by three other tracks: the Title track, the audio track, and the music track. The horizontal pointer that covers all four tracks is the *timeline*; it shows you what's in each track as you go along. You can move along by dragging the timeline left and right, or by selecting individual items in any track.

The Effects tab, shown in Figure C.18, lets you add special effects like wipes, dissolves, and fades to your clips. Like the other editing tabs, it displays the entire track list; however, it also shows you a magnified version of the Video Track in the upper-right corner of the window. The Effects list contains all the 40+ effects Cinema understands, along with space for an animated preview of the selected effect.

When you choose an effect from the Effects list, Cinema will draw a box in the magnified Video Track to show you where the effect will apply; you can drag the box to lengthen or shorten the effect duration. If you click the Apply button, Cinema will add the effect to the Video Track at the specified point—but you can always remove it later.

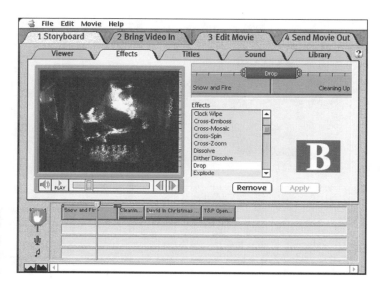

Figure C.18

Add cool effects with (what else?) the Effects tab.

The Titles tab (shown in Figure C.19) lets you add professional-looking text titles to any part of your video. The current video frame is shown twice: the left-hand version is full-size, but the right-hand copy is smaller and shows any titles for that frame. The buttons surrounding the right-side frame allow you to change the title's font, color, face, style, and alignment, as well as removing titles you don't want. When you add titles, they show up as separate entities in the Titles track.

You can add voice-overs, background music, or whatever other type of audio you want with the Sound tab, which appears in Figure C.20. Each frame of video can have three subtracks of sound: the original sound from the video source, a music track, and a narration track. You can control the relative volumes of these subtracks with the sliders on the right-hand side of the window.

The Record, Stop, and Import buttons let you get sound from other sources. You can import sound from QuickTime movies, but at present you can't import a MIDI-only movie file. Whatever you import or record will show up in the appropriate track so you can see where it's positioned relative to everything else on the timeline.

Figure C.19

Title your videos with the Titles tab; make sure to use a big enough font to make your titles legible on a regular TV.

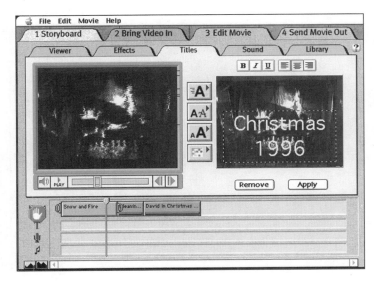

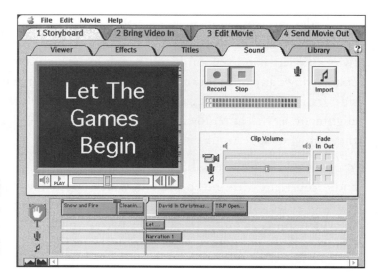

Figure C.20

You can add voice-over narration, background music, or MIDI files in the Sound tab.

The Library tab (see Figure C.21) shows all the audio, video, and music clips that make up the current movie. Each clip has a small thumbnail to show you what it looks like, and you can switch into Preview mode to see (or hear) a full-size preview of any clip. Dragging a clip from the list onto

Figure C.21

You can store a library of clips and use them in many movies with the Library tab.

the Video, Audio, or Music track will place it at that position on the track. You can also use the Import button to pull in any QuickTime file (except MIDI-only movies).

Video Output with Cinema

The final step in producing a video with Cinema is to get it into a form that the rest of the world can see and use. Cinema stores each movie as a movie data file plus a folder that contains the audio and video clips for that movie. Before anyone else can see your movie, you need to assemble all the pieces into a sequence. Cinema does this for you in the Send Movie Out tab.

Before you can preview or save your movie in its final form, Cinema has to render the titles and effects you added in their final forms. When you first select the Send Movie Out tab, Cinema alerts you that it needs to prepare the final movie. When you click OK, it does the rendering while you go get a diet Coke or glass of juice. When you come back, you can use the Start and Stop buttons with the radio group below them to do three things:

- Select Preview full-screen to see a full-size, 640×480 preview of your movie, with all effects and sounds intact. This shows you exactly what the people who view your movie will see.

- Select Make videotape to "print" your movie onto a VCR. You'll have to connect your video equipment first, but the process is quite simple and lets you share your movies with anyone who has a VCR.

- The Save movie for button turns on a pop-up menu that lets you save your movie in one of several formats. Each format represents a set of compression settings and frame rates that will work well in a certain environment—for example, the 4x CD-ROM format uses roughly twice as much bandwidth as the 2x CD-ROM format. The Internet/WWW choice optimizes movies for playback over the net. Avid has indicated that in the future they'll support streaming video formats as options too.

When you're finished, you'll have a movie to be proud of!

Where to Learn More

Desktop video can be a confounding subject—you probably understand the "desktop" part, but videographers speak their own language, and it can take a little while to crack the code. Here are some places to help you learn more:

- The crew at Pixelfreak (**http://www.pixelfreak.com**) produces an excellent site with lots of links and useful data on digital video editing and capture.

- Nels Johnson's *Web Developer's Guide to Multimedia & Video* (Coriolis Press; ISBN 1883577969) is a somewhat dated but still useful guide to getting video from the "real world" onto your Web site. It covers choosing equipment, learning the buzzwords, and capturing video for download or streaming.

- The `rec.video.desktop` Usenet newsgroup has a lot of discussion of PC- and Mac-based capture and editing solutions. Be sure to read the group for a while before posting.

- Companies like Netvideo (**http://www.netvideo.com/**) offer one-stop video services. If you need a lot of video work done, or if you need professional-quality work, consider hiring it out.

INDEX

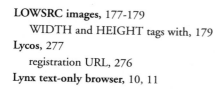

OTHER BOOKS
FROM PRIMA PUBLISHING
Computer Products Division

ISBN	Title	Price
0-7615-1175-X	Act! 3 Visual Learning Guide	$16.99
0-7615-0680-2	America Online Complete Handbook and Membership Kit	$24.99
0-7615-0417-6	CompuServe Complete Handbook and Membership Kit	$24.95
0-7615-0692-6	Create Your First Web Page in a Weekend	$24.99
0-7615-0743-4	Create FrontPage Web Pages in a Weekend	$29.99
0-7615-0428-1	The Essential Excel 97 Book	$27.99
0-7615-0733-7	The Essential Netscape Communicator Book	$24.99
0-7615-0969-0	The Essential Office 97 Book	$27.99
0-7615-0695-0	The Essential Photoshop Book	$35.00
0-7615-1182-2	The Essential PowerPoint 97 Book	$24.99
0-7615-1136-9	The Essential Publisher 97 Book	$24.99
0-7615-0752-3	The Essential Windows NT 4 Book	$27.99
0-7615-0427-3	The Essential Word 97 Book	$27.99
0-7615-0425-7	The Essential WordPerfect 8 Book	$24.99
0-7615-1008-7	Excel 97 Visual Learning Guide	$16.99
0-7615-1193-8	Lotus 1-2-3 Visual Learning Guide	$16.99
0-7615-0852-X	Netscape Navigator 3 Complete Handbook	$24.99
0-7615-1162-8	Office 97 Visual Learning Guide	$16.99
0-7615-0759-0	Professional Web Design	$40.00
0-7615-0063-4	Researching on the Internet	$29.95
0-7615-0686-1	Researching on the World Wide Web	$24.99
0-7615-1192-X	SmartSuite 97 Visual Learning Guide	$16.99
0-7615-1007-9	Word 97 Visual Learning Guide	$16.99
0-7615-1083-4	WordPerfect 8 Visual Learning Guide	$16.99
0-7615-1188-1	WordPerfect Suite 8 Visual Learning Guide	$16.99

TO ORDER BOOKS

Please send me the following items:

Quantity	Title	Unit Price	Total
_____	_____	$_____	$_____
_____	_____	$_____	$_____
_____	_____	$_____	$_____
_____	_____	$_____	$_____
_____	_____	$_____	$_____
		Subtotal	$_____
		Deduct 10% when ordering 3–5 books	$_____
		7.25% Sales Tax (CA only)	$_____
		8.25% Sales Tax (TN only)	$_____
		5.0% Sales Tax (MD and IN only)	$_____
		Shipping and Handling*	$_____
		TOTAL ORDER	$_____

Shipping and Handling depend on Subtotal.

Subtotal	Shipping/Handling
$0.00–$14.99	$3.00
$15.00–29.99	$4.00
$30.00–49.99	$6.00
$50.00–99.99	$10.00
$100.00–199.99	$13.00
$200.00+	call for quote

Foreign and all Priority Request orders:
Call Order Entry department for price quote at 1-916-632-4400

This chart represents the total retail price of books only
(before applicable discounts are taken).

By telephone: With Visa or MC, call 1-800-632-8676. Mon.–Fri. 8:30–4:00 PST.

By Internet e-mail: sales@primapub.com

By mail: Just fill out the information below and send with your remittance to:

PRIMA PUBLISHING
P.O. Box 1260BK

Rocklin, CA 95677-1260

http://www.primapublishing.com

Name_____ Daytime Telephone_____

Address _____

City _____ State _____ Zip _____

Visa /MC# _____Exp. _____

Check/Money Order enclosed for $_____ Payable to Prima Publishing

Signature _____

License Agreement/Notice of Limited Warranty